The
NLP Practitioner
Manual

Peter Freeth

GeniusMedia
CREATING KNOWLEDGE

2020

The NLP Practitioner Manual

Peter Freeth

First Edition: August 2011

Second Edition: August 2014

Third Edition: August 2017 (May 2021 3.11)

ISBN 978-1-9082930-3-9

Published by:

Genius Media
B 1502
PO Box 15113
Birmingham
B2 2NJ
United Kingdom

geniusmedia.com

books@geniusmedia.com

For information about NLP training programs, visit:

wwwgeniusnlp.com

Contents

Exercises

The Format of This Book

This book contains:

- Text that explains the principles of NLP

- Exercises that teach the techniques of NLP

- Space to write your own notes

When I'm talking about the principles of NLP, I've written in plain text, like this.

> When I'm explaining a technique with step by step instructions, I've written in a slightly different style, like this, leaving space to the left of the exercise for your notes.
>
> There are two or three roles in each exercise; Practitioner, Client or Observer.

And when I want you to think about a question and note down your own answers before moving on, I've used a box, like this.

Finally, I might refer to "coaching" at various points, simply because that's easier than listing all of the professional scenarios within which you would use NLP.

The NLP Practitioner Manual

1 NLP Practitioner

NLP stands for Neuro Linguistic Programming; a study of the mind and nervous system (Neuro), language and the way that we build a linguistic map of the world (Linguistic) and our learned behavioural responses (Programming).

NLP is a study of how we can use language to map the connections between internal experience and external behaviour.

People describe NLP in different ways; a study of excellence, a model of human communication and behaviour or a toolkit for personal change are ones you may have heard. Some NLP trainers even present NLP as a panacea for all ills; it can give you confidence, wealth, contentment, good health and more. Because of this, NLP has earned a reputation from some critics as a hyped up, pseudo-scientific cult that tries to pass itself off as a branch of psychology, or neuro-science, or psychiatry, depending on which website you're looking at.

Many years ago, I ran a large practice group operating out of London. A trainer came over from America to run a short course, and he graciously joined us for the evening. I forget the subject of his workshop, but half way through, he began talking about why NLP is not a cult, and spent the rest of the evening trying to convince the audience that this was the case. The members of the audience, about 40 people, stared at each other in confusion. Who had said that NLP was a cult? No-one had. The trainer was answering a question that no-one had asked, because he had anticipated that someone would ask it. Was he trying to be too clever? The fact was that 40 people had turned up, either because they thought that NLP was not a cult, or that it was and they liked that, or they didn't care either way. In any event, the trainer possibly made life too complicated for himself.

In this Practitioner manual, I am not presenting NLP as something it is not. NLP is a powerful toolkit, and it is well worth the time and effort required to learn and master its subtleties. NLP should never be used to influence or manipulate, and if anything, subversive intentions do have a habit of surfacing quite clearly in a person's behaviour.

NLP is currently used in business, sports coaching, therapy, counselling, coaching, training, teaching, sales, advertising - in fact in any area where people want to achieve better results for themselves and others.

At the heart of NLP is a set of linguistic tools for understanding the intuitive mindset and behaviour of excellence in any field.

Whether you are an athlete, sales person or teacher, you have certain perceptions, certain skills and an attitude that enable you to achieve results within your own environment. By tapping into the intuitive excellence of experts in the field of personal change - therapists - the creators of NLP, Richard Bandler and John Grinder created a broad and flexible toolkit for personal change. It works with our fundamental perceptions of the world, from which we form our beliefs and generate the behaviours that we hope will get us the results we want.

NLP at Practitioner level comprises these techniques, and certainly they are highly valuable in many different everyday situations. Yet we shouldn't overlook the value of those core modelling tools too, because they are the means by which we can continually generate new techniques and increase the flexibility and effectiveness of NLP. NLP is a generative approach, meaning that we are always seeking to build on what is already working.

This modelling toolkit is the subject of 'The NLP Master Practitioner Manual' which is also the manual for my Master Practitioner training programs.

NLP is not an abstract theory. NLP is a study of real people achieving real and tangible results in their real lives. NLP is a way of sorting and organising our mental and behavioural skills, allowing us to understand and refine those skills so that we can achieve more, easily and consistently.

NLP was originally the modelling toolkit by which intuitive talents were extracted and coded, but because the first people modelled were therapists, NLP has become confused with the techniques that it produced.

You might like to think of the techniques as being NLP's footprints. By following in those footprints, we can retrace the steps of the people who created NLP and experience their journeys for ourselves, always remembering it's the journey that is important. Getting your feet precisely into every one of those footprints is not, perhaps, a good use of your time, because whilst you're looking down at your feet, you're missing the scenery.

The people who come to NLP training wanting to improve their lives and their relationships have already taken the first critical step - taking responsibility for change, and for the effect they have on other people. These people already know that it is they who must adapt, not others. Perhaps, in the past, they learned the hard way that you can't make other people do what you want. They learned that you can only do what you want, and if you need other people's help then you need to be better at expressing what you want, or change the action you are taking to get it.

NLP is about you. It's not about what you can do to other people. If you try to learn NLP with an attitude of, "I'm already good at this, I want to learn to do it to other people", then NLP training will magnify that attitude so that it's even more apparent to others.

If you are curious about yourself and other people, and if you are hoping to find new ways to get better results more consistently then you will definitely benefit greatly from learning about NLP.

The three levels of licensed training; Practitioner, Master Practitioner and Trainer have quite distinct aims. At Practitioner level, the key aim is to give you a personal experience of change. Before you start learning how to change other people, it's very important that you have a personal reference for the way that people change and how the tools work. You will learn some basic change tools and by the end of the course you will have experienced some kind of personal change such as solving a problem or curing a phobia.

At Master Practitioner level, you gain more insight into the structure and application of the tools so that you can create new tools and refine your use of techniques. At Trainer level, you will learn how to learn NLP so that you can train others.

You don't need any training at all to use NLP, but you'll only get a license to practice if you complete the course. You need to decide for yourself if that's important to you but I would say that the experience of Practitioner training is far more useful to you than the certificate will be, and it is totally different to just reading a book, because reading a book doesn't give you a first hand experience of what happens in other peoples' minds. As an absolute minimum, I strongly recommend that you work through the exercises in this book with a friend or colleague.

All Practitioner course content is prescribed by the NLP licensing bodies, of which there are now several. The original licensing body is the Society of NLP. All of the other worldwide licensing bodies essentially derive their content and licensing criteria from the SNLP, with differences on course length or additional content.

This book contains everything that is in the SNLP core Practitioner syllabus, and it also covers a number of other topics which are taught by various trainers as part of an extended Practitioner course.

I've seen courses as short as 7 days and as long as 30 days. Neither is right or wrong, because I would suggest that you can only truly learn NLP when you are applying it in the course of your daily life, and you can begin to see how it operates for you. NLP Practitioner training is simply the beginning of the process, and no matter how long that beginning takes, you must give yourself every opportunity to practice thoroughly and attend further training.

There has been a long history of politics in NLP training, as there has been in many fields as soon as money is involved. Various trainers fell out with each other and set up their own competing licensing bodies, many of which have now failed or merged.

In the UK, this would be like a doctor being struck off from the BMA's register and, in response, setting up his own, competing professional association.

The history of these political battles is well documented, and we have no need to discuss them here because what we are primarily interested in, the tools and techniques of NLP, are broadly shared by all of the licensing organisations.

One of the key responsibilities of any NLP trainer is to provide a safe environment where, if you choose to take part, you will learn what's useful and important to you by exploring new ideas and approaches to situations which previously you, or others, may have found difficult.

Sometimes you might find a particular approach seems more comfortable for you. Take this as a sign that you are learning within your comfort zone. If an approach or idea seems new or confusing, take this as a sign that you are stretching your experiences, increasing both your flexibility and your ability to get the results you want.

In pursuing your journey to learning NLP, you've read this far, and in doing so, you have taken a valuable and vital step forward that most people have not taken.

That's not because I'm saying that this is the best book ever written on the subject of NLP, it's because in reading these words, believe it or not, you are taking action. And one way of looking at the importance of NLP in personal change is that it is about getting people to take action.

I can't even tell you that, when you put these tools and techniques into practice, you will achieve outstanding results, because I have no control over what you're going to do with the information in this book.

All I know is that in reading this book, you have taken a step towards achieving your goals. It really doesn't matter what you do, what is important is that you do something, because to take action is the ultimate expression of intention.

Many people in your position would have some goals, yet not many of them are doing anything to achieve them. They're saying, "One day...", and, "When I have enough time..."

Self-help books are certainly big business, with new titles hitting the shelves almost every day. Entrepreneurs, coaches, therapists and even TV celebrities want to share what they feel are the keys to a successful and happy life. Unfortunately, for most of them, this is what most of their readers will do:

1. Feel the need to solve a particular problem

2. Self diagnose the problem

3. Read a book for easy answers and instant recipes

4. Imagine trying the techniques

5. Put the book down because it doesn't work

What happens in step 4 is that the reader isn't really trying the techniques, they are simulating the techniques in their current "map of the world" where no technique can work, because the whole situation doesn't work.

If you're in a hurry then, yes, you might get some take-away food on the way home or buy a "ready meal" that you can just warm up in the oven. But would you want to live off that? Anything that's "ready made" is, by definition, made to someone else's recipe or agenda, not yours. That's why, throughout this book and throughout NLP Practitioner training, I encourage you to think for yourself and, above all, try something out, test it for yourself before judging it.

New ideas are disruptive by nature. What makes a new idea work isn't always the idea in itself, it is the fact that it disrupts the current situation. When what you're doing isn't working, it's usually a good idea to try something else. When the "rules" of the current situation constrain you, new ideas and a new perspective enable you to break free and overcome obstacles that had previously hindered you.

Anything, no matter how small, that you can put into practice, will make a huge difference.

Therefore to put anything into practice and benefit from it, you must disrupt your normal routine. You must let go, even temporarily, of "what works", even when it isn't working. You must step out of your comfort zone, let go of your preconceptions and be willing to accept that, if something isn't getting the results you would like, it's not your fault. You just need to try something new.

There's one important idea that I want you to keep in the back of your mind as you read this book, or any other book.

Nothing in this book is true. Does that sound strange? You may find that a great deal of it is useful to you, and you may find that many of the ideas and stories correlate very closely with your own experiences. You may even find yourself practising the techniques of NLP and getting great results. This does not make them "true" in any universal sense. Everything has many alternative explanations.

We don't really understand how our minds and bodies work. Different people have created different models, and those models may be useful for us in getting certain results. For example, if you want to run faster, a model of how your muscles and bones function is useful, even though you may not understand how your mind makes your muscles and bones move. If you want to lose weight, a model of your metabolism may be useful. If you want to know if it will rain tomorrow, a model of the weather might be handy.

Models allow us to make useful predictions, but we must always bear in mind that every model has inherent inaccuracies, because a model is a generalisation.

If you want to get better results in your interactions with other people, a model of how your behaviour and communication relate to the outside world is useful. None of these models are true, yet they may all be useful.

Whilst none of this is true, there is one thing that I can promise you. It's the one thing I can absolutely guarantee.

All of the ideas, techniques and concepts in this book will only ever work if you put them into practice. If you read something and decide it wouldn't work, then you're right. You form a belief which you then reinforce by deliberately taking action to prove it, by not doing the thing that wouldn't work.

Therefore, all that I ask of you is that you suspend belief or disbelief until you have truly found out for yourself. You will only know what works for you by doing it.

The techniques of NLP are simply its footprints, remember.

Being able to read a recipe book and follow the recipes to the letter doesn't mean you can hold a dinner party. To do that, you have to think systemically, creating the right atmosphere for your guests and serving them dishes that complement each other and arrive in the right order. A dinner party is more than just eating, it's the whole experience of an enjoyable evening with friends.

Similarly, learning the tools and techniques of NLP is neither the beginning nor the end of your journey. Learning to use a saw doesn't make you a carpenter, and learning to be a carpenter doesn't make you a craftsman.

Coaches, therapists, counsellors, managers, consultants, doctors, athletes, recruiters, actors, teachers, sales people, authors and entrepreneurs all benefit from learning and applying NLP. In fact, anyone who has to deal with people in the personal or professional lives can benefit. Is NLP a panacea, a cure for all ills? No, of course not. Nothing is. But it is one of the most versatile and valuable tool kits that you will ever discover, and learning NLP is a journey that will bring you value, insight and reward beyond what you may have first imagined.

I'm privileged that you are joining me for this part of your journey, and I hope that you enjoy exploring and learning NLP as much as I do.

^{2} Who Can Use NLP?

Since NLP is a process for modelling thought patterns, language and behaviour, it is useful for anyone wanting to:

- Improve the quality of communication within their professional relationships

- Identify and change patterns of behaviour

- Set and achieve goals more effectively

However, I would add that this does not mean that NLP is for everyone, which is the stance of many trainers. Since NLP is for people, and you're a people, NLP is for you.

That's like saying that people eat food, and Marmite is food, so you'll love Marmite, or shellfish, or cabbage. There is nothing wrong with those foods, but to assume that everyone will like something that you like is a fault of logic.

NLP is a technology, and technology should be invisible. Do you think about the technology in your computer? Can you say that you love magnesium, or thin film transistors, or dynamic link libraries?

I strongly urge you to tell your clients exactly what you are planning to do when you work with them, but that is not a reason to believe that the technology is a panacea. People need rituals and causes. They want to understand where they are and where they're going.

As I said earlier, throughout this book, for the purpose of brevity, I have used the terms "coach" and "coaching" to encompass any professional activity where you are working with a client or client group to effect change.

I could have used 'Practitioner' instead of the noun 'coach', but it's a bit cumbersome to replace the verb. What I'm trying to say is that, if you don't see yourself as a coach, please don't take it personally. This book is still for you. It's for everyone! No, not really, it's for you because you're already reading it.

The professionals that could fit within this broad description include, in my view, the following:

- Any kind of coach; life, business, executive etc.

- Counsellor

- Therapist

- Alternative therapist

- Doctor

- Health practitioner

- Sports coach

- Teacher

- Trainer

- Manager

- HR professional

- Sales professional

- Mentor

- Parent

3 Your NLP Learning Plan

Let's begin this journey by exploring exactly what you want to achieve in learning NLP. Take the time to write some brief answers into the following boxes. You can add to your answers at any time, and it's a good idea to revisit your answers from time to time to find out how well you are achieving your goals.

---

1. What do you want from this learning experience?

To have people hear what I'm trying to say. To know how to speak differently when I'm not getting through. To see me as others do

---

2. How will you know when you've achieved it?

People hear me & understand what I want to communicate

---

3. What exactly will you see, hear and feel?

---

4. What are you going to do to get it?

---

5. What can other people do to help you?

6. What difference will having this make in your life?

7. How will you put it into practice every day?

8. What difference will other people notice in you?

9. How will you continue to develop your skills?

^{4} The Presuppositions of NLP

When Bandler and Grinder first modelled people like Erickson and Satir, they found that they had certain beliefs about their clients, beliefs that seemed to make it easier for the client to change.

In the context of NLP training, some trainers, regard the presuppositions as the "rules" of NLP that you must learn by heart. Our view is that they are like any other belief, useful, if they help you to achieve an outcome more easily. Therefore, think of the presuppositions as "useful concepts to believe if you want to help someone to change easily". Just don't presume that everyone wants to change.

The original language of the presuppositions was devised about 30 years ago in California, so it seems a little strange today, to say the least. Although you might see other versions and even other presuppositions elsewhere, these are the original ones as they were worded by Bandler and Grinder.

I'll translate each one into something that may be easier to understand, and I've given examples where I can of the impact that each belief can have. My translations are neither true not complete, they're just my translations. You might add your own to make them more complete for you.

The ability to change the process by which we experience reality is more often valuable than changing the content of our experience of reality.

It's easier and more useful to change your perception of the world than it is to change the world, especially when the problem is something that has already happened.

The meaning of the communication is the response you get.

Judge the effectiveness of your communication by what other people do, rather than what you think you say. **Yes.**

All distinctions human beings are able to make concerning our environment and our behaviour can be usefully represented through the visual, auditory, kinaesthetic, olfactory, and gustatory senses.

Everything that is in your head has a picture, sound, feeling, smell and taste, including abstract things like "happiness", "professionalism" and "work".

The resources an individual needs in order to effect a change are already within them.

You already have everything that you need to get everything that you want, so the job of the NLP Practitioner is to help you access those resources easily.

The map is not the territory.

The representation that you hold of the "real world" is a map, not the world itself, where any experience is deleted, distorted and generalised differently than other people's. Disagreements show us that we are looking at different maps of the same territory.

The positive worth of the individual is held constant, while the value and appropriateness of internal and/or external behaviour is questioned.

Your value as a human being cannot be determined by your behaviour, which only represents part of your rich and varied capabilities applied in a variety of contexts.

There is a positive intention motivating every behaviour, and a context in which every behaviour has value.

Your behaviour is motivated by your desire to have or get something useful for you, and there is nothing intrinsically wrong with any behaviour, there's just a time and a place for it.

Feedback vs. Failure - All results and behaviours are achievements, whether they are desired outcomes for a given task/context, or not.

Some people translate this into "there is no failure, only feedback". In fact, I would add that there is no success either. Failure and success are judgements made against a desired outcome. The important thing is that you take action and notice what happens.

5 Coming to Your Senses

What equipment do you have for gathering information from the outside world?

Obviously, I can't hear you, so I'll pretend you said:

My five senses!

And I'll say, "Good start!", because that there are more than five. Here are some of the senses that you have:

In fact, the 'five senses' is an idea that was first put forward by Aristotle, whereas today we know that there may be at least 22 senses, plus a significant number that we don't share with animals and plants such as echo location and the ability to detect gravity and electromagnetic fields.

Now, this may appear obvious, and therefore trivial, but this is in fact the most important thing you will learn today.

Why? Because all of the rich memories, ideas, thoughts, pictures, sounds, poems, songs and desires that are in your head got there by coming in through your senses. They didn't appear magically, they didn't arrive through intuition and they weren't "hard wired" into your brain before birth.

You might think that this is obvious, but it has an important meaning for our communication. The colour green, the sound of a car horn and the smell of lemon juice are easy to think of in terms of sensory inputs. What about honesty, professionalism and danger? What do these mean in sensory terms? What exactly does honesty sound like?

Almost everything that is in your head got there through your senses. Therefore, your senses are what you use to represent memories to yourself. You see, hear, feel, taste and smell memories using the same processing systems that allow you to gather real time information from the outside world.

Almost everything? Yes, except for certain instinctive knowledge that you were born with, such as how to breathe, beat your heart or swallow milk. If you remember that far back then you'll know that it took you a while to learn how to regulate your body temperature and even longer to learn how to walk and speak.

Our senses are our only tool for gathering information from the world, yet as we grow older we ignore sensory information more and more and replace it with "experience" or what we "know" [It will help you a great deal to gather more information if you try and forget what you think you already know.] Intuition is one way that you notice subtle sensory information that gets missed in the fog of all the stuff you "know" about.

Over the years, you have taken in vast amounts of sensory data and attached linguistic labels to it. We don't fully understand this process, so we can't tell computers how to copy it. We can teach a computer to understand that an object is both a table and wood, but if we smash the table up the computer struggles to understand that whilst it's still wood, it's not a table any more.

Of course, humans sometimes have the same problem. If you go to a rubbish dump on a Sunday morning, you're sure to hear someone saying, "Look! A perfectly good table! All it needs is a new top! And three new legs!"

Take a look at these two tables. Which one is bigger?

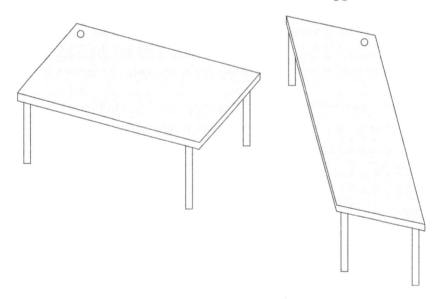

Have you ever lost your car keys, only to find them right in front of you?

Have you ever pushed a door that was marked "PULL'?

Are the horizontal lines curved or straight?

And what about these?

And is this image moving?

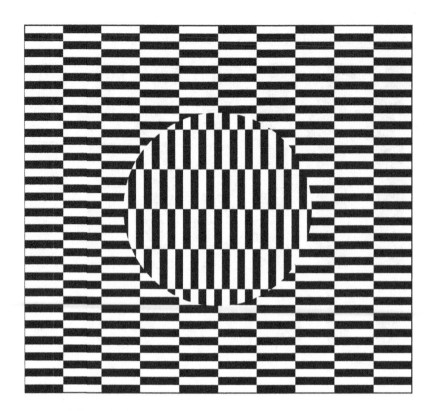

Look at this next image.

Hold the book at arm's length and, with your left eye closed, look directly and only at the left face. Move the book slowly towards you until the right face disappears. What is happening? Do the same by closing your right eye and looking at the right face.

Try these next two; can you explain what's happening?

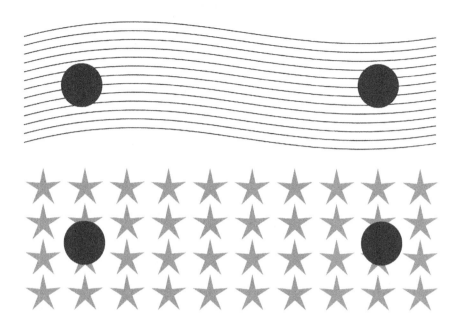

Have you ever heard someone say something totally different to what they actually said? Have you ever daydreamed? Have you ever dreamed at night?

Well, if you answered, "Yes!" to any of those, where did that voice come from? Was it the one in your head? Don't worry, we've all got one. Some of us have many, and they can come in very handy.

Here's the first useful tip for you, and I can guarantee it is a very useful thing to know about. In fact, if you ever feel nervous or if you ever worry, or if you ever tell yourself you should have known better, then this will be a very, very useful thing to know. Are you ready?

Did you know that you have total conscious control over that voice in your head?

Did you know that if it nags you or criticises you, you can change its tone of voice to be anything you want. If it sounded really soothing and supportive, would you be more inclined to listen to its advice?

If it sounded really excited and enthusiastic, how do you think you would feel? Try it out now. In a really critical, harsh voice, say, "That was rubbish, you should have known better". Next, use a really kind and supportive voice to say, "Hey! That didn't work so well, what can you do differently next time?"

Pay attention to the difference in how you feel about those two voices.

Just so you're familiar with the NLP jargon, the voice inside your head is called your "Internal Dialogue". If you find that you criticise yourself when you get things wrong and that this makes you feel bad, just try this really simple exercise.

Next time you make a mistake and the voice says, "that was stupid" or, "that was a bad idea" say, in a genuinely curious way, "Thankyou! Now, how does that information help me?" You can try any variation on this, such as, "Thankyou! What do you suggest I do differently next time?" You will find that the results are quite different to when you just nag yourself. You can make up any form of words that are right for you as long as you follow the basic structure of "acknowledge value" then "redirect to a positive course of action". You probably already apply this structure when other people offer you criticism - don't you? It just helps bypass the emotion of criticism and get to the real value - the feedback.

Everything that you "know" is represented to you using one or more of your senses. For example, you "know" the colour of your front door by seeing a picture of it. We also know that your senses may not be giving you the full picture, the whole story or a real handle on the situation.

The only way that you can gather information about the world is through your senses. As you get older and have more experiences, you filter your senses more and more and over time, what you think you see, hear and feel about the world gets further away from reality. Often, this is a good thing and helps you to deal with the huge amount of sensory information that comes into your brain every moment of every day and night.

When you went to school and learned about nouns and verbs, you didn't start speaking differently - you simply acquired a new labelling system for what you already knew about. You didn't start thinking, "I must remember to use a noun in this sentence". That labelling system only serves the purpose of letting two or more people share information using a common language.

All of our experiences and memories are based on sensory inputs, and those sensory inputs are filtered to reduce the volume of information that we need to process. Therefore, we develop an incomplete understanding of the world and our experiences in it through this filtering process.

Whilst the filters reduce the volume of information available to our conscious, rational minds, our unconscious minds are open to all available information.

This raises a fundamental principle in NLP, coaching and change work in general, when a client is operating from an incomplete map of the world, the information they need to complete it is already within them.

This means that we don't need to teach or give advice, we just need to ask the right questions to draw that information out.

NLP is, in part, a toolkit for reorganising and completing our experiences so that they can be more useful to us in the future, enabling us to make better decisions and be more effective in our everyday lives.

I also need to consider that, together, these filters work to ensure you only become aware of a world that supports your beliefs. If you believe that the world is out to get you, you will delete anyone who helps you, distort a few interactions so that they mean that people are out to get you and then generalise those instances so that everyone is out to get you.

Reality

For millennia, philosophers have debated the nature of 'reality', and we could broadly say that there are two schools of thought.

The first proposes that reality is "out there", whether we are observing it or not. Reality is like a theatre, where the play is always running, regardless of who is in the audience.

The second proposes that we create or project reality based on our needs, desires and expectations. Reality is like a cinema, where we can choose to see whichever film we want.

It's entirely possible that these philosophical debates arose from disagreements over objects and events. The question is; do objects have fundamental, immutable qualities which are merely perceived differently by different people, or is an object defined by its observer?

To understand where this fits in with NLP, we have to look at the history of the debate.

Philosophers were the first scientists. They put forward theories to explain what could be observed, but in ancient times, they lacked the ability to gather the kind of experimental evidence that even a primary school student takes for granted today. Hence, various philosophical or scientific theories which are unquestionable today were unthinkable a thousand, or even a hundred years ago.

The motion of the planets and stars, the origin of diseases and even the creation of life itself are topics that have been hotly debated over the ages, with the proponents of new ideas being labelled as radicals, heretics and even lunatics.

The ancient Greeks coined the word "Atom", meaning, "indivisible". They were able to work out that every physical material can be constructed from these basic "elements", and we could probably say that the great age of science began with their experiments.

However, more recent discoveries show that atoms are not, in fact, indivisible. They are made up of smaller particles. But as our ability to measure and quantify observations continued to improve, scientists found that even the discoveries of the Electron, the Proton and the Neutron did not explain everything that they could observe.

Classical Physics

Classical physics is based on rules, constants and certainty. We know the constants of gravity and electromagnetism. We can predict the motion of the planets so accurately that in 2005, NASA launched a probe called Deep Impact that, seven months later, crashed into the "Tempel 1" comet. The comet is essentially a lump of ice, 4 miles across and travelling at about 23,000 mph. The probe was about the size of a washing machine.

NASA's analogy is that the probe hitting the comet is like a pebble hitting a truck. A pebble that you threw seven months ago. Don't underestimate classical physics.

A pivotal experiment was conducted in 1803 by Thomas Young. He placed a light source behind a piece of card with a hole in it and looked at the light that shone through.

Up until this point, it was accepted that light, like everything else, is made up of tiny particles. Photons, as light's particles are called, carry consistent amounts of energy. The more photons, the more light.

Young found that when he placed a light source behind a hole or a slit, he saw a band of light on the other side.

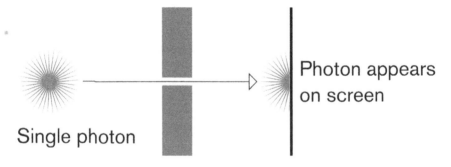

But, to his surprise, when he placed the light source behind two slits, he didn't see two bands of light. He saw many.

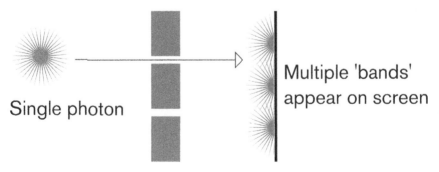

This is the famous 'double slit experiment' which every physics student carries out at school, and it is the foundation of "quantum physics".

What he saw as dark and light bands was known as an 'interference pattern'. Here's another example of an interference pattern, where two rows of stripes combine to give the illusion of a third row, a signal with a frequency which is a function of the two combined frequencies.

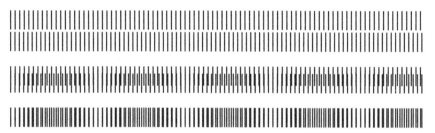

Scientists even developed a way to produce and measure only one photon of light. Logically, it can only pass through one of the slits, not both, producing a single band. Yet passing through both, at the same time, is exactly what it did, producing multiple bands.

This experiment is important because it produces a result that cannot be explained with classical physics. If light is packaged in photons then a single photon can only go through one or other of the slits. The only explanation for the multiple bands that Young observed is that light is not packaged in particles.

Experiments like this revealed that the world isn't quite as neat and predictable as it seems, and that the world around us can be explained in more than one way.

At the same time as scientists were forming a new understanding of the world, people such as Dr Franz Mesmer exploited the public's lack of understanding of these principles to further their own careers. Mesmer developed his theory of "animal magnetism" and made a considerable fortune taking his mysterious yet utterly ineffective magnets to paying clients around the world.

Today, we use Mesmerism as a term to describe a pseudo-scientific con artist who uses the public's lack of understanding of scientific principles to further their own interests. Unfortunately, Mesmerism is far from dead.

Quantum Physics

Young's experiment showed that light is not a particle but a wave; a continuously varying flow of energy. Yet in other experiments, light did indeed behave like a particle, a discrete 'packet' of energy. How can it be both?

Quantum physics introduced the idea that light is both, depending on how you look at it. Quantum simply means a precise amount, as in quantity.

Or more accurately, the location of a wave depends on how, and when, you look at it.

When physicists developed tools capable of looking inside an atom, they discovered some very strange things. For example, they discovered that you can't tell where something is until you look at it. For example, the classical view of an atom looks like this:

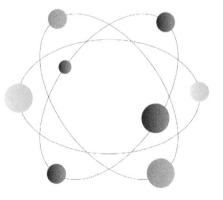

It's a tiny little solar system, with particles orbiting around inside the atom's "nucleus".

But quantum physicists know that this is a very simplistic model, and they represent an atom like this:

This is called a "probability cloud". We don't know for certain where the electron will be at any given time, we just know it's in there somewhere. We won't know exactly where it is until we look for it.

Sadly, modern "Mesmers" have seized on quantum physics as proof of new-age theories such as the "law of attraction" and "cosmic ordering".

Their logic is that since an electron only manifests itself to the scientist's whim, and matter is made of electrons, and money is made of matter, with enough concentration, you can manifest money into your life. That's an abridged version, but you get the point.

Reality and NLP

Is reality an objective, fixed arrangement of objects and events which we can only observe?

Or is reality a subjective arrangement that can be influenced by the observer?

And if you believe in a higher power, where does that fit in?

We have discussed the origins of scientific observation and outlined the fields of quantum and classical physics because this is a discussion that you will no doubt become involved in at some point in your NLP journey. You'll encounter people who believe that they can manifest their dreams just by thinking about them, and they use the "facts" of quantum physics to "prove" their claims.

I am not saying that they are wrong, I am saying that you must apply the principles of the great philosophers and scientists and test these claims for yourself.

Ultimately, you will adopt whatever beliefs work for you, we simply urge you to believe in what is happening, not in what you would like to happen.

Let's instead look at where NLP, or anything that helps you to critically analyse your own perceptions, can make a difference – in forming relationships with other people.

Let's imagine for a moment that we can't change the world, just by thinking about it.

However, let's imagine that we can change our perceptions just by thinking about them, and by changing our perceptions, we can change our reactions, and by changing our reactions, we will change our behaviour, and by changing our behaviour, we change other peoples' beliefs, and by changing other peoples' beliefs, we can change the world. Even Depeche Mode agree with me:

"You can't change the world

But you can change the facts

And when you change the facts

You change points of view

If you change points of view

You may change a vote

And when you change a vote

You may change the world"

Imagine what would happen if you thought that:

- People are untrustworthy

- It's hard to get what you want in life

For you to get what you want means someone else has to lose something And now, just imagine what you could achieve if you knew that:

- People are helpful

- Anyone can get what they want if they focus on it

Getting what you want means everyone can get what they want at the same time So there are at least two possibilities that we can explore:

- If we create 'reality', we might as well make it useful and enjoyable

- If we create 'reality', any map is not the territory and we need a way to bypass our filters and get to "reality"

If we combine all of these filters together and refer to them as the "critical filter", in that it is noticing critically, judging, deciding, then we can see that there are at least two mechanisms that we can practice and use to bypass the critical filter.

Whilst you may think it's useful for someone to believe that the world is a) a loving place and b) safe, if they are experiencing that hallucination within a burning building then that hallucination is no longer useful. They need to temporarily see the world as a hot, threatening place so that they can organise their behaviour appropriately.

The final piece of this puzzle is the way that we then communicate this internal representation to other people:

If we believe the world is safe, we don't say so, we simply act as if it is. If we feel unsafe but don't want to let other people know that we think that, we try to say, "I feel safe" whilst our remaining 93% of communication says, "no I don't". The result is that we say something like, "Don't worry".

If we are to effectively step into someone else's world, we have to pay attention to as much of their communication as we can as well as having techniques to bypass their critical filters.

Understanding the overlooked but vital role that our senses play in forming our most fundamental understanding of the world is key to understanding NLP.

Our Early Development

Children take a relatively long time to develop to full mental maturity. Humans, as a species, are unusual in that our babies are unable to fend for themselves when born. Many other mammals can stand and walk within minutes of birth, but a human baby is born with a brain that is not yet fully developed. Our mental capacity comes at the cost of an extended development phase after we are born, and many months of learning must pass before a human baby can do the things that a lamb can do almost immediately after birth.

This extended developmental period gives psychologists ample opportunity to study how children learn, how they perceive the world, how they think and how they develop.

This has also created dozens of different and often competing theories, many of which you will see manifested in the teaching methods of different schools and nurseries.

The Swiss scientist Jean Piaget conducted extensive research and described a number of development stages that a child will normally progress through. These form the basis for much of child psychology today and are widely recognised.

Learning by Doing

Children live in a concrete, sensory world. If you have ever played a game of 'peek-a-boo' with a baby, you will have seen its surprise and delight when your face or the toy reappeared. Why is a baby so surprised by this? Surely, the baby or child must know the toy was still there, just hidden out of sight.

In fact, a young child's experience of the world is so concrete, so built upon its primary senses, that when the toy is hidden, it ceases to exist.

Think back to where we started this chapter, in talking about the role of sensory information in understanding NLP. As adults, much of our world is imaginary. We imagine other peoples' intentions. We imagine that our car keys have disappeared. We imagine that the boss is going to be in a bad mood this morning. We imagine what's for dinner tonight.

The irony is, of course, that where an adult's world is largely imaginary, a child's world is anything but.

As a child gets older, it explores and begins to create abstract 'maps' of its surroundings. There comes an age when a child is no longer surprised by the reappearing toy, and you will see a different behaviour – when you hide the toy, the child will look for it. This is an important test in child development, and marks the child's developing ability to create a mental model of its surroundings. Later on, the child also learns to model people.

Beyond the 'mapping' stage, when you hide a toy, there is a conflict between the data available to the child. Its senses say that the toy no longer exists, but its experience says the toy does indeed exist. The child then takes action to resolve this conflict, guessing that the adult has hidden the toy.

Between 4 and 12 months old, the child has started to call upon its internal map, and is valuing its own internal data above external data.

Many years later, at a magic show, that early surprise and delight is rekindled when the child looks for the coin in the magician's hand, only to find it empty.

The more you expose a child to rich, sensory experiences, the more information it has to build new maps and develop new ways of thinking about the world.

Let's look at the stages of child development, and compare them to what we know about the role of NLP.

The Sensorimotor Stage, 0 to 2 Years

At this time, the child is developing its sensory awareness and its motor skills. It is learning to sense the world around it and take action in order to meet its needs.

Age	Developmental stage
1-4 months	"Primary circular reactions" - an action, such as thumb sucking, becomes its own stimulus which leads to the same action.
4-12 months	"Secondary circular reactions" - an action, such as squeezing a toy, leads to an external stimulus such as a sound which leads to the same action.
12-24 months	"Tertiary circular reactions" - an action is repeated in different situations, such as hitting different objects to hear the different sounds they make.

Pre-operational Stage, 2 to 7 Years

At this time, the child develops the ability to use symbols to represent objects and events in the 'real world'.

A symbol is used to represent something, and you can have many different symbols to represent the same thing.

The child develops a sense of past and future at this stage, and the ability to mentally manipulate symbols. This marks the child's progression to the next stage of development, and is what Jean Piaget called the ability to 'decentre', which he investigated with the following experiment.

Piaget sat down at a table with a model mountain range on it. He asked a child to tell him which view of the mountain range Piaget could see. Younger children indicated their own point of view, older children indicated Piaget's point of view, demonstrating their ability to see the model from an imaginary angle.

Here is an overhead view of a version of Piaget's mountain range (two spheres and a cube) showing the positions of Piaget and a child.

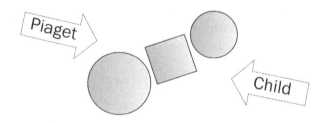

Which of these would the child see, and which would Piaget see?

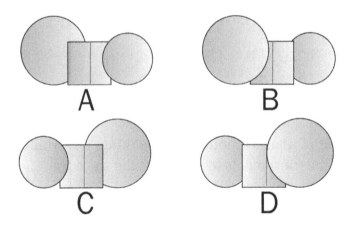

If you have a child of your own, or you can borrow one, try this test with some objects on a table.

This test is important because it is the foundation of a very human ability; empathy. The ability to see things from someone else's point of view requires significant mental acrobatics. Later in life, the ability to see yourself from other peoples' points of view forms the basis of concepts such as self-awareness and moral standards.

Learning by Talking

One of the most important abstract maps that a child learns to use is that of language. Language is a symbolic representation of the world, in that the word 'apple' is not an apple, it is a symbol that represents an apple. When the child learns to use the symbol, it can communicate its needs to a parent or carer.

At around 18 months old, you will see a child develop the use of other symbols too. For example, it will use objects as toys to represent other objects, such as play food or toy villages with cars and people.

When the child learns that the square thing with coloured buttons on can make the TV change channel, it will try to influence other household objects too, perhaps trying to turn the cat into something more interesting, like a puppy.

The ability to assign symbols to objects is the beginning of the process of abstraction, the ability to create complex mental maps or models of objects, places and people.

Concrete Operations Stage, 7 to 11 Years

The word 'operations' refers to logical calculations or rules that are used in solving problems. At this stage, the child can understand symbols and can manipulate those symbols mentally to solve problems, although at first this will still need to be within the context of concrete, real world situations. Children learning maths at school still work with objects rather than purely abstract ideas.

Around the age of 6, most children will know that a quantity of something stays constant, even when it is a different shape or in a different container.

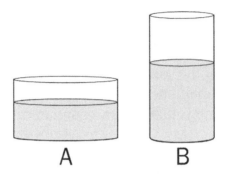

Prior to this stage, a child will tend to see glass B as being the most full because the level of liquid in it is higher, when in fact both have the same amount of liquid in, which a child at this stage will understand.

The amount of liquid is 'conserved' regardless of how it is stored.

An older sister might 'give in' to her younger brother's demands for the large piece of cake, in return for her 'making do' with four smaller pieces. You can see that the ability to perform concrete operations depends entirely on the child's ability to manipulate imaginary constructs. The child can visualise the amount of cake or modelling clay and perform mental calculations. This requires the ability to hold a memory and manipulate it in various ways.

Formal Operations Stage – 12 years onwards

At this point, the child is developing adult thinking abilities, particularly the ability to use logical and abstract operations and form theories about how things work.

At this stage, the child is not only creating and interacting with mental models, they are also able to abstract and discuss these models as entities in their own right.

A young child would have difficulty understanding an abstract concept such as 'counting", hence the use of play money or counting toys in schools. But, once the child has developed the ability to create abstract models, more advanced mathematical concepts can be learned without having to use any 'real world' examples.

Psychology and NLP

Possibly in an attempt to gain credibility, many NLP trainers claim that NLP is a branch of psychology; it is not. Both relate to our understanding of the mind, but they are very different. Psychology is a huge field of scientific study, whereas NLP is just one field of practice.

Psychologists and NLP Practitioners do not compete when they operate from a mutual understanding of how the two fields fit together.

By understanding what psychologists have discovered about the way that our minds develop, we can understand how and where NLP can fit in, and by understanding how psychologists form and test their theories, we can conduct our own experiments and form our own, unique understanding.

The very foundations of our ability to operate as human beings lie in these development stages. The ability to form a mental map of the outside world, represent that map using abstract symbols and then communicate with other people using those symbols is the basis of a human society. NLP offers one set of tools to understand how those processes of abstraction and communication influence our behaviour and the results that we achieve in our lives.

Long before children enter formal education, they learn by watching, listening and copying. They observe their parents, grandparents, siblings, friends, people on television and anyone that they come into contact with. They experiment by emulating what they have observed and they notice the results that they get.

If the result is that their parents are pleased and give them positive feedback, they discover that the behaviour is valuable and they repeat it.

If the result is that their parents are angry and give them negative feedback, they discover that the behaviour is valuable and they repeat it. They probably do it even more, depending on how they benefit from their parents' anger.

If the result is that their parents ignore the behaviour, they discover that the behaviour has no value and they are more likely to stop it.

For example, let's say the child learns to emulate an actor on television. Their parents find it highly amusing and the child gets lots of attention. If what they learn is some offensive language, the child still gets lots of attention. A child tends not to differentiate between 'good' and 'bad' attention, so the child gains either way. 'Bad' attention also usually lasts longer, and can even end with a reward for a promise not to do it again, or a reward to appease the parents' feelings of guilt about the punishment.

Fundamentally, children learn in order to have more independence, because independence gives them control, and everyone has a need to have control over their environment.

Again, this is completely natural and is a sign of normal development. It can also be very frustrating for parents.

Needing a sense of control over our surroundings is probably what led our ancestors to worship natural Gods and create rituals. Even today, we still rely on rituals to control events in the outside world.

We use a lucky pen to fill out the lottery ticket, footballers wear their lucky boots and we discretely try to avoid walking under ladders without making it look like we're superstitious, which would of course be ridiculous.

Every morning, you follow a ritual to exert some control over the day ahead. What you wear, what you eat, what you see and what you hear all influence your day, because they influence how you feel.

⁶ State

You tend to perform well when you feel like it. No surprise there.

"State" means your present physical and mental condition, so you might be tired, happy, curious, careful or fascinated - all of these are states. Your state is partly influenced by your thoughts and partly influenced by your reaction to what's going on around you in the outside world. You'll realise by now that this really means that your state is wholly influenced by your thoughts.

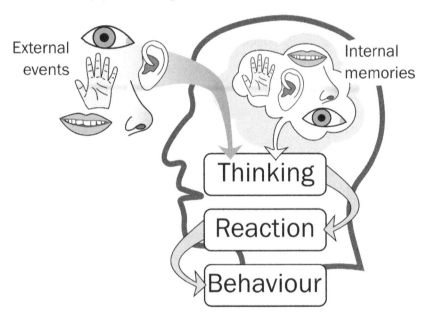

The two key ways to quickly influence your state are through your physiology and your focus of attention.

First, I'll mention the role of physiology as it's simple, powerful and easy to overlook. If you are alert and have plenty of water and oxygen, you will feel energetic and perform well. If you are lacking in any basic physiological needs such as sleep and light, you will perform below your best.

Getting the right physiology for an activity is the first thing you can do to improve your performance. In a warm, cramped room with no natural light, you'll be lucky to keep your customers or colleagues awake, let alone in a productive state.

In a room with lots of fresh air, light and water, it's much easier to keep people in an attentive state.

People have all kinds of methods and routines for controlling or maintaining states. Perhaps you have a routine for getting ready for work, or for going out on a Friday night. Perhaps you have a lucky charm or item of clothing that helps you get into a certain state. Perhaps you can just think of a state and you're there. The reality is that everyone has total control over their state, yet most of the time we just go with the flow, letting external events and people cheer us up or put us down.

Here's an exercise you can try with a friend that influences their state through their physiology:

6.1 Physiology

For this exercise, you'll need some space to walk side by side, perhaps along a corridor or quiet footpath, or in your garden.

Ask your client to name three states that they would like to explore. Have your client come up with a single word that describes each belief – usually a state adjective such as proud, relaxed or alert.

Now ask your client to picture a situation in their lives that they would like to see differently.

As you walk together, coach your client to find the pace, breathing, posture and full physiology of the first belief.

For example, "How do you walk when you feel alert", "Where do you breathe from when you feel alert?", "Where are your hands as you feel alert?"

Your role is to direct their attention to details of their physiology as they walk. This creates a positive feedback loop which reinforces the physiology and therefore the state.

Having fully settled into the first belief, have them now adopt the second one.

Continue with the third until they have tried on all three.

Finally, have them try on aspects of all three to create a new state, for example, "Notice your breathing as you're proud, relaxed and alert, and notice your hands as you're proud, relaxed and alert."

Ask your partner to once again picture the situation that they thought of and notice what looks different.

Find out how that feels different for them.

State is an important starting point in NLP because, in a way, state is everything. Your state defines the meaning you make of the world, the choices you make, the risks you take and the language you use. The differences in your behaviour between a great day and an awful day may be tiny, yet they add up over time creating a state that builds throughout the day, reinforcing itself.

When you wake up, knowing it's going to be a bad day, you program your sensory filters to notice things that go wrong. Anything that goes well is set aside as an accident or coincidence. When you plan for bad things to happen, they often do.

When you wake up, knowing it's going to be a great day, you notice everything that goes well for you. Anything that doesn't go your way is set aside as just a temporary setback. When everything seems to be going your way, it probably is.

You might say that you can't predict or control what happens to you, and you might be right in saying that. What you can control is your response to what happens. Here's an example.

A salesman leaves a message for a customer to call him. After two hours, the customer hasn't called back. The salesman knows that the customer always returns calls promptly, therefore something must be wrong - the customer must be avoiding the salesman. Self doubt starts to creep in and the salesman's state changes to reflect his negative mood. When the customer finally calls (he had lost his mobile) the salesman's voice tone reveals his state and the customer thinks something is wrong. The customer's state changes accordingly, confirming that salesman's suspicion and they descend in a spiral of emotional states.

The only thing that the salesman can say for certain about this situation is that he has not spoken to the customer since leaving a message. The salesman's response presumes that he has read the customer's mind; the customer has heard the message and has made a conscious decision to not call back. None of this is true, so it's just as acceptable for the salesman to imagine the customer going to the dentist, or just taking a quiet afternoon out to make an important decision. Neither this nor the pessimistic version is "true" in an absolute sense, so which is the more useful to believe?

Let's say the customer has gone away to decide whether to buy the salesman's product or not, and currently the customer is undecided. When the customer calls back for more information, the salesman's state could be the deciding factor. You may think that no customer would make a decision so lightly but in fact everyone does exactly this - we all buy from people we like to do business with. A friendly voice on the end of the telephone could be all the customer needs to decide. Conversely, a negative or pessimistic voice could swing the decision the other way by making the customer more aware of their doubts.

You've probably read adverts for instant, cure all influence techniques that will guarantee sales. The reality is that people succeed in any area of life by consistently being one tiny step ahead. A salesman who is consistently positive, helpful and persistent will succeed a little more than a colleague who lets his state reflect his worries. Those small changes are iterative over time and they build on and reinforce each other.

Mind and Body Connections

The medical scientists of the twentieth studied the human body in great depth, dissecting it,naming the parts and studying their functions. Bones, muscles, nerves and brain tissue were all distinct from each other.

However, if you look in a medical text book like Grey's Anatomy, or if you have the chance to visit Gunther von Hagens' BodyWorlds exhibition, you will see that the reality is quite different.

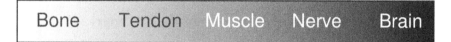

It's actually very difficult to say precisely where your nerves end and your muscles begin, or where your muscles connect to bones through tendons and other connective tissues.

The implication of this is that what happens inside your mind directly affects the actions of your body. You can't separate them physically, and you can't separate thoughts and behaviour either.

When a parent says to a child, "Don't drop that!", the child responds involuntarily to the parent's suggestion and drops whatever they are holding. As the child's mind tries to think about not dropping, the child's hands relax through something called an ideomotor response. Literally, a thought that becomes an unconscious action. The same thing happens when you see someone sucking a lemon and experience your mouth watering, or when you're a passenger in a car and feel yourself pressing down on an imaginary brake pedal.

Your body is an extension of your mind, allowing your thoughts to act upon the world, and your senses feed the results of those actions back into your mind. You are inseparably part of a feedback loop comprising you and the world around you.

6.2 Mind-Body Connection

Ask your client to think carefully of a time when they felt not so good about themselves.

Invite them to pay attention to their body posture. Do they notice any tension in their body? How are they breathing? What are they doing with their hands?

Get them to sit up straight, shoulders back, chin up, smile and try as hard as they can to remember that memory.

What's different?

People talk about a 'red mist' when they're angry, or seeing something with 'fresh eyes' when they have taken a break, or even 'rose tinted spectacles' when they're feeling optimistic.

The way they feel literally changes they way they perceive the world; not only seeing it differently but hearing, feeling, tasting and smelling it differently too.

Conversely, your physical posture affects how you think. Sitting up straight and smiling when you're on the phone changes your attitude which changes your voice tone which changes the other person's response to you.

An emotional state is therefore a unique set-up of your mind and body. To change just one aspect of that set-up changes the whole thing, just like changing one word in a sentence can change the entire supermarket.

Try this exercise too. Just be careful where you do it.

6.3 Change the World

Choose a situation that you are in regularly, such as a team meeting or your journey to work on public transport, where you can compare two instances of the same event.

Read the instructions and imagine the situation, just before you walk into each instance of it.

In the first instance, the people around you are idiots. They are utterly feckless morons. They have nothing better to do with their time. You may know them well or they may be strangers. Either way, notice their blank faces and know that absolutely nothing of any value is going on in their minds. Luckily, you are there to save the day. Without you, the whole situation will grind to a halt.

In the second instance, the people around you are exactly like you. Fortunately, they look very different, otherwise you wouldn't be able to tell them apart, but on the inside, they have pretty much the same knowledge, needs, fears and hopes. Individually, one person can achieve a little, but when you just stop for a moment, look around you and really notice, you can be truly amazed at what all these people can achieve together. You can be proud of the part that you play in this and know that everyone around you is counting on you to do your best.

How did you feel as you walked into each instance?

How did the other people look to you?

How did you feel about them?

What did you think was going on in their minds?

How did you behave compared to 'normal'?

How did the other people look at you?

What were they thinking as they looked at you?

How did you feel about the outcome of the event?

What would you say you achieved?

7 Communication Models

The simplest communication model looks like this:

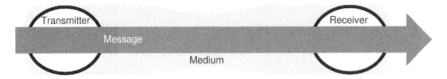

However, communication in the real world doesn't quite work like that. First of all, the system will always contain noise which reduces the quality of the signal:

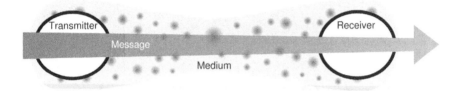

In some systems, the effect of noise is cumulative; it adds up the more times you pass the message through the medium, so it becomes harder and harder to extract the message from the noise.

Imagine a system whereby we need to communicate in code. I have a codebook, and you have a codebook. In my codebook, it says that the code for "today" is "55". In your codebook, it says that the code "55" translates into "tomorrow". It sounds ridiculous! Yet that's the way it works. How can we ever make ourselves understood?

If I have an experience in my head that I want to convey to you, I look in my codebook and translate those sights, sounds and feelings into words. Some of them translate easily, like "apple" or "table". Some of them translate very badly, like smells that I had never experienced before, so I translate those vague experiences in reference to other, more familiar experiences. So I might say that a smell was like a cross between floor polish and smoke. But what kind of smoke? And what kind of floor polish? How can I convey those experiences accurately when I can't even convey the right kind of apple. No, not that one. Not that one. Yes, that one. As for tables, it obviously doesn't matter. Any table will do. A dining table, a coffee table, a table of contents or an operating table. It doesn't matter. Just put the apples on it. No, not those apples, the computers. Oh, never mind.

So I translate my experience into the code of language and then hope that the original experience is recreated in your head.

And I don't even check. I just carry on as if the message is received by you exactly as I intended it. And you carry on as if the message you're receiving is exactly what I intended to send. As you nod to indicate "message received", your nod also indicates to me "I'm thinking what you're thinking".

There is always a sender and a receiver in communication, who have different personal realities. They each have their own "map of the world" formed by their experiences, perceptions, ideas, relationships, beliefs, cultures etc. They will perceive, experience, and interpret things differently. A single event will be perceived differently by different people.

We could regard noise as being analogous to a noisy environment like a factory or busy street, where it's literally hard to hear what someone is saying. Or we could consider those differences in culture and experiences as being noise, in that they affect communication in the same way. We could also say that the transmitter is a source of noise, in that they transmit lots of information which may distract from the message they are trying to convey!

For communication to take place at all there must be some kind of shared space, a medium through which the participants believe it is possible to communicate.

Based on what the receiver perceives, and their interpretation of the verbal and non-verbal input, they will form a concept of the meaning of the message. It will mean something to them, and it may or may not be what was intended by the sender. We could say that effective communication is when the receiver has the same understanding as the transmitter, or at least that the understanding is close enough to lead to the same result.

In communication systems like the internet, a receiver signals a transmitter to say that the message has been received and that it makes sense i.e. that it contains no errors.

Human communication works in the same way, so if I say something that makes grammatical sense, you will probably nod. If I say something that makes no sense, you might look confused or say, "I don't understand".

The problem is this: the receiver nods to signal "I understand what you just said", but the transmitter acts as if the nod means "I agree with you", when the result could actually be very different.

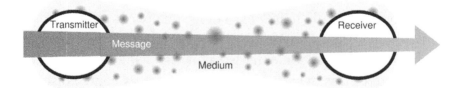

If a transmitter says a word such as "trust", she has a certain meaning attached to it in her reality based on her experiences of it. However, because words also have dictionary definitions it might appear as if the word is something very precise. Of course, a dictionary does not define a word, it merely translates it into other words. Those other words give us points of reference so that we might form an understanding of the word we're looking up.

Not all of the associations that the transmitter made about the word travel across the communication medium. What crosses the medium is the symbols, just like the codes I mentioned earlier.

When the receiver hears the word or sentence he will interpret it based on his experiences, perceptions, beliefs, expectations and opinions. He might also add in information from his own experiences in order to make it mean what he thinks it is supposed to mean.

There may be some agreement, at least within a particular culture, on some common experiences and objects. When you say "house" or "airport" or "happy" or "sad" most people will have an understanding very close to yours. But if you say words for abstract qualities, like "best", "right", "wrong", "tasty" and so on, then there is huge margin for error.

To have effective communication we need to understand this process so that we can compensate for its inefficiency and potential for error and misunderstanding.

Is there a simple solution? The first step is to be aware of this process. The second step is that when someone says, "I understand", bear in mind they don't really mean that they understand, they mean that they have processed something which sounds grammatically correct and which they have made some sense of. If your message is important, it's worth checking that what they received bore some relation to what you think you transmitted.

Noise could be one of the leading contributors to the breakdown of personal and professional relationships. That noise doesn't come from passing traffic, it comes from the noise within each person's own mind; the noise of assumptions, suspicions and conclusions. The noise of not saying something for fear of upsetting the other person, or the noise of having to say something because their silence obviously means that you've upset them.

In NLP there is a presupposition, "The meaning of the communication is the response you get", which applies here, because we can determine the effectiveness of communication simply by observing what happens as a result and comparing it to what we intended to achieve.

Feedback

Feedback is important in every technique, so I just wanted to take a moment to explain something important.

Often, when people use the word "positive" they mean "good", and by "negative" they mean "bad".

In NLP, we're using the strict definition of these terms instead of the more widely used ones.

In other words, positive simply means that something exists, or that you have more of it.

Negative means that something is in an opposite state or that you have less of it.

Positive feedback is not encouraging and does not focus on a person's strengths, because all feedback should be informative and neutral. Positive feedback simply means, "When you do more of x, y happens".

Negative feedback means, "When you do less of x, z happens".

For example, a driving instructor might tell a student to hold the steering wheel with their hands at a "ten to two" position (positive feedback) and to relax their grip on the steering wheel (negative feedback).

You'll find the word "positive" throughout this book, in the instructions for techniques. This always implies the strict definition; "explicitly stated, stipulated, or expressed".

8 Submodalities

Submodalities are the components (sub) of our senses (modalities) and help us to describe the qualities of our sensory experiences in a way that we don't do everyday, although other people will show you their submodalities non-verbally. If you haven't noticed this before, you'll be amazed when you begin to pay attention to people more literally.

Think about a time when you felt a bit down in the dumps. When you observe the mental image closely, do you notice if it seems brighter or darker than 'real life'?

Does it seem distant? Do any sounds seem distant too? Do the physical feelings feel heavy or cold?

Now think of a specific time when you felt happy, that you were enjoying yourself.

Is the picture bigger than before? Brighter? Are the sounds clearer? Louder?

Perhaps it even feels as if you're not looking at a picture at all, it's as if you are really there?

Why do you think that you don't remember events exactly as they were at the time?

I can't say for certain why this is, but we can map out the submodalities, which are the qualities we are comparing, and discover strong correlations between the submodalities of similar memories.

In general, for most people, pleasant memories tend to have bigger, brighter, closer, moving images, clear sounds and light, rising, warm feelings. Unpleasant memories tend to have dark, fuzzy, distant images, quiet, muffled sounds and cold, falling, heavy feelings.

Whilst submodalities appear to form as a result of the way that we naturally store memories, they do tell us about the distortions that we make in forming our perceptions.

A memory contains a huge volume of sensory information, but what interests us most about our memories is their meaning. We can easily think up examples of memories, given a label such as "surprised" or "confused", and what marks that memory as such is the unique combination of submodalities.

It's as if you have a mental filing room, and when you open the drawer marked "surprised", all the memories inside have the same brightness, temperature, weight, clarity and so on.

8.1 Compare Submodalities

Choose specific memories of two very different states; disappointed and proud.

Elicit and compare the submodalities of those states, starting with "disappointed".

Visual

Big	↔ Small
Close	↔ Far
High	↔ Low
Left	↔ Right
Moving	↔ Still
Colourful	↔ Black and white
Bright	↔ Dim
Focused	↔ Blurred
Associated	↔ Dissociated (you can see yourself)
One image	↔ Many images

Auditory

One location	↔ All around
Loud	↔ Soft
Fast	↔ Slow
High pitch	↔ Low pitch
Clear	↔ Muffled

Kinaesthetic

Moving	↔ Still
Growing	↔ Shrinking
Turning clockwise	↔ Turning anticlockwise
Rising	↔ Falling
Intense	↔ Subtle
Heavy	↔ Light
Warm	↔ Cold
Location in body	
Breathing fast	↔ Breathing slow
Breathing high	↔ Breathing low
Breathing deep	↔ Breathing shallow

Submodalities are one aspect of what constitutes a state, and the link works both ways. When the state changes, the submodalities change. Conversely, when you shift the submodalities, the state changes.

8.2 Try On Submodalities

Take your client's proud state and have them help you to 'try on' those submodalities.

Choose any thought and adjust the submodalities to match those of your client's.

How does that state feel to you? What name would you give it?

8.3 Change Submodalities

Take the disappointed state and play with the submodalities, like tuning an analogue radio or old fashioned TV.

Find the submodalities that seem to have the biggest effect on the overall state or the intensity of the response. If your client is happy to no longer feel disappointed about this memory, experiment with the submodalities, for example moving the picture closer or further away, turning the sounds up or down, moving the feelings around. Be prepared to try anything and notice what has an effect on their emotional state.

Your client may have neutralised their feelings naturally, corresponding to the submodalities.

Focus on changing their perception of the memory, for example,

- Tear the picture in half

- Move the picture to the location that corresponds to "things I no longer do"

- Separate the picture into a "bad" layer and a "learning" layer, then throw away the "bad" and integrate the "learning"

8.4 Swap Submodalities

Take the submodalities of 'proud' and apply those to the experience of 'disappointed'.

For example, let's say that the content of 'disappointed' was you standing in a room talking to someone. Let's say that the submodalities of 'proud' were visual bright, big, colourful, close, moving, auditory loud, clear, kinaesthetic warm, lifting, spreading.

Take the 'disappointed' picture and, one by one, invite your client to shift the submodalities to match those of 'proud', asking them to turn up the picture brightness, bring it closer, turn up the feeling temperature and so on.

How do they feel about that experience now?

8.5 Translate Submodalities

Submodalities are analogue, and can therefore increase and decrease in relative intensity. 'Bigger' is analogous to 'louder' or perhaps 'heavier'.

As you listen to your client talk about a current issue, translate submodalities from one sense to another.

For example, if they say, "It just feels heavy" then respond, "Does it also look dark and sound dull?"

Once you have set up a number of references, find out which are easiest for your client to change, e.g. they might not find it easy to make the problem weigh less, but they might be able to brighten the image or clarify the sounds.

8.6 Confusion to Understanding

Elicit your client's submodalities for a time when they felt confusion, and also for a time when they felt understanding.

Ask your client to choose a subject that they feel confused about and help them to shift the submodalities of their thoughts on that subject to those of understanding.

How does this affect their feelings towards the subject?

Internal Dialogue

One of the interesting aspects of our auditory sense is our ability to hold internal conversations, known in NLP as "internal dialogue" and in other fields as "self talk" or "the inner critic".

Do you ever pay attention to the vocal qualities of your internal dialogue, or do you simply take it for granted and act upon its instructions?

It's possible that your internal dialogue is actually a simulation of specific people. Listen carefully when you are being self critical, whose voice is it?

8.7 Internal Dialogue Modelling

Have your client describe a specific instance when they feel self critical. Have them describe it in detail so that they can get into full flow, and you can listen out for the signs of internal dialogue, including:

- Marked change in vocal qualities
- "I said to myself"
- "I told myself"
- "I thought..."

Play back the snippets of internal dialogue and ask your client to analyse who they might be role modelled from.

8.8   Internal Dialogue Tonality

Repeat the previous exercise, then invite your client to change the qualities of the dialogue.

Try changing the pitch, pace or intonation.

Also try out different characters, including:

- A news reader
- An angry teacher
- A cartoon character
- A caring friend
- A comedian
- Someone annoying

What effect does that have on how they feel about their internal dialogue?

8.9   Internal Dialogue Questioning

Have your client describe a specific instance when they feel self critical. Have them describe it in detail so that they can get into full flow, and you can listen out for the signs of internal dialogue, as in the previous exercise.

For each item of critical dialogue, invite your client to say any of the following to themselves.

- "Thank you"
- "Thank you. Can you tell me how that helps me?"
- "Get lost!!" (or similar)
- "Thank you. What do you suggest I do differently?"
- "Can you put that in writing please?"

What responses, of any kind, does your client experience?

You'll notice that questioning the internal dialogue validates it, whether you say "thank you" or not. Consider a colleague who is always pointing out what could go wrong. Before long, other people can't stand to listen to them and their voice becomes whinier and whinier. If you suppress your internal dialogue, it could be that the same thing happens.

Watch TV advertising for the next few days and notice any ways in which the advertisers manipulate the various submodalities to imply emotional relationships such as a feeling getting stronger regarding a product.

Notice how visual submodalities are manipulated to imply preference or desirability.

Notice examples of words such as bigger, brighter, clearer, sharper and notice how these words might connect with a change in your emotional response.

^{9} Anchoring

Your state is the basis for everything you do, so in NLP there are many techniques for managing your, and other people's state. Possibly the most well known is anchoring, which is the process by which Pavlov famously got his dogs excited at the sound of a bell ringing. Of course, we don't like to think of ourselves as being as easily influenced as animals so we don't like the term "conditioned response" yet it's exactly the same principle, and advertisers know this only too well.

You can be certain that the music and imagery in advertising are designed to invoke a specific emotional response which you will then associate with the brand which is shown at the end of the advert. Many brands have 'sound logos', designed to influence you, even if you're not watching the TV.

To understand anchoring, we must first understand a couple of concepts relating to our emotional state. Firstly, our memories are important in accessing states, and secondly, we respond most strongly to changes in state rather than the state itself. If a state does not move or change, it ebbs away.

There's a picture in the original NLP Practitioner course manual and many NLP books that looks like this:

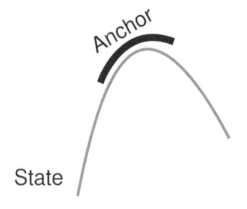

This is misleading as it only relates to states that increase in intensity, and it tells you to anchor when the state "peaks".

Unfortunately you have no way of knowing when the state will peak!. To wait for the peak implicitly means that you have missed it. You only know you've reached the top of a hill when you're on your way down again.

The more effective way to think about anchoring is to anchor a state change or transition. Your computer (or any device in your house with electronic control) uses a clock to synchronise the processor with the other parts of the system, memory, disc drives and so on. The entire system is synchronised to the clock pulse's transition, like this:

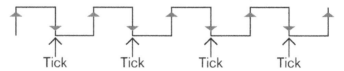

Every part of the system is synchronised to this central clock so that data can be moved around the system efficiently.

It's exactly the same with anchoring, The key to making anchoring work is to set the anchor at the moment of a state transition, not at the moment of a state 'peak'.

With anchoring, we are not aiming to control the maximum intensity of a state, we are aiming to control the moment that a particular state is triggered or accessed. Intensity can be built later if required.

In order to understand the process of anchoring, we must first understand why it is useful or even necessary to anchor.

Many people see anchoring purely as a method for accessing a state, so they would use it to make themselves feel good or energised, for example. While anchoring certainly can help with state management, that is not the reason that a NLP Practitioner needs to be able to do it. Recalling a 'resourceful state' is actually a trivial use of anchoring. In fact, it's useless because, by the time you have thought to access your chosen state, you are already in control and thinking about how you choose to feel in that scenario. You have already triggered the state, merely by thinking about it. The purpose of this type of anchoring is mainly to impress the audience during training; it's a parlour trick.

As a NLP Practitioner, you know that your clients already have the resources they need in order to effect change. They don't need any new ones. You therefore use anchoring as a way of managing the process of change.

Imagine the situation. A client walks into your office and says, "I have this terrible fear of flying, but it's preventing me from doing things that I want to do. Can you help me?"

"Sure". You say. "But first of all, I need to understand exactly how your fear works. Fears are usually driven by something useful, like a protecting instinct, and I want to make sure that I understand exactly what's happening."

"Um... OK then. I guess that's OK"

"Great, thanks. So, could you get scared of flying for me?"

"Well... it's difficult in this office. It's not like a plane."

"I see. OK. Book two seats on a flight for tomorrow morning, and we'll go take a look together."

Not very practical, is it?

Notice also that there is, in this interaction, a fundamental principle of operation in NLP which is somewhat different to other therapeutic approaches. In NLP, we don't seek out how the fear began, we only want to know if it is happening now.

Some people see this as a superficial approach; dealing with the symptom of the problem and not the 'root cause' which may be 'deep rooted'. In many other forms of therapy, understanding the cause of a behaviour is the key to understanding and then modifying it. In NLP, understanding the trigger for a response or behaviour is all we need. Therefore, NLP can be used as a 'content free' approach, in which the client doesn't actually need to put the problem into words. This is very useful when the problem is embarrassing or traumatic.

I'm not saying that the historical cause of a behaviour is not important, only that it is just one example of what triggered the behaviour. Fundamentally, behaviour is learned, but we can't change how or when you learned it. We can only change how you respond now, so by building more choice into the point at which you would usually respond, you generate new behaviours, hence the use of the word "generative" to describe NLP's approach.

Back to our example, how can you understand a client's fear of flying without actually taking them on a plane? Maybe you could get them to talk, in detail, about what happens when they fly. They might 'relive' the experience and feel it as if it's real. That's a good start, but we can't get our clients to keep talking through the whole story, over and over again.

Anchoring is the solution.

The primary reason that a NLP Practitioner uses anchoring is to be able to control a client's response to a stimulus in order to change that response, to manage the process of change.

Here's another example. My computer has a problem. When it's most inconvenient, my computer crashes and I lose my work. I have no idea why, but I wish it wouldn't do it.

I need to reproduce the problem, so I turn off various add-ons until the computer is running in a simple configuration. Then I keep a note of what I'm doing when it crashes. Then, when I think I know what's causing the problem, I perform that action on purpose. If the computer crashes, I've found the cause. I have a much better chance of fixing my computer if I can consistently reproduce the problem. This is a better approach than "Do a clean reinstall". Computers, like people, do not behave randomly. Also, you can't reinstall people.

Anchoring is usually taught by using a memory of a time when you felt a particular emotional state. Often, on a NLP course, people will pick "relaxed" and will then have trouble anchoring the state, and there is an important reason why; imagine yourself sitting down during a training course. From there to "relaxed" is not a big change, and anchoring works by associating an event with a state change. Think back to the analogy of the 'clock pulse'. The change needs to be big enough that every part of the system clearly recognises it. In this example of "relaxed", your brain is picking up too much background noise for the state change to really stand out.

Here's a picture of the transition from "rest" to "relaxed":

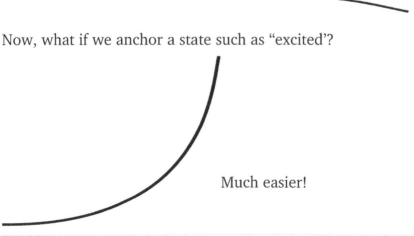

Now, what if we anchor a state such as "excited'?

Much easier!

9.1 Anchoring

We're going to start with a "touch" anchor because it's easy to set up while talking to and observing your client.

Ask your client where they would be happy having an anchor applied - to their arm, hand or shoulder, perhaps?

Ask your client what state he or she would like to experience, and make it something energetic such as excited or even angry. Imagine being in that state yourself to lead your client in.

Ask your client to recall a specific memory of that state.

Explore the submodalities of that memory, and when you notice your client begin to go into the target state, apply the anchor; touch their hand, squeeze their arm etc.

Break state, then have your client imagine experiencing the state strongly as you apply the anchor again. Repeat the reinforcement as many times as you feel you need to, asking the client to work with you to intensify and build the state each time.

Each time you reinforce the anchor, decrease the delay between asking your client to recall the state and applying the touch. Their nervous system is trying to make shortcuts, you have to stay one step ahead.

Break state, then test the anchor. Distract your client by talking about something else for a moment and then set off the anchor. Ask them what they notice. It may be a subtle or strong feeling, or even a sound or image.

A break state is a very important part of the process, because you need to reset your client's state, ready to set the anchor again.

To break state, either ask them about something in the room, the colour of the carpet, for example, or ask them to remember something that's hard to remember such as which side their hot tap is on at home.

The more times you reinforce an anchor, the more consistently it will work and the longer it will last. Your aim is to leave your client's brain in no doubt about what to do when you trigger the anchor. To test, just reproduce the anchor and ask if the memory or state comes back.

You may have seen 'life change' TV programs in which the resident coach gave the participant an anchor for confidence, getting the participant to squeeze their finger tips together. Whilst this is usefully visual for TV, it is not, in fact, a very effective way to anchor. An anchor ideally needs to be something unique. If it is not, it will easily become 'over-written' by other day to day experiences.

Language is a powerful anchor, and you can easily recall a state if you have anchored it with a word.

9.2 Translating an Anchor

A touch anchor is a good start, but it might not be very practical for every day use. If we are also to use an anchor as a way to access a particular state, we must be able to do it in a way that is more discrete and versatile.

An anchor can be any stimulus in any sensory system. A smell or a piece of music might all elicit certain emotions. What about a word?

Does the word "happy" make you feel happy? Probably not. What about words such as "tickle", "smile", "bubbles", "ice cream" or "sunshine". These words relate not to the label for the state but to our emotional experience of it. They therefore make much better anchors than the labels we usually apply.

To start, you'll need your touch anchor from the previous exercise. Test it again, and take some time to reinforce it. Now, ask your client to choose a word that represents their target state. They might choose a colour too.

On the count of three, set off the touch anchor as the client says the word. Break state and repeat.

Test the anchor by asking the client to say the word to themselves, observing the external signs of the state.

Invite your client to continue reinforcing the new anchor.

> List some inputs or triggers that you recognise are already anchors for you

I've covered the setting of a basic anchor, and I'll return to anchoring again later on.

Remember, anchoring is the basic process of making a connection, and that is also the process of learning. Therefore, anchoring is the first step towards learning, perhaps a new behaviour or a new attitude.

Many mnemonic techniques use anchoring to teach amazing feats of memory, such as remembering a long shopping list, names at a party of even counting cards in a casino.

The ancient Greeks called one mnemonic tool the "method of locus" or the method of places. To remember a sequence of information such as a shopping list or a speech, they would imagine walking a familiar route, seeing reminders along the way that marked a particular point in a speech that they wanted to memorise..

Because anchoring is such a fundamental part of NLP, it is far more valuable and versatile than just a state change tool. Anchoring is part of every NLP technique, as a way of controlling the process of change.

For now, you've now learned a number of ways that you can influence your state, and all of these techniques fall into two broad categories; focus of attention and physiology.

In reality, both work to influence our state and also as elements of our state. You know that if you smile while on the telephone, your voice tone changes. You also know that when you feel miserable, other people can see it because you sit and move differently.

To get people to move in their minds, for example, in a learning or negotiation context, it's important to get them to move in their bodies. If a meeting is proving to be hard going, suggest you all get some fresh air and a drink. Get people moving and their minds will move with you.

Many high level, professional negotiators have said that they rarely make any progress when sat around a table. The time when the negotiation really moves forwards is when they take a break, go for a walk and end up chatting at the coffee machine.

Do not underestimate the importance of physiology, because your mind and body are part of the same system so getting someone moving on the outside is often the easiest way to get them moving on the inside.

Finally, the simplest way to recall a specific state is to think of a time when you felt that way. If you want to relax, remember a specific time when you felt relaxed. In order to process the memory, you feel the relaxation not in the past but right now.

More Anchors

I have shown you some different methods for basic anchoring, and we have seen that associations can be made between any input and any output. An output doesn't have to be a state as in a generic state of happiness or confidence, it is in fact more useful to think of an output as being a specific response. People don't wander around feeling happy, something makes them happy, even if that is the process of choosing to think happy thoughts.

A response from an anchor could be an internal feeling such as happiness or confidence, or it could be a more overt behaviour, such as closing the fridge door instead of picking up a snack, or standing up to deliver a presentation instead of cowering in the corner.

Also, anchors are not only on/off switches that trigger a response, they allow analogue control over the intensity of a state.

Because we have focused on triggering simple states, it's easy to miss the fact that what we've actually also done is build the intensity of states. Reinforcing anchors achieves this, and there are other ways to do it too, giving you a much finer degree of control over the intensity of a state or response.

In what situations might this be useful?

9.3 Sliding Anchors

Ask your client to come up with a state to use in the exercise, and find a specific instance of them experiencing that state.

Now choose a means of setting a basic anchor so that you can vary the anchor, for example anchoring at various points up their arm, or with a word at various volume or pitch levels.

Set the first anchor in the middle of the range.

'Tone down' the state and anchor at a lower position.

Now move up and down the anchors so that you trigger the state at its middle and lower intensities.

High

Middle

Low

When you can control the intensity at these points, begin to creep up towards the 'high' point. Let your whole physiology, expression, language and voice tone reflect the growing intensity. Occasionally bring the state back down to the first two anchor points and then intensify it again.

Remember throughout that each anchor is a trigger. Imagine each anchor as a 'bounce' on a trampoline. When you time your 'bounces' just right, you can bounce higher and higher; much further than you would have bounced just by jumping.

How much can you intensify the state?

How many uses for a sliding anchor can you think of?

There are more interesting things that we can do with anchors. For example, we can stack anchors on top of each other so that one trigger leads to a number of responses.

The 'translating anchors' exercise is a form of stacking anchors. We don't take the original touch anchor away, we just add a word on top of it so that both can trigger the state.

We can stack anchors in two ways; firstly, we can assign more inputs to the same output. Secondly, we can join two similar states by triggering them at the same time.

The very first exercise in this book, where you used physiology in walking to access a state, was a form of stacking anchors. Do you remember trying to combine the three states into one?

9.4 Stacking Anchors (Inputs)

Add more anchors to the first basic anchor that you set. Try different locations, words, sounds, colours, music, smells, anything that you can think of.

9.5 Stacking Anchors (Outputs)

Choose two complimentary states that you think would be useful to combine. For example, happy and energetic, or determined and focused. They should have similar energy levels.

Set basic anchors for both states using touch and in locations where you'll next be able to read both at the same time. Or example, one on each wrist or elbow.

Test both anchors, breaking state in between, so that they work reliably.

Now trigger both anchors at the same time.

What do you experience?

Circle of Excellence

This is a popular technique with many trainers, although it is not actually part of the Practitioner syllabus.

Circle of Excellence is essentially an anchoring exercise. It relies heavily on existing associations such as colour, and on movement to create 'spatial anchors'.

9.6 Circle of Excellence

Think of a resource that you would like to access, such as a state or belief.

Place an imaginary circle on the floor in front of you.

Imagine that within that circle lies the resource. You might add a colour which seems appropriate for the resource.

When you are ready, and only when you are ready to fully take on the resource, step into the circle.

As you cross the boundary, feel the resource flowing into you. If you chose a colour, see it washing over you.

Circle of Excellence

Start

Take a moment to allow the resource to settle in and then, when you are ready, step back out of the circle, leaving the resource behind.

Step into and out of the circle a few times so that the boundary is clearly marked and you can feel the resource only within the circle.

Now, take a situation that you would like to feel differently about or approach with a new perspective. When you are ready, hold the situation in your mind and step into the circle.

What seems different?

The 'Circle of Excellence' technique uses 'spatial anchoring' to mark out the states that correspond to the circles. For the next few days, look around you and notice other ways in which 'spatial anchors' are marked out.

Anchoring at Work

If you've practised the use of kinaesthetic anchors, you might be thinking that you can't just go around touching people, especially at work. Well, it's quite likely that you already do. You just do it accidentally, without a clear purpose other than to make a social connection with someone. Anything that you do or say, consistently, becomes part of another person's experience of you, and that is an anchor.

Any time you ask someone to recall an experience, you are accessing their anchors. As they recall the details, they will move into the emotional states connected with those details.

Think about a time at work when you've felt frustrated, perhaps undervalued or not listened to. What happened? What words did you hear? Or not hear? How does that make you feel? Now think about a time at work when you created something new and other people really noticed what you'd contributed to the team. How did that feel?

Eliciting an emotional state is as easy as asking someone to think of it. You actually don't need to set up anchors by touching people or assigning colours, their own words are already powerful anchors, and are all you need if you're paying attention. You are paying attention, aren't you?

To elicit a particular emotional state, it's very helpful if you first set some constraints, and we could call this 'setting the scene'. Let's try an exercise to practice this.

9.7 Conversational Anchors

1. Set the scene

This is essentially a pace and lead, and you're also doing something very important in terms of building rapport, which is to share your intentions. If you launch straight in with questions, your client will most likely be wondering why you're asking them. You also want to constrain their responses, which makes it easier for them to think of a specific instance.

"I'm interested in learning how you've dealt with frustrations in the past, because that's something that I think we all face, and I feel you're someone who can be quite creative in overcoming obstacles, can I ask you about that?"

2. Ask for a specific memory

"Can you remember a time when that has happened? What can you tell me about it?"

3. Listen and watch

Whilst they're talking, pay attention to their:

- Words - particularly words that they mark out with an emotional response, a pause, emphasis etc
- Voice tone - particularly when they're marking out words, or when their voice tone changes
- Movements - particularly any movements to mark out certain words, or points when their body posture changes
- Rhythm - the general pace and rhythm or their words and movements, particularly any changes of speed

4. If necessary, ask for meaning

If they're describing the situation in a dispassionate, dissociated way with little emotional connection, you can force an emotional response by asking for meaning.

"And what did that mean to you?"

"And how was that important for you?"

5. Play back and test

All being well, you will have seen a number of states, starting with an undesirable state and ending with some kind of resolution state.

Play back the sequence you've heard, as a set of instructions, using the anchor words of the different states in your summary. As you say each anchor word, watch your client's state follow.

Ask them to confirm if you've understood them correctly.

For example, "So, let me check that I understand you, there was a project at work that had been *dropped* on you, and you *felt* that you were already *chasing your tail*, and then when your computer crashed and you had to *step back* and give yourself some *air*, you realised that the *heavy feeling* of *pressure* was because of your need to *show* that you could handle it, and once you could *see yourself* trying to please others, you realised that you could create that *space* any time you want, and you don't even need an excuse, you can just go and get some *air*, take a break, whatever you need. Is that right?"

Keen-eyed readers will notice a sequence here, moving from kinaesthetic to visual dissociated. That's what changed the client's state, not the computer or the project or the facts of the story, but something that led them to dissociate from the feelings. That's the change you're reproducing using the conversational sequence of anchors. If you see that person at work getting stressed, you can use that anchor word, *air*. You don't even have to tell them to get some air, you can refer to yourself and the word will still affect their state and behaviour.

"Wow, I was feeling heavy today, I'm going to get some air"

"I really enjoyed getting some fresh air at the weekend"

"Is the air conditioning working today?"

Swish

Sometimes, people will act in a certain way through a habit or other unconscious process. No matter how hard they try, they always wind up acting or responding in the same way because by the time they realise they're doing it, it's already too late.

Anchoring was the process of connecting together a sensory input with a physiological output. It would be useful if we could also reverse the process of anchoring to break existing associations, but we can't, because your brain's connections can't be broken, they can only be replaced with more favourable or well used connections.

The advent of aerial photography revolutionised archaeology. Features, invisible on the ground, could clearly be seen from the air. Roman roads and buried buildings could easily be seen from this new perspective, giving archaeologists clear direction for their research.

Just because those ancient roads aren't used any more doesn't mean they're not there. It's simply more convenient to use the new routes.

However true that may be, it is much easier to simplify the situation, and say that anchoring is a technique for making connections, the swish is a technique for breaking them.

The swish can be used to change almost any habitual pattern of behaviour where the behaviour can be traced back to a specific trigger. For example, if you're having trouble dieting, your desire to raid the fridge can be traced back to a single thought or event.

9.8 Swish

Find something that your client would like to be different which involves some kind of reaction to someone or something. You need to track down the precise moment that the undesirable response is triggered.

For example, if you want to swish a fear of mice, don't picture standing on a chair, make it the very instant the mouse appears. Hold one hand up in front of the person's face and ask them to put the picture there. Let's call that the 'old' hand, it doesn't seem to matter which you use.

Now create a picture of a desired outcome which can be anything that is different to the "problem". Hold your other hand up and ask your client to place the outcome image there. Let's call this the 'new' hand.

Put your hands down by your side. By attaching the images to your hands, you have created a visual anchor.

With your 'new' hand ready, bring your 'old' hand up into the client's field of vision. Only wait long enough for the reaction begin, perhaps no more than half a second.

Swap your hands over, quickly growing the 'new' outcome picture to replace the 'old' picture as the 'old' picture shrinks away.

As the images swap over, make a "whoosh" or "swish" sound to surprise the client and get their attention.

Swap the images over as quickly as you can, and bring your 'new' hand, the outcome picture, right into your client's face, almost hitting them on the nose.

Hold the outcome image in front of your client's eyes for a few seconds.

Break state and repeat three times, using different 'new' pictures to disrupt the old reaction.

To test, ask your client to try to remember the way they used to react.

What seems different?

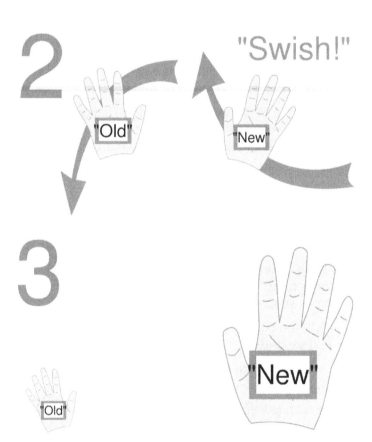

How does the swish work?

You can use the swish pattern in many different ways, and it is one of the most powerful and important techniques in NLP.

With the swish, we are setting up a new response pattern, a new "habit" which is preferable to the old one. People continue to have habitual responses that no longer serve a useful purpose for them, simply because the unwanted response has become so familiar. Because the swish is about rewriting unconscious responses, the faster you do it, the better it works.

One more thing to remember with the Swish. This is the first technique we've covered that needs you to see things from the client's point of view.

Different cultures around the world understand the concept of time differently. In Western cultures that read and write from left to right, people generally see the future in front of them or to the right. Therefore, in many NLP techniques, you have to reverse your normal view of the world so that your behaviour enhances the technique rather than working against it.

The swish makes use of another basic principle; the pattern interrupt.

Have you ever been interrupted half way through doing something and completely forgotten what you had been doing? Whenever you are doing something on "auto pilot", your behaviour is following a well rehearsed pattern. Changing gear in your car, typing your computer password and shaking hands are all common examples of patterns. In fact, if you have seen stage hypnotists or TV mentalists, you have probably seen them using a "handshake interrupt" to get their subject's attention.

Normally, a pattern runs so quickly that there is no way to change it. Hearing your boss' voice or seeing a spider leads you to react so quickly that your reaction is almost the first sign of the problem.

By controlling the trigger with a visual anchor, you can control the timing of the pattern, which means that you can interrupt it. When you both interrupt the pattern and replace the outcome, you create the possibility for change. It's as if you have prised open the pattern to discover its inner workings.

> Does a swish have to be visual? What else could you try?

A visual swish is very fast and easy to do, but you may feel a little self conscious waving your hands in peoples' faces in a restaurant.

Of course, if you know to expect a pattern then you can interrupt it, so you can either anchor the trigger or you can perform the interrupt in "real time".

An auditory swish can be as subtle as an interruption and suggestion in the middle of a conversation.

A kinaesthetic swish is essentially the collapsing or chaining of anchors that I covered earlier.

Keys to getting the swish to work every time are:

- Know what you're doing in advance so that you don't have to stop to think half way through.

- Do it fast. Very fast.

- Hold the undesired current state only as long as you need to trigger the "old" response, less than a second.

You may not get your "old" hand anywhere near your client's face before you see their reaction starting.

- Continue to reinforce the desired state and fade out the undesired state.

- Don't be tempted to swish in the "correct" response, just go for anything that's different.

You only need to break the old pattern, a new fixed pattern is no more useful than the old fixed pattern, since our aim is to introduce choice. In practising the swish, you will learn how to change habitual behaviours. There is a sequence of events here that happens very quickly because your brain only learns things quickly. Slow learning does not work, because it gives you time to think and thinking is not always helpful!

Friends and colleagues often try to help by getting you to talk about the problem which usually makes it worse, because you get more of what you focus on. From a NLP point of view, the problem is already in the past and the swish pushes it even further behind you, focusing you on the present and future. A traditional counselling and therapeutic concept is that if you understand why you have the problem, you will be closer to solving it. The NLP concept is that understanding why you have the problem is of no use in solving it because the problem is not happening in the past, it is happening now. You feel your fear of public speaking now, not in the past when you recall a presentation that went badly for you.

In order to solve the problem, we need only to understand how it is operating now, the sequence of mental steps that operate now to lead you from the first thought to the emotional response that is the hallmark of the problem. In fact, we could say that the problem is not public speaking, or cold calling, or spiders, the problem is that you feel bad when you think about those things.

By finding the choice point in the process, you are finding the point at which it is easiest to introduce change.

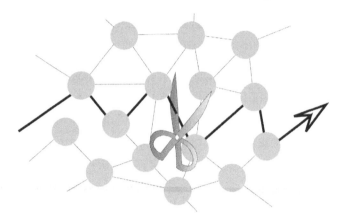

There's no point trying to manage stress once you are stressed, as it's too late and trying to manage your stress (or anger) just makes you more stressed. Instead we need to focus on what happens before you get stressed so that you can go off in a different direction altogether.

It makes a lot of sense when you think about it. There's no point looking at the map for directions to London when you're already in Edinburgh. It's easier to plan your route before you go in the direction you don't want to go in.

The second important part of the swish is the outcome. You cannot replace something with nothing. You cannot just take a thought out of your head. It's like trying to stop thinking about an annoying piece of music. You cannot turn it off, you can only replace it. The swish does not take away the unwanted thought, it simply offers a more desirable one.

You can swish with a piece of paper, by writing down aspects of the problem and then, when the person is really focussed on the paper (their state is anchored to it) just screw it up, throw it away and start again on a blank sheet.

The simple process to remember for adapting the swish technique to any situation is:

- Find the point at which the person has choice

- Interrupt their normal, habitual thought process

- Focus their attention on what they do want Remember, state is not just the trivial matter of how you feel, it is the mental, physical and perceptual foundation for everything you do, and it will greatly affect the results that you get.

Here are some more suggestions for ways to use the swish:

- In a restaurant, anchor the undesired state to the plate and let the waiter take it away

- Use a flipchart or notepad to swish, tearing the edge of the page beforehand so that it rips off neatly

- Swish in a business report by turning the page, having the current situation on one page, followed by the desired outcome on the next

- Swish in a computer presentation by clicking from one slide to the next

Squash

A simple light switch is a digital component of an electrical system. It has two states; on and off. There is no in between. A dimmer switch has on, off, and many levels in between.

Can a simple light switch be both on and off at the same time? What would happen if you tried to set it to that position? You might hear a crackling noise as electricity tries to jump across the contacts. This is not an in between state. Either current flows through the contacts, or it doesn't.

What about a dimmer switch. Can you set it to 'high' and 'low' at the same time? What if you rapidly move it from high to low, is that an 'in between' state?

You're essentially trying to get two different energy levels to coexist in the same system at the same time, which is generally not possible. What if we try that with anchoring?

We've looked at various ways to use anchors, and because anchoring is a "building block" of NLP's tool kit, you'll find it in most of the techniques. In the squash, we combine anchors to generate a new state or response.

The swish works by interrupting a habitual pattern and introducing choice. The squash works by resolving a conflict or dilemma, creating an alternative choice.

You've no doubt seen people naturally "weighing up their options" in their hands like this before, so this is a great example of a technique that you can use in everyday situations without people thinking you're strange.

9.9 Visual Squash

To start with, you take the two choices, or the two sides of the conflict, and hold one in each hand. Let's call them A and B, just to break with tradition.

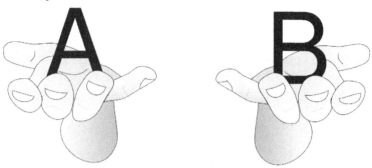

With one option in each hand, take a moment to really clarify each one, imagining something that represents the option in the palm of your hand. Take some time to call to mind all of the images, sounds and feelings associated with each option.

When you've got a clear understanding of what each option is, just gently bring your hands together, slowly. Some people find this part incredibly difficult! Just allow your hands to come together at whatever speed feels right, and when your hands are close together, just squash the two options into each other, like this:

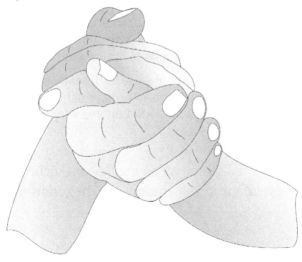

Many people, at this point, experience some very odd feelings, tingling across the back, the release of tension, conflicting feelings ebbing and flowing. It's really interesting that these simple techniques can have such a profound physical effect.

If you have experienced such a response, wait until it subsides, and then open your hands. As soon as you do so, the very first thing that comes to mind, perhaps that you even see in front of you, is the result, option C:

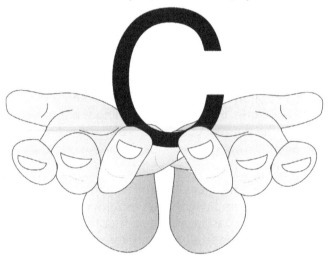

The end result of this is that option C combines the important elements of A and B and "feels right" as a course of action. The result could be a combination, or A, or B, or something completely different, or nothing at all. Just see what happens and consider what it might mean.

While this is called the visual squash, it really combines both visual and touch, or kinaesthetic, anchoring. It's one of the few NLP techniques that you can use very effectively by yourself.

The visual squash is known as a 'negotiation technique'. How could you adapt it to a commercial negotiation?

9.10 Spatial Squash

Imagine two circles on the floor, just big enough to step into, quite close together.

Consider the two parts of the dilemma or compromise and get a clear idea of how you might represent each of them, what images come to mind, any sounds or feelings and what name you might give each of them. For now we'll call them options A and B - you can call them whatever you like.

Place option A in one circle.

Place option B in the other circle.

As you get ready to step into circle A, bring to mind the images, sounds and feelings that you associate with option A, and when you are ready, step into the circle and fully immerse yourself in this option.

Step out of circle A.

As you get ready to step into circle B, bring to mind the images, sounds and feelings that you associate with option B, and when you are ready, step into the circle and fully immerse yourself in this option.

Step out of circle B.

Once you've tested both spatial anchors and you have a reliable response from stepping into each circle, you can combine them.

Step into both circles at the same time, one foot in each.

What do you notice?

9.11 Kinaesthetic Squash (Collapsing Anchors)

First, you'll need to anchor an undesired response; a reaction that your client has but wishes they didn't.

As with the stacking anchors exercise, use a touch anchor and choose a location that you can easily reach for both anchors at the same time. The shoulders are ideal.

Let's say that it's a state of anxiety prior to a presentation or interview. Anchor the anxiety and test the anchor to make sure it works consistently. No matter how bad your client feels as a result of you setting the anchor, it's not real.

Break state. Get up and walk around the room and really take your client's mind off the anchor you've just set.

Choose a new state to anchor, something very different. Do not anchor the way that the client would like to feel in the difficult situation, because that would be finding the 'right' state, which will definitely be 'wrong'.

Find a totally new state, such as getting the giggles or crossing the finishing line of a race, exhausted.

Anchor this second state and test it.

Set off both anchors at the same time, the undesirable response a moment before the second response, and holding the different response a little after you have released the undesired.

Hold both anchors and squeeze the anchors very gently just to keep the states in place. After a few seconds, release both anchors.

1. First down
2. Second down
3. Hold and reinforce
4. First up
5. Second up

Imagine that the anchors are flowing like a wave from the first to the second anchor. The delay between the first and second should be perhaps half a second to a second, only long enough for you to see the first state being triggered.

Allow a little longer, perhaps a second, between lifting the first and second anchors.

The whole process of collapsing the anchors will last for maybe 5 to 8 seconds.

Allow your client a few moments to take in what just happened. They'll let you know when they're ready to talk.

> How can you explain what happens when you collapse anchors?

Fortunately, you are not a light switch. By triggering two anchors at the same time, you force two states to coexist in the same system, which they cannot.

Collapsing anchors is not about "overwriting" a "bad" state with a "good" state. Presuming the "right" response is one of the biggest dangers in NLP. NLP is a generative process; you disrupt problematic patterns and provide an environment within which a more useful result emerges. But you can not and must not dictate that result.

Furthermore, neither of those states or responses was bad or good; both were appropriate at some time in some situation. Just because the client would prefer that something didn't happen doesn't mean that it didn't happen for a reason.

Let's take a common response; fear of spiders. For some people, this problem develops to the level that it is utterly debilitating. They won't even go into certain rooms of their own house. Yet in itself, their response is not wrong. It is merely less appropriate in some parts of the world than in others. If you live in the UK, the chances of being in danger from a spider bite, or a bite from any animal, are slim. For some people, even thinking about spiders is unpleasant. Yet thinking about a roller-coaster ride, or a day at the beach, or a walk in the countryside is much more enjoyable. Yet they are all simply thoughts.

In the UK, we don't check under the toilet seat for spiders, as some people say they have to do in Australia. If I went to the toilet in Australia, I would want someone with me who had a fear of spiders. They would be the first person to spot one!

One of the operating beliefs, or "presuppositions" of NLP is that no behaviour is right or wrong in itself, you just have to remember that there's a time and a place. Our goal as NLP

Practitioners is not to change peoples' behaviour, it's to give them more choice over their behaviour.

Being afraid of a spider and being pleased to see a spider are two different states or configurations of the same system. Your pulse rate cannot be high and low at the same time. You cannot move away from and towards the spider at the same time.

The result of collapsing together these two, very opposite, states is that the system, namely your client, goes into a brief period of confusion, then reorganisation. A new state emerges that is neither of the two original states but something new. The fear state has not been "overwritten", like your computer's hard drive, it has been added to, extended, grown, enhanced and reorganised. This is what makes NLP a 'generative' approach.

You can still see a spider; they haven't gone away. You can still feel fear; that is a vital survival instinct. But the connection between the two has changed.

You've tried a visual squash and a kinaesthetic squash. Could there be an auditory squash?

The squash relies on triggering two conflicting anchors at the same time. We can do that by merging two images, or by triggering two touch anchors together. But how do we play back two sounds or words at the same time?

A verbal anchor is, of course, not just the word, it is the word, plus the voice tone, plus the context, plus the facial expression. The word is only 7% of the anchor. Does this give you any clues for how we might create an auditory squash, so that we can integrate conflict in a natural conversation?

I do like to say that your job as a NLP Practitioner is not to solve your clients' problems, it is to break those problems so that they don't work any more.

9.12 Auditory Squash

Ask your client to talk about a situation that they would like to feel differently about. Notice the words that they repeat or emphasise and make a note of these, including the voice tones, facial expressions and gestures.

Break state, then ask your client to talk about a situation where they feel a very different state such as positive, energised, optimistic or excited. You choose the state, otherwise they will choose something which is constrained by the undesirable state. Again, notice the words that they repeat or emphasise and make a note of these, including the voice tones, facial expressions and gestures.

Break state, and then talk to the client about the possibilities for change and learning, and use their anchor words, combining the word of one state with the tone and visual non-verbal aspects of the other. Mix them both ways. You'll need to prepare for this, it can be tricky to juggle the combinations the first time you try it. Keep going, though, and play with it. Make up a story, talk about a future scenario in which the client is achieving more and enjoying the change, whatever comes to mind.

Finally, ask your client to try to recall how they used to feel in the first situation and ask them what seems different.

10 Outcomes

The secret to getting what you want is knowing what you want.

Of course, that's obvious, yet you'd be surprised how many people don't have a clear idea of what they want. When you have a very clear set of outcomes, every action and thought reinforces those outcomes and takes you a step closer to achieving them.

When you don't have clear outcomes, your thoughts and actions tend to be more random, so you have to think consciously about what you do, and you have to waste time correcting actions that take you in the wrong direction.

Frequently, people have a very clear idea of what they don't want, and they only know when things are going wrong for them. They tend to bounce from one wrong course of action to the next, never settling on a clear direction.

You can see how this works for yourself by asking a decorator to paint your bedroom, "not blue".

In business, we think we set clear goals, yet mostly these goals are not phrased in language your brain understands, so they're actually quite useless.

What I mean is that people often express goals in abstract, symbolic terms rather than concrete, sensory terms.

A goal like "To complete this project by September 1st" sounds very specific, but it really doesn't mean much in concrete terms until you look at a calendar. The various people involved in the project will have different definitions of "complete". Although we use dates and times as fixed, absolute markers, your brain treats them as very elastic concepts because we all have a different way of coding and representing time. In particular, the concept of "now" is different for each of us.

In order to process a goal like "To complete this project by September 1st", your brain has to create a representation of a completed project (different for everyone) and to imagine it as if that were happening right now (different for everyone) so when September 1st comes round, people disagree over the status of the project for two main reasons. Firstly, definitions of "completion" differ from one person to the next. Secondly, and more importantly, in the time coming up to September 1st, people differ in their sense of urgency. You can imagine how disagreements can arise so easily when you don't specify goals.

Setting a clear outcome is fundamental to NLP, both for choosing a direction to move in and more specifically in undertaking change work. If you begin by getting the client to set a clear outcome, you will have far more flexibility and scope to explore than if you begin by looking for a problem to fix. You'll also often find that setting an outcome is all that you need to do.

In the following exercise, you will help your client to come up with a goal. It might be something short term or something long term and aspirational. You may want to write the goal down, if you do so make sure you write it down precisely as they say it - don't be tempted to paraphrase or restate it. Always use other people's words, especially when their dreams are involved.

Finally, there are spaces after the questions so that you can try the exercise yourself.

10.1 Well Formed Outcomes

1. What do you want?

2. Is that something you want to achieve rather than avoid?

3. When, where, with whom do you want it?

4. How will you know when you've got it? What will you see, hear, feel, taste and smell?

5. What will you gain or keep by achieving this outcome?

6. What might you lose by achieving this outcome?

7. What will you gain or keep if you don't achieve this outcome?

8. What might you lose if you don't achieve this outcome?

9. What is the first step that you can take that is under your control?

10. What resources do you have to support you in this?

11. Offer your hand, palm up, to your client and ask, "If I offered [outcome] to you right now, would you take it?"

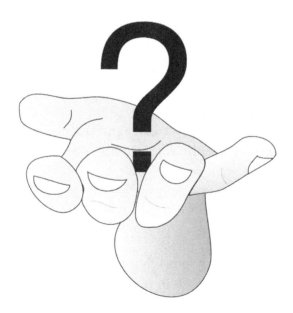

PURE

Just to remind you of the four criteria for a "Well Formed Outcome":

Positively stated: What you want to achieve, not avoid

Under your control: Achieving the goal is solely down to you

Real: See, hear, feel and perhaps taste or smell the outcome

Ecological: The outcome is valuable for every part of you as a balanced system

A goal doesn't have to be well formed, it's just that if it is well formed you are more likely to get what you want. What are the implications of a goal not satisfying those criteria?

Positively stated: You'll move away from what you don't want, but you may not get quite what you do want.

Under your control: You can't put 100% of your energy into achieving the goal, so it will seem more difficult or frustrating to achieve.

Real: You'll get something, but it won't be exactly what you want.

Ecological: You may get what you want but at some point an unplanned side effect will pop up, or you may lose something that you didn't expect to.

So if what you want is some chocolate, and you don't have a clear representation of the outcome, it probably doesn't matter what kind of chocolate bar you get. If you want a new job then you can't afford to be so vague. You can determine how well formed a goal needs to be, based on how important it is to you.

Of course, since it takes only seconds to create a Well Formed Outcome, why should you go through life not getting exactly what you want more easily?

People often ask how Well Formed Outcomes relates to a goal setting tool like SMART.

Simply, Well Formed Outcomes is a tool for setting a direction when you can't control the precise end result. SMART is a tool for specifying an end result without the means to get there. It's a good tool to use when delegating a task, because it allows room for the person performing the task to figure out the best way to complete it.

Well Formed Outcomes is about setting a direction because, for a long term goal, you can't be certain that things will stay the same along the way. For example, you could set yourself a goal for promotion but be made redundant before you can achieve it. However, you can be sure that you will make progress in your pursuit of the goal; more progress than if you simply focused on the end result.

SMART is more objective, Well Formed Outcomes is more subjective, and both are important.

In practice, a good project manager will follow up a SMART objective with an action plan to achieve it.

A Well Formed Outcome appears to contain a specific end result which you can see, hear and feel, however the reality is that you can control the destination or the journey but not both, when the world is not under your control.

For example, if I give you a set of turn by turn directions from your house to a meeting venue, you may or may not arrive, depending on what factors have arisen that make those directions obsolete. A road may be closed for directions, and if you don't know where you're supposed to be, you can't get there.

Specifying the destination means that you have to work out the route for yourself, which is fine as long as you have a map.

How would you plan such a route? First you might open up a road map. Where would you look next? Would you locate the destination, or your present location?

Most people look for the destination first and then work back to their point of origin, and this is precisely what happens in Well Formed Outcomes, and also in a collection of techniques known as "timeline" which I will explore later.

In practice, the only real difference between Well Formed Outcomes and SMART is that Well Formed Outcomes does not have an explicit timeframe, although I recommend that you always create one, preferably by connecting the outcome to a future event such as getting home from work or sitting down to Christmas lunch.

On the other hand, many successful change programs such as the 12 step programs based on the work of AA are based on the principle that you cannot do something or change something tomorrow. If you want to achieve major change in your life, you cannot put it off. You cannot wait until tomorrow to change the course of your life, even if you can't see an opportunity to take tangible action until tomorrow. You could start planning today. You could write out your change plan right now. There are countless things that you could do right now to set your life in the direction you want.

If a pilot were off course, when do you think he or she would make the correction?

The underlying principle of Well Formed Outcomes is that, if you focus on what you can do today, tomorrow will take care of itself.

Earlier, we discussed the perceptual filters that reduce the sensory complexity of the world.

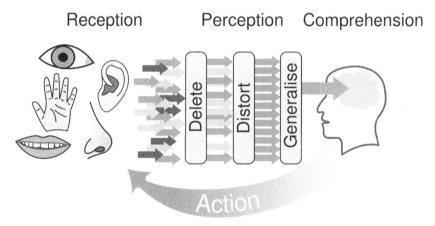

Reception   Perception   Comprehension

How do those filters know what to filter in and what to filter out? Simply, you program them. Mostly, you program them unconsciously so that you are more aware of opportunities to satisfy your current interests and needs.

Your beliefs are an essential component of your filters. What you know to be true about the world tends to influence the world, or at least it seems that way. You see and hear things that are true for you, and only when a situation conflicts with your beliefs do you become aware of the way that your beliefs shape and influence you.

Your beliefs allow you to delete what is contrary to them and to distort and generalise the world so that it conforms to your beliefs. For example, if you believe other people to be intelligent and considerate, you will interpret their behaviour and respond differently than if you believe other people are generally stupid and selfish. Therefore, your beliefs mould your behaviour by colouring your perceptions.

Another important component of these filters is your state. Depending on your state, you will perceive the world differently. When you are feeling overly critical of yourself, a colleague's praise sounds like sarcasm. When you feel good about yourself, a colleague's sarcasm is shrugged off and you might even feel sorry for them. Your state influences how you interpret the world and the actions of people around you, so when you feel like doing something, you notice more opportunities to do it.

Finally, you can program your perceptual filters with Well Formed Outcomes. When you have an outcome, you notice more opportunities to achieve it.

This could be one reason why, when you realise what you want, chance seems to act in your favour, coincidences bring you new opportunities and your efforts seem to have a greater influence on the world and other people.

As Louis Pasteur said, "Chance favours the prepared mind".

10.2 PURE Outcomes

Here's a simple version of the outcomes exercise.

Ask your client for a goal. Thinking about what they tell you, is it:

Positive — What they *do* want

Under their control — Entirely down to them to take the first step

Real — They can tell you what they see, hear and feel in primary sensory terms.

Ecological

Pay careful attention to their congruence when you ask the final test question, "If I could give that to you now, would you take it?"

Remember, anything other than a clear "yes" is a "no". Any pause, translation (definitely, of course, sure, absolutely etc) or unnecessary emphasis is a sign of incongruence.

In the words of the Radio 4 game show, 'Just a Minute', you're listening for hesitation, deviation or repetition.

As a hint, their first response will almost always be incongruent, you just have to figure out why.

Allowing them to dwell on the incongruence will generate new information which you can use to repeat the exercise, refining the outcome until you get a congruent response.

11 Rapport

Rapport isn't something you do - it's a measure of the quality of a relationship.

You could think of rapport as being that sense of having something in common with people you like, when you're on the same wavelength, see eye to eye and feel a real connection with them.

Rapport is a communication medium, a conduit for effective communication. Without it, it's very difficult to engage the processes of agreement and compliance. In other words, people are more likely to do what you want if they like you. Having said that, and assuming that you're a naturally likeable person, there are still many things that people do to stifle natural rapport.

In general, in most situations, it is more useful to have rapport than not.

Let's first discuss what rapport is not.

Rapport is not body language. Body language is a phrased coined in the 1970s by Allan Pease to attribute meaning to particular gestures and body postures. Most of Pease's work has since been discredited as having been made up rather than proven through experimental evidence,

Rapport is not a means to influence someone. You cannot "get into rapport" with someone so that they act against their will. Rapport is a two way process, and the other person is influencing you as much as you are influencing them.

Rapport is not good, in itself. In fact, there are many situations when rapport is a barrier, and I will give you some examples later on.

Finally, rapport is not a "one to one" phenomenon. Groups have rapport, and an individual can have rapport with a group.

Most of the time, we get into and out of rapport with people unconsciously, so our beliefs and thoughts are revealed non-verbally, regardless of our efforts to hide our true feelings. Regardless of what people say, they will show you who and what they agree and disagree with.

11.1 Rapport

In small groups, discuss the question of what rapport is, how you know when you have it and if it is possible to influence it.

Each person should contribute one personal example of having rapport.

What do you conclude from this?

11.2 Rapport Within Rapport

In the same group as for the previous exercise, now discuss how rapport formed within your group during your discussion about rapport.

How did rapport make you feel?

How did it influence your point of view?

Matching and Mirroring

You have probably heard of matching and mirroring. People often ask what the difference is, and as far as I can tell, there doesn't seem to be one. It's possible that matching means you copy the other person's posture and gestures, like for like, whereas mirroring means that you copy them as if you're looking in a mirror.

Having tried it both ways, I can't find a significant or consistent difference, so from here on, I'll just use the term 'matching' to mean "the purposeful and deliberate emulation of a person's body posture, gestures, facial expressions, language and vocal intonation for the purpose of establishing or increasing rapport."

Having said that, I absolutely do not suggest that you ever match someone in 'real life' for the purpose of gaining rapport. It's largely a waste of time; you either have rapport or you don't, if you don't then there's a good reason, and if you do then you don't need to spend any time worrying about it, because you'll be missing far more important things.

But as NLP Practitioners, there is value in matching. Let's begin with a few experiments.

11.3 Matching

Work in pairs for this exercise, with an optional observer.

Choose two conversation topics; one that you might expect to agree on such as holidays, and one that you might expect to disagree on such as sport or religion.

We're going to test four different permutations of conversation topic and rapport, and find out what happens.

Repeat this basic procedure four times:

1. Break state
2. Take a moment to match or mismatch each other
3. Discuss the subject for five minutes
4. Break state
5. Reflect on how you felt about the topic, your own views and the other person

Here are the four permutations:

1. Agreeable topic, match
2. Contentious topic, mismatch
3. Agreeable topic, mismatch
4. Contentious topic, match

11.4 Mismatching

You can work in threes, or in pairs if the trainer can help out with the timing.

Practitioner and client: spend a moment matching each other and building rapport. Then start a conversation about anything - the weather, sport, your jobs etc.

Observer: Sit where only the Practitioner can see you. When you sense that the conversation is "in flow", signal for the Practitioner to break rapport by mismatching.

Practitioner: Watch out for the Observer's signal. When you see it, mismatch by changing the direction or posture of your arms and legs and, most importantly, break eye contact.

You can do this gently, by looking at your Client's chin, or shoulder, or more obviously by looking away completely.

Observer: Make sure that the Practitioner continues to break eye contact, even though they will be desperate to restore rapport.

Finally, match again, because the mismatch will likely feel quite uncomfortable.

Discuss what happened and why.

Is breaking eye contact a pattern interrupt? If yes, how?

11.5 State Matching

You'll need a group of 3 (A, B & C) for this exercise. It's easier if you all stand up.

Person B recalls a specific, strongly emotional memory.

C matches B.

A coaches C to match B even more precisely, guiding C to match B's physiology as exactly as they can, including: Eye movement Breathing location, depth and speed Finger location Foot and toe movement Centre of balance

A now asks C to describe their state - how they feel and what they're experiencing B comments on how close that is to their own state and experience

11.6 Voice Matching

Your client speaks a short phrase which you repeat back, paying more attention to the volume, pace, pitch, rhythm etc. than to the words.

The phrase should be something short that you can repeat consistently, allowing you to focus on the tonal qualities.

Your client coaches you to make the matching more accurate and you continue until it's as perfect as you can make it.

Rapport is generally thought to be a good thing. Certainly, it's difficult to develop any kind of relationship without it, as you have seen from these exercises.

But should a NLP Practitioner only be concerned with building and maintaining rapport? Is it also valuable to break or reduce rapport, and if so, why?

What else can you do to encourage rapport?

List some reasons for reducing rapport in coaching.

Congruence

In 1969, the social psychologist Albert Mehrabian and his assistant Michael Argyle performed a study which has come to be famous in the field of communication and influence; even infamous.

Mehrabian and Argyle gave their test subjects words and phrases to read to each other and paired those words with different intonations and facial expressions. What they deduced from the results was that the overall meaning of a message is a combination of factors; some verbal and some non-verbal.

The purpose of their research was to find out how we deduce specific meaning when these different elements contradict each other, and the context they used was of 'liking'.

The verbal elements of language are the words and their underlying structure of grammar and syntax.

The non-verbal elements include tonal components such as voice tone, volume, pitch and intonation and visual components such as facial expressions and body movements.

The conclusion of Mehrabian and Argyle's work can be shown in this famous pie chart:

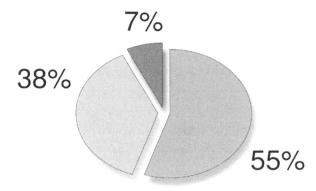

Visual Non-Verbal	Tonal Non-Verbal	Verbal
55%	38%	7%
Facial expressions	Pitch	Words
Hands	Volume	
Body	Intonation	
	Pace	
	Rhythm	

Not everyone agrees with these figures, and some people even dispute the original research. We can perhaps at least agree that words are not the only form of communication between human beings. If you don't agree, then just ask yourself if you have ever been misunderstood, or if you have ever picked up on an unspoken signal from someone, or if you have ever been blind to someone's sarcasm or sincerity because of your own point of view.

Although the original research has been reinterpreted and even misinterpreted over the years, perhaps what we can conclude is that Mehrabian and Argyle did show that there are multiple communication channels and that we can deduce a great deal of information from paying attention to the non-verbal elements as well as the verbal.

11.7 Congruence and Facial Expressions

Here are a few simple facial expressions. Pick some random words or phrases and imagine that each one is being spoken with these expressions.

How does the meaning change?

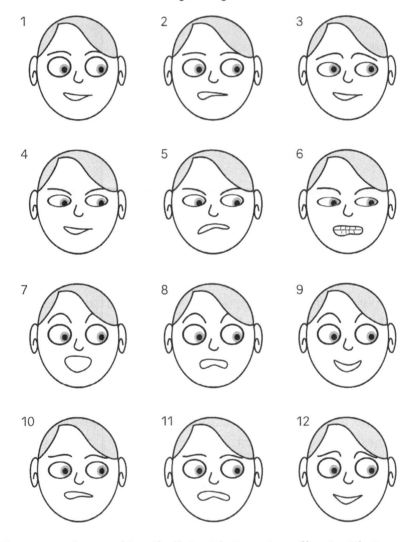

For example, combine 'hello' with 5, or 'goodbye' with 9.

How about 'Are you busy?' with 12?

Here's an experiment that you can conduct to test Mehrabian and Argyle's research for yourself.

11.8 Non-Verbal Communication

You'll need a group of people for this, perhaps ten or more. The bigger the group, the more accurate the results will be. If possible, the presenter should be someone who the group does not see presenting regularly.

Ask a volunteer to present to the group for 20 seconds on a subject of their choice.

Ask the group to write down the first five things that they notice, which can be anything at all.

After 20 seconds, stop the presenter and ask everyone to count their observations.

Add up the total number of items that they:

- Saw
- Heard, as in specific words
- Heard, as in tone, pauses, accent, ums and ahs

You can convert the totals into a percentage or a pie chart quite easily.

Let's say that your numbers are 28 'saw', 19 'tone' and 3 'heard'. Add them all together, that's 50. Now divide each one into the total, so that's 28/50 = 0.56 for 'saw'. That's 56% of the overall communication. In this example, 'tone' is 38% and 'words' are 6%.

If you want to draw a pie chart, just multiply your results by 12 and draw imaginary hands on a clock face. That puts 'saw' at about half past six (12 x 0.56 = 6.72), 'words' at just past eleven o'clock and 'tone' is the space in between. Easy!

In trying this exercise over many years and with hundreds of students, that these figures remain fairly constant. The only thing that really affects the result is when the presenter is speaking about a particularly relevant subject. On a very hot day, the presenter was talking about ice cold beer. Everyone heard the words "cold beer"!

Strictly speaking, this experiment doesn't reproduce Mehrabian and Argyle's research, because their research was conducted in the specific context of 'liking'.

However, isn't it odd that the results from this experiment match Mehrabian and Argyle's results, time after time?

Let's do some more experiments and find out how good you are at recognising incongruence.

11.9 Congruence

Ask your client 10 questions to which you both know the answer, e.g. what colour is the sky today?

Your client will reply truthfully. Watch out for anything that they do consistently, such as move their eyes a certain way.

Next, ask your client 10 questions to which you both know the answer, e.g. what country are we in?

Your client will reply untruthfully. Watch out for anything that they do consistently, such as move their eyes a certain way.

When you think you have picked up their subtle, unconscious patterns, ask them another 10 questions to which you do not know the answer, such as "what car do you drive?" and they can choose whether to answer truthfully or not.

Tell them if the answer is true or false. Don't think about it, just say what feels right, the first thing that comes to mind.

Did you find that, the more you tried to analyse their behaviour, the more you tried to find 'tells', the less effective you were at spotting the incorrect answers?

Why do you think that is?

You've probably seen TV mind readers telling people in the street what their computer passwords are and where they live. Is it a trick? If so, how is it done?

This next exercise uses rapport to emulate mind reading. On one course, a student was thinking about a recent event in her life, namely her driving test. The person she was working with didn't know her and didn't know that she had just passed. He was struggling. He said, "I'm getting nothing. Not a thing. All I can see is white zigzags." More out of desperation than a serious guess, he asked "Is it a driving test?"

At first, students think that this exercise is a little strange, but when typically 50% of the group get a "direct hit" and most of the rest get at least the feelings and sensations right, there is certainly something interesting happening.

> How can you explain what happens in this exercise? Is there a relationship between this and the feeling that you get when you know what someone close to you is thinking?

11.10 Direct Mind Reading

Client: Think of a recent event, something with a strong emotional connection, good or bad. Just think about this event or experience and really amplify it. Really amplify the feelings you get from the memory. Keep running it through in your mind, over and over, like you're watching a looped video. Hear the words and sounds, see the images bright and clear. Don't allow the feelings to fade, keep reinforcing them, focusing on different details of what you see, hear and feel.

Your partner is going to get into rapport with you and then share with you their internal experiences. Don't prompt or guide them, but also don't be awkward. Just genuinely explore your own experience, and if your partner gets close to it, let them know.

Practitioner: Just allow yourself to relax and enjoy being in rapport with your client. At first, take time to match their posture, breathing, movements. Then just relax and concentrate on your own feelings or sensations. Start to daydream about the kind of experience that could lead to those feelings. For example, if you feel a little out of breath, why would that be? If you feel heavy, what would cause that?

When you are relaxed and ready, start to put your ideas, images, intuitions into words. Think about the kind of feeling you can feel, describe the feeling and notice your client's response as you get closer to understanding what your client is thinking about. Just start guessing and refine your ideas as you go. Do not sit there and think until you have got it right, you never will.

This is an interactive process. Test your thoughts and uses your client's responses to guide you.

If you feel movement, just say what you feel, don't try to explain. Say what you see and feel, and make as many guesses as you like, no matter how strange they seem.

Pacing and Leading

Rapport is a fairly static process. You get into rapport with someone and, before you know it, you're both in a loved-up little world of your own and you're away with the fairies, as they say. Your hour is up, you've put the world to rights, but your client is no further forwards.

When you're meeting a close friend for a catch-up, this is fine. When you're a NLP Practitioner and you're supposed to be keeping your client on track, it's not fine.

Being in rapport is a good feeling, when you are in rapport with someone who feels good. When a client is talking through a feeling, there may be a great deal of 'negative' emotion, and, whilst it is vital to empathize with the client, it serves neither of you to get into a downward spiral. The client needs you to understand them yet they also need you to maintain your professional position.

You can empathise with a client to the extent that they feel that you really understand them, but if they ask, "So what do you think?" and you answer, "I've no idea. I just feel so frustrated by the whole situation that I can't think straight" then they'll probably be looking for a new coach or consultant within the hour.

When a client asks, "What do you think?", an appropriate answer might be, "Well, to begin with, I really feel your sense of frustration. Believe me, if I were in your position, I would feel the same way, and I'd probably be looking for someone to show me that there is a way forward."

Of course, when you say 'someone', you mean 'you'.

This is an example of pacing and leading. Essentially, you're saying, "I understand how stuck you feel. Let's look for a way out together"

When a client describes a problem, you'll see their whole body posture change. You might see their shoulders drop, their breathing change, their eyes look down more and they might frown. They look exactly how they feel, and it's very easy for their energy level to drop to the extent that they really can't see a way out of their problem.

When you're in rapport with a client, your body posture will look very similar, and it is important that you are mindful of the situation and stay in touch with the overall process, otherwise you can easily lose your sense of direction and be drawn into the client's state. Before you know it, you're out of time and have moved no further forward.

Pacing and leading gives you a means to join the client in their present situation, building trust and understanding, whilst also showing them that their desired solution is not only possible, it is readily achievable.

Pacing is the process of maintaining rapport over time, through its ups and downs.

Leading is the process of directing a person's state and responses using rapport as a communication medium.

The principle is to get rapport first, then pace, then lead.

Why would you want to lead someone? Well, firstly, NLP is not non directive. It is not person centred counselling. It is outcome oriented, and to achieve an outcome means to go somewhere other than the present state.

Secondly, the problem is not the problem as the client states it, the problem is that they have been unable to resolve what they think the problem is. Some aspect of their undesired behaviour is based on a world view which perpetuates the problem. To get them out of this, at their request, requires you to be a guide to alternative possibilities. Therefore your first task in achieving change is to introduce the possibility of change, and that can be in any form. A simple change in state, a joke, a different point of view can be the first step in the process of change.

11.11 Pacing and Leading Part 1

Practitioner: Ask your client questions that are taken from their current experience, that require a yes or no answer, such as:

- Are you sitting down?
- Can you see a window?
- Are you looking at me?
- Did you travel to get here?
- Are you wearing shoes?
- Can you hear my voice?

Client: Respond no to each question. Notice how, over time, your state changes along with your responses.

Practitioner: Gradually shift to questions about things that are possible but not necessarily true, such as:

- Are you enjoying the course?
- Are you learning a lot?
- Do you like the other students?
- Do you like me?
- Would you like to give me some money?
- Will you buy me lunch?

Client: Notice how you feel towards these questions.

11.12 Pacing and Leading Part 2

Repeat the exercise, but this time the client will reply yes to every question.

Practitioner: Ask your client questions that are taken from their current experience, that require a yes or no answer.

Client: Respond yes to each question. Notice how, over time, your state changes. Notice what happens inside, and notice what happens to your responses.

Practitioner: Gradually shift to questions about things that are possible but not necessarily true.

Client: Notice how you feel towards those questions

Compare what happened in the two parts of this exercise.

11.13 Matching, Pacing and Leading

Loosely get into rapport with your client by matching their body posture.

Invite them to begin talking about a situation that they have found difficult and as they do so, continuously pace their changing posture, eye accessing and facial expressions. As you give them ongoing feedback and prompts to continue, match their voice tone.

When you sense that your client is really 'in flow' and their attention is very much on what they are talking about, begin to lead.

Change your posture gradually, testing as you go. If they don't follow, pace a little longer. Once they start to follow, direct your changes in posture and voice tone towards a more resourceful state.

Notice any state change and differences in their language.

Ask your client what they noticed.

11.14 Pacing and Leading in Conversation

Have your client describe a problem, perhaps a frustrating or confusing situation. Only let them talk for long enough to give you a sense of the problem's 'headlines'.

Whilst they're talking, pay attention to their:

- Words - particularly words that they mark out with an emotional response, a pause, emphasis etc

- Voice tone - particularly when they're marking out words, or when their voice tone changes

- Movements - particularly any movements to mark out certain words, or points when their body posture changes

- Rhythm - the general pace and rhythm or their words and movements, particularly any changes of speed

Pace what they have given you, beginning with your intention, for example "So to make sure I understand you, what I'm sensing is...."

Then reflect back their key words (which are, of course, anchors), using their voice tone, movements and rhythm,

Wait for them to acknowledge your feedback, for example by saying, "yes, that's it".

Redirect their attention with the PURE principles of well formed outcomes (exercise 10.2). For example:

What is it that you *do* want? (P)

What *can* you do? (U)

What would a good result *look* like for you? (R)

As you continue to pace and lead, reflecting back their words, redirecting to PURE outcomes, notice their state and focus changing. When you see that their focus has moved past the problem, end with an Ecology question:

"And how do you feel about all of this, now?"

12 Calibration and Strategies

Calibration means fine tuning your awareness to the person you're working with, so that you can pick up their conscious and unconscious information. Often, if a Practitioner is struggling to get a technique to work, it's because they're focusing on what should be happening instead of noticing what is happening.

A strategy is a sequence of mental and physical steps that a person goes through, consistently, to produce a certain behaviour and achieve a result. Programming (the P in NLP) refers to these strategies and the way that we learn and assemble them to produce complex patterns of behaviour. You'll usually find that the words program, pattern and strategy are interchangeable in NLP.

As a telecoms apprentice, I learned a basic fault finding procedure that now enables me to fix pretty much anything that breaks around the house.

It turns out that it's also a very useful process for coaching with NLP, because NLP is about processes, interconnected systems and systemic change. When one part of my dishwasher failed, a small relay in the control electronics, it wasn't just the relay that didn't work. That in turn meant no hot water which in turn meant that the dishwasher didn't wash the dishes. One small component affected the whole system, so no matter what it is that we're working on, we must always think in terms of systemic change.

If you've ever had something repaired, only for it to have something else wrong with it as a result, then you've experienced the effect of not thinking systemically. The problem is rarely in the same place as the symptom, a blown fuse being a good example. Many household fires have been caused by the home owner replacing old fashioned fuse wire with a bit of coat hanger to stop it from blowing. The modification doesn't address the reason that the fuse kept blowing, with the result that the wire gets red hot and something close to it catches fire.

Here's the basic fault finding process.

1. Find out what the user thinks is wrong. The most common fault is "user error".

2. Reproduce the fault. You need to make sure that the system is doing what the user says it's doing

3. Verify normal operation. You need to know what the thing is supposed to do when it's working!

4. Isolate and replace faulty component. A gradual process of working back from the symptom until you find the root cause.

5. Test the system fully to make sure it's all working the way it should be. Steps 4 and 5 loop until the system is working as it should.

6. Get the user to test the system to make sure they're happy with it and that they understand what went wrong and how they might avoid that in the future.

This sequence of steps, whilst useful as a process for finding a faulty component in a system, is also an example of a strategy. If you observed a good engineer, you wouldn't necessarily see them performing these steps in an explicit sense. You would see the same consistent results, but to get to the implicit steps, we need to elicit the unconscious strategy – the bits that they do without thinking.

Recently, I had a conversation with someone about business processes in relation to knowledge and experience. In one particular aspect of an engineer's job, there is a twelve step process that defines how to terminate an electrical cable. The person I was talking to said that he watched an experienced engineer terminate the cable and noticed that he only performed nine out of the twelve steps. This proved that experienced people don't necessarily follow documented processes.

I asked if the engineer had really skipped three of the steps, or if it only looked that way to a casual observer. It turned out that the engineer had followed all twelve steps, but that something very important had happened for three of them - he had done them in his head. For example, one of the implied steps was to measure 25mm from the end of the cable. The engineer didn't need to do that because he had a visual strategy for accurately estimating that distance. Can you hold your finger tips about an inch apart? If you can, then you have learned a similar strategy.

Any repetitive task that you can perform without having to think about it is an example of a strategy, and what's absolutely fundamental to NLP change work is your ability to figure out what that underlying strategy is before you do anything that resembles a technique. In fact, the better you are at figuring out these strategies, the less reliant you will be on techniques because by understanding the strategy you will have everything you need to influence the results that the person gets.

Let's see how we can begin to map out these strategies.

12.1 Strategy Elicitation

Practitioner: Ask your client to talk about any memorable event. As they do this, pay attention to their language, specifically words that indicate they are recalling visual, auditory or kinaesthetic elements of the memory.

As they relate the story of the event, make a note of the sequence, noting any patterns or connections that seem interesting to you.

Next, ask your client to talk about something that they would like to be different in their lives, something that they would perhaps describe as an ongoing problem.

As they do this, pay attention to their language, specifically words that indicate they are recalling visual, auditory or kinaesthetic elements of the memory.

As they relate the story of the event, make a note of the sequence, noting any patterns or connections that seem interesting to you.

A conversational strategy elicitation is nice and relaxed, and you can ask your client to stop and go back if you want to double check something.

The one thing missing is when there's a step that the client is themselves unaware of. How can we identify a step in a strategy if the client doesn't know that it's there?

Eye Accessing

Observing and interpreting non-verbal communication is the subject of an entire book in itself, and there is one small part of this field of study which is of particular interest in NLP, and that is the subject of 'eye accessing cues'.

This is one of the most hotly debated topics in NLP, with arguments on internet discussion forums being commonplace. Some people think that eye accessing cues are gospel, others that they are heresy. Various people even claim to have 'discovered' eye accessing cues.

Probably the biggest problem is the spreading of the rumour that the police use eye accessing cues to tell when someone is lying. You cannot deduce something as vague as a 'lie' from eye accessing alone. What you probably can deduce is the overall pattern of a person's thought processes. When they break that pattern, it might be a lie, but it might equally be something else, which I'll get to in good time.

The reality is that no-one understands or can verify the eye accessing phenomenon, but we all know that it happens. There doesn't appear to be any particular physiological reason for it, and it may even be learned. We are not, therefore, interested in absolute truths that apply to all people, we are interested in understanding a client better.

Our thoughts are a constant stream of information, some external and some internal. When we are processing internal information, we could call that 'thinking', and when we think, we use many of the same parts of our brain as we use for taking in new, external information.

Researchers have put volunteers into MRI scanners and made direct comparisons between internal thoughts and external stimuli. At least I think they were volunteers.

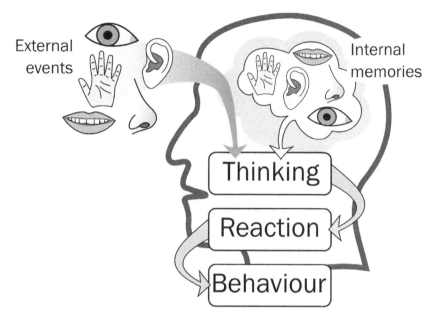

Increased blood flow infers increased activity and the latest 'functional MRI' (Magnetic Resonance Imaging) scanners can produce videos of the brain working in real time.

If I ask you to think about what you had for breakfast this morning, I can be fairly confident that if you say, "Porridge", then you did indeed have porridge, and therefore in between you hearing the question and saying the answer, you thought of porridge.

However, knowing what you thought of is not very important for a NLP Practitioner. Knowing how you thought of it is much more important.

Ask someone a question and, most of the time, you'll find that they don't maintain eye contact with you. Specifically, in the split second between question and answer, they glance up, or to the side, or down.

Why is this? I don't know. No-one knows.

What does it mean? I can only guess. No-one knows.

Is there a pattern? Yes, for an individual, although some generalisations seem to hold true for a majority of people.

Does it even matter? Oh yes. Let's explore why.

12.2 Eye Accessing

Practitioner: Memorise each question and then look your client right in the eye as you ask it. If you read from the page, you will miss the eye access as it will happen as soon as your client understands the question - which is long before you have finished reading it.

You can make a note of what you see with an arrow, like ↗ or ↘ remembering that what you see will be reversed.

1. What colour is your bedroom carpet?

2. Where is your kitchen?

3. What colour is your can opener?

4. What does your front door handle feel like?

5. What does wet grass feel like?

6. What does wet grass smell like?

7. How bright is your bedside lamp?

8. What's the first sound you heard today?

9. How did it make you feel?

10. What's the best smell to wake up to?

11. How do you brush your teeth?

12. Is your hot tap on the left or right?

13. What does your bathroom soap smell like?

14. What does a dog's bark sound like?

15. Describe the smile of someone you love

16. Have you ever felt sad?

17. What reminds you of your last holiday?

18. How heavy is your mobile phone?

19. What shoes did you wear yesterday?

20. Were they comfortable?

21. What's your favourite colour?

22. How does confusion feel?

23. Who was the last person you spoke to on the phone?

24. How would a mouse sound if it could sing?

25. What letter is next to L on a computer keyboard?

26. When were you last cosy?

27. How does it sound to walk in snow?

28. When did you last hear your name?

29. When were you last in trouble?

30. What is the eighth word of one of your favourite songs?

31. What clothes were you wearing yesterday?

32. What clothes will you wear tomorrow?

33. What did your first school smell like?

34. In your car, how do you turn the windscreen wipers on?

35. What was your first taste of alcohol like?

36. On a telephone, where is the number 7?

37. How would you write your name backwards?

38. What was the last phone number you dialled?

39. How does it feel to wade through water?

40. What mobile ring tone is most irritating?

Hopefully, you noticed three things in this exercise.

1. Your client's eyes moved before they answered

2. They seemed to move consistently for certain types of question

3. Sometimes, there were a number of movements that seemed to be in a sequence

> When you saw a sequence, what did you theorise was happening?

When your client's eyes moved about rather than going to one place and staying there, you were seeing something known as a 'pattern'. For example, if you asked the question, "What does a robin's song sound like?", they may look up to the left, then up to the right, then across to the right and across to the left before answering. This indicates that they first pictured a robin before trying to recall what its song sounded like. You can check your interpretation with them after they answer the question.

For some questions, you may also have seen your client physically moving, for example brushing their teeth or closing a door. This is interesting, but it's not eye accessing.

Here are the traditional NLP eye accessing cues, drawn as a client's eye accessing cues, seen from your point of view as you look at the client, so if you were recalling and image, you would look up and to your left.

Visual Recall

Visual Construct

Auditory Recall

Auditory Construct

Auditory Digital

Kinaesthetic

I like to simplify eye accessing, which also gets round the problem of the two downward accesses not seeming to fit the symmetry of the others. The way that I simplify it is as follows:

Right now, you may be thinking one of two things. Either, "eye accessing is cool and amazing", or "what on Earth is the point of eye accessing?"

So far, we have worked with the building blocks of NLP, the elements of anchoring, submodalities and so on. These are basic principles, but they tell us nothing about how a person creates a situation that they would like to change.

In order to experience a "problem", your client has to run through a certain pattern of thoughts and actions. They will be largely unaware of the fleeting thoughts, so how can you ever hope to help them change something if you don't even know what it is you're changing.

Here's a genuine example from a client who wanted to deal with his frustration caused by his family's eating habits.

"I get mad at my kids for eating the wrong things or at the wrong times."

"Who was it who was harmed by eating the wrong things at the wrong times?"

Client looks up.

"I don't know."

"Who did you just see?"

"My mother."

"What happened to your mother?"

"She had a very bad diet and had a lot of stress and she got diabetes."

"So you want to save your kids from getting diabetes?"

"Yes."

"OK, well that's a good thing. Are you approaching that in the most effective way?"

"No, probably not!"

All of that came from observing eye accessing.

Strategy Elicitation and Modelling

Modelling is a part of everything you do with NLP. It is the means by which all of these techniques were created.

What we are modelling is a series of mental steps which are sensory representations. Since our senses are the means by which everything gets in to our heads, they are also the references by which we process information and respond accordingly.

It is these learned responses to external or internal perceptions that we want to get at with modelling. The word "strategy" refers to a specific sequence of steps that generates a behavioural result.

Bandler and Grinder used a particular way of writing down sequences of representations, and it's useful to learn that notation, firstly so that you can understand their books more easily and, secondly, so that you can very quickly capture strategies when working with a client.

The notation is very simple; V for Visual, A for Auditory and K for Kinaesthetic.

Then you add two modifiers; I for Internal or E for External, and R for Recall or C for Construct. The only odd one out is Ad for Auditory Digital or internal dialogue, which means that A is for Auditory Tonal; sounds rather than speech. You might see this written as At.

Here's what you end up with:

Vi	Visual Internal	Ve	Visual External
Ai	Auditory Internal	Ae	Auditory External
Ad	Auditory Digital		
Ki	Kinaesthetic Internal	Ke	Kinaesthetic External
R	Recall	C	Construct

The final result might look something like this:

Ve → ViC → Ad → Ke → Ki

For a strategy that goes like this:

See a new sofa, picture it in your house, ask yourself if you can afford it, sit on it, feel good.

I'd suggest that you mostly ignore R and C, because a construct will usually be a composite of recalls. To picture a new sofa in your house, you have to recall your house and then overlay the sofa that's in the shop.

> Can you think of a strategy that one person would call a problem but which would be useful for someone else?

> If your job involves selling, do you think it would be useful to know your customer's decision strategy? How would that be useful?

12.3 Model a Decision Strategy

Ask your client to recall something that they bought recently, which they had to make a decision about.

Identify the starting point of their decision, perhaps seeing something in an advert, or feeling that something needed replacing, or hearing someone talk about something, or whatever the first step was for them.

Work gradually through the decision, at each stage identifying whether it was Visual, Auditory or Kinaesthetic and Internal or External.

What seems to be the pivotal point in the decision process?

12.4 Model a Talent

Ask your client to identify something that they would describe as a skill or talent and apply the same strategy modelling process as before.

Be very specific about what you are modelling. If your client says they are good at time management, that's far too big a set of behaviours for this exercise. You might narrow that down to their ability to choose which of two tasks is the higher priority.

12.5 Model a problem

Ask your client to identify something that they would describe as a current problem and apply the same strategy modelling process as before.

Remember that what they describe as a problem is in fact a talent taken out of context, so treat it with the same respect as the decision and the talent.

Every behaviour has a positive intention, it is designed to achieve something. Whether that something is desirable or not depends only on context.

NLP and Transactional Analysis

Transactional Analysis, the work of Eric Berne, amongst others, contains the concept of 'scripts'; self perpetuating patterns in behaviour which are analogous to an actor's script in a play. The same parts say the same lines, over and over again. The central figure will even manipulate other people to play those necessary parts so that they can deliver their lines, much like children playing and telling each other who to be and what to say.

NLP's strategies are not scripts, but they could be triggers for them, and they could be components of them.

NLP's strategies are sequences of representational systems, starting and ending with an external stimulus or action.

Scripts are far more complex, and NLP is not a replacement for Transactional Analysis in itself, perhaps more a set of tools to assist in TA.

Some of the more complex NLP techniques such as the Six Step Reframe certainly operate on the more complex level of scripts and transactions, and can be used to provide insight into a person's behaviour and choices. However, TA, in itself, is more a framework for understanding the role of scripts and transactions in a normal and healthy personality, whereas NLP is more a collection of techniques that can assist in bringing about the changes that a person desires.

If you have read the original NLP book, Frogs into Princes, by Bandler and Grinder, you may recall that the NLP Practitioner program, of which the book is essentially a transcript, was a complementary training program aimed at experienced therapists. Bandler and Grinder had created, or plagiarised, a new set of tools for change, and they offered them to the therapeutic community to complement mainstream approaches such as Transactional Analysis, Gestalt Therapy and even Freudian Analysis.

Today's NLP Practitioner courses are usually offered to anyone, not just to people with therapeutic or counselling experience. Some very short courses offered by some NLP trainers can be as little as 5 days long. Compared with the original training programs, something is inevitably missing.

Short courses are like the user guide for a power tool. They allow you to put new blades or drill bits in and change the battery, but they tell you nothing about how to approach the concept, design and construction process. They tell you nothing about craftsmanship. And this is the biggest criticism of NLP; that it is sold as a panacea when it is only the user guide for the tools.

13 Language

Earlier, we discussed the stages of a child's mental development and found that a child develops abstract maps and then attaches symbolic labels to that map.

For example, what is this?

That's right. It's a book. Or a picture in a book. Or a pattern of ink on a sheet of paper. Or a pattern of light on a screen.

Did you think it was a compass? Try using it when you're lost and you'll soon find out if it's a compass or not.

Our entire mental map of the world is based on linguistic labels. From the moment we learn to talk, we want to know what things are called.

When we learn a foreign language, we start by asking, "What is French for hello?" or shop, or bus, or more likely, two beers please. Or as the dancers in the Japanese combined workout and language learning video teach, "Spare me my life". I don't know where they're expecting viewers to go for their holidays.

Words are labels that represent our rich sensory experiences, or handles that we can use to pull those experiences from our memories. And as we listen to language, these rich metaphors are streaming through our minds, which is one reason why stories and metaphors are so powerful. And it also raises the question of what happens when a label is ambiguous and could represent any of a number of experiences.

Imagine that, in your brain, you have a bucket full of memories. Each memory can be pulled out of the bucket and experienced by pulling on the appropriate string. The label lets you know what kind of memory it is, and the more labels that are attached to a memory, the easier it is to pull out. You might say that some memories have "strong associations" or that you are particularly "attached" to some events in your life.

We could say that the more labels a memory has, the stronger it is.

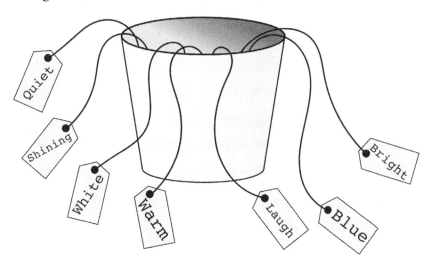

All of these labels are attached to the same memory; they are synonyms for an experience. You can take any of the strings and pull out the same memory.

As you read the labels, what memory might be in the bucket?

What memories might these labels be attached to?

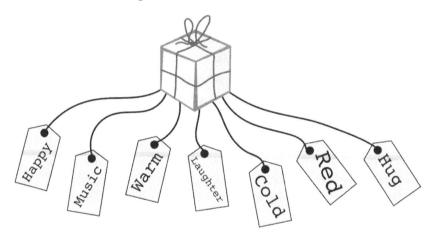

We make new memories by connecting new experiences to what we already know. We make sense of new experiences by comparing them to our memories.

I'm sure you've heard people say, "Oh, it's just like..."

When you introduce a new idea to someone, no matter how innovative or revolutionary it is, they can only make sense of it by comparing it to what they already know.

13.1 Memory labels

Read the following list of labels to your client. Give them enough time to bring to mind a memory based on each word. Ask them to stay with that memory and explore deeper within it as you move to the next, or at least find a connecting memory that is somehow relevant.

- A childhood memory
- The colour red
- A boy's name beginning with C
- A sound
- A feeling

What memories are evoked by these words?

What does that mean?

Here is a different list so that you can both try the exercise.

- A childhood memory
- The colour yellow
- Something you eat
- A sound
- A feeling

Our ability to encode the world using our linguistic labelling system is central to our society, our culture and our working lives. Language is the means by which we are able to communicate knowledge, enabling us to share information, solve problems and explore our surroundings. We can cure a disease and transfer that information to a doctor on the other side of the world, instantly. An explorer on the moon can describe what it's like for the viewers back home. You can tell the people you are close to how you feel about them. You can read a book and learn useful things.

We can include visual communication such as icons, graphical user interfaces and even semaphore and Morse code in this too, as these are extensions or representations of linguistic labels or coding mechanisms. We could call these "second order" signalling systems in that they are representations of words which are representations of experiences.

In NLP, there are broadly two models of language, the Meta Model and the Milton Model. They just about fit together as the converse of each other.

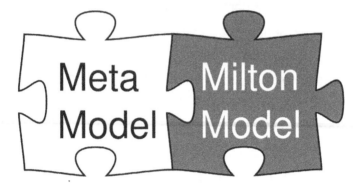

From people like Virginia Satir and Gregory Bateson, the Meta Model was created. Simply, we construct sentences which are grammatically correct yet which delete, distort or generalise information. For example, if I tell you that you shouldn't eat chocolate, it's bad for you, you might believe me. But why? What makes the statement "true", other than the fact that I've said it?

Parents pass their beliefs on to their children every day; some are useful, some are not. The Meta Model therefore allows you to explore and unpick beliefs, assumptions and rules that have simply dropped off the edge of conscious attention and become accepted as facts.

Milton Erickson was a Hypnotherapist in Arizona. He can perhaps be credited as the person who made hypnotherapy acceptable in western medicine, using it in a wide range of situations and helping patients that other therapists had declared "incurable". The story goes that Erickson suffered from polio in his early life and found himself able to spend many long hours paying attention to the effect that words had on people.

Erickson's language was the opposite of the Meta Model, it was full of deletions, distortions and generalisations, carefully crafted to influence the listener in a certain way.

If you listen to any statement or speech prepared by a politician, you will hear a lot of Milton language. For example:

"People will understand that the solutions to these kinds of problems are to be found not in the past but in the future, and everyone will appreciate what a difficult task this can be. You can also be absolutely certain that the government you have now is in a far better position than any other to tackle these problems and to resolve them in a way that is economical, effective and respectful to the local community".

Does that sound familiar? Perhaps you remember hearing that before, about asylum seekers, or racial problems, or local policing policy? Actually, I just made it up.

Milton language is a vague framework within which the listener can place their own meaning. If someone tells you that you will be richer if you make a certain decision, you may or may not agree depending on whether money is important to you or not. If they say that you will enjoy even more of the things that are so important to you, you can only make sense of the sentence if you insert something of importance to you. The sentence, whilst sounding vague when we analyse it in this way, actually becomes totally unique and personal to each listener.

In this way, politicians, leaders and storytellers can communicate directly with every listener or reader in a very personal way.

Milton Model is often hijacked by sales people who can teach you to write "hypnotic sales letters" that command your customers to reach for their wallets.

This is, of course, nonsense. A customer who is even half awake will recognise such contrived attempts to influence them, and a customer who is fast asleep will soon wake up and realise what they've done. Maybe enough are so embarrassed that they don't ask for a refund.

Milton Language is a therapeutic, or at best, a coaching language for use with permissive clients; people who actually want you to influence them.

Consider these two scenarios.

Scenario 1: A sales person calls you up and you don't put the phone down immediately, because they sound like they might have a service that you're interested in. They say:

"That's right, and as you listen to my words and begin to imagine, in your mind, now, the many wonderful benefits that you will continue to enjoy when you buy this product now, and you can imagine the joy that is in your life from buying this product and as you give me your credit card number, aren't you, wondering how soon you'll receive your product and excitedly open the packaging and begin enjoying all of those wonderful, safe, reassuring benefits..." And so on.

Scenario 2: You are having difficulty in getting the kind of job that you want, and you know that you let yourself down in the interview by trying to be all things to all people, so you go to a career coach for help. Amongst other things, they say:

"You know, it's really interesting, isn't it, when you're sitting in front of someone who you really want to work with, and sometimes, I know that you find yourself trying too hard, and maybe you used to worry about what they would think of you, yet you can, if you choose, imagine stepping across the room, and into their chair, and looking back at yourself, and begin to wonder now, for you to be there, sitting right there now, means that you could be the right person for the job, couldn't you? And the interviewer, you don't know that until you've met them, and you really hope that they have questions for you, because who do you want to hire most? It's the person who shows the most interest, isn't it? And now as you imagine hearing the interviewer's questions, they become a conversation, and before long, you're asking your own questions and feeling that you're part of this process of exploring, and choosing..." And so on.

From a technical, Milton Model point of view, neither. From a moral, ethical point of view, the first example is unthinkable, yet there are lots of people out there who continue to try to use the Milton Model in that way.

I can't stop you. No-one can stop you. I can't stop you buying a gun and using that to persuade your customers to buy from you. It's entirely up to you how you use these tools.

So what I'm really saying is that yes, there are lots of resources out there for using these tools in ways that I don't agree with from a moral point of view. I can't control what other people do, I can only control what I do. How you apply NLP is up to you, simply remember that NLP tends to amplify your intentions and reveal them more clearly to others.

14 Meta Model

The Meta Model is based on linguistic rules and structures which are not specific to NLP, you'll find them in everything from books on transformational grammar to school books. However, what is specific to NLP is the way that those rules reveal lost information beneath them.

If language didn't have a structure, we would have no way to know if something was missing or not. Yet because language has a structure, that structure gives us the information that we need to understand and even change underlying thought processes.

The Meta Model recovers information lost through our sensory filtering process.

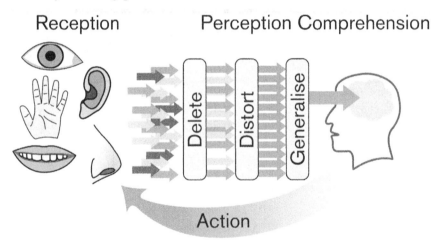

We don't just filter sensory information coming in, we also filter information going out as language. With a client, I'm not so interested in what they say, what I'm more interested in is how they have converted their experiences and perceptions into language, as that gives me an understanding of how they perceive the world differently than I do. By understanding their mental map, I can work with them to change it more effectively.

Let me just demonstrate how important this point about structure is.

According to linguists such as Stephen Pinker, we are born with the "hardware" for language already installed. He demonstrates this by saying that all languages in the world, even those found in remote valleys that have had no contact with other cultures, follow the same basic structures; either Subject Verb Object (SVO) or Subject Object Verb (SOV).

It's also quite possible that language is not hard wired, but events in the outside world tend to follow the same pattern. Something is in one state, then it's in another state, and we notice the difference, relative to our own position.

Hence, if a friend drove past your house, they would probably recognise that they were moving, but your house wasn't. However, have you ever been in a traffic jam and experienced a moment of panic when the cars to the side of you start to move and you grab the handbrake? Of have you being sitting on a train and the train on the next platform moves, and you think that you're moving?

Albert Einstein realised that we can only measure the qualities of objects when we compare them to other objects. We can't say that your friend's car is moving at 30 mph, it is only moving at 30 mph relative to your house. If we compare the car's motion to the axis of the Earth, its speed is about 1070 mph, and if we compare the car's speed to the Sun, or a nearby galaxy, the speed could be anything up to 666,000 mph.

Therefore, everything that we are aware of implicitly contains the thing that we are aware of (the Object), ourselves (the Subject) and something that changes over time (the Verb).

What is important to note is that our experience of the world is relative to a frame of reference. Comparative words such as "higher" and "lower", "warmer" and "cooler", "better" and "worse" clearly imply a frame of reference, others are much less obvious.

So here's our first simple Meta Model exercise. Since English is a SVO language, a grammatically correct sentence will be something like:

- The cat climbed the tree

If we take out one of those components:

- The cat climbed the

- The climbed the tree

- The cat the tree

Then it's quite obvious that something is missing, right?

What about these examples:

- The cat climbed

- It climbed the tree

- What's the cat doing in the tree?

Same deletions, but now it's harder to spot them. And since the clues aren't so obvious, we're more likely to fill in the gaps from our own experiences. If the cat climbed, I can call to mind an image of a cat going up a tree. Yet the cat could have climbed a telegraph pole or the curtains or my trouser leg. If the cat climbing is the point, does it matter what it climbed?

Well, if my daughter runs in and shouts, "the cat's stuck" I need to know whether to call the fire brigade, coastguard or mountain rescue, depending on where the cat is stuck. If it's stuck up a tree, I need the fire brigade. If it's stuck inside the postman's trousers then I don't think a dozen burly firemen are going to help the situation.

On the other hand, if the cat is helping her with her homework and it doesn't know the answer, that's a different problem altogether. Then the solution would be to get a video of the cat on YouTube as quickly as possible.

Here's another way to demonstrate this idea. Can you tell what is missing from this diagram?

No?

OK then, how about this one?

Or this one?

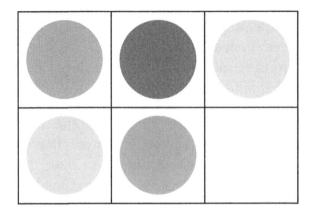

So the problem is that we communicate half formed half truths, and the listener fills in the gaps from their own experiences and makes their own meaning from that. And in doing so, the speaker also reinforces the half truths of their own experiences. So what we need to do is recover the lost information to give both the speaker and listener an opportunity to discover more fully what is being communicated. In the case of the cat, a simple question such as "Where is the cat stuck?" will do nicely. In the case of the more complex transformations of language that we churn out, we need a few more questions. Our ability to fit information into structure is what underpins our ability to distinguish Meta Model patterns.

Each of the following categories is a specific form of deletion, distortion or generalisation. Of course, natural language contains all of those, so the Meta Model as covered in Practitioner training is a good way to train yourself to recognise the potential for missing information. You can then choose where to focus your questions to recover the most useful information.

I'm sorry to say that many NLP trainers don't really understand the Meta Model themselves, and they don't understand why it is important. They teach Meta Model as a set of clumsy, superficial questions to challenge a client's assumptions, which does nothing to loosen the issue that the client wants to work on. Perhaps the most annoying example is when someone says, "Oh, I'm always doing that", and half a dozen freshly minted Practitioners leap from dark corners, crying, "*Always???????*"

Yes, always. What's it to you?

The Meta Model lies at the heart of modelling, and modelling is the foundation of NLP. Without the Meta Model, you will be unable to effectively and consistently map out a client's 'problem', which means that you will be ineffective in dealing with it. At best, a Practitioner who doesn't understand the Meta Model will randomly throw techniques at the problem until either something works by chance, or the client just gives in to make life easier.

You can recognise a poor trainer by phrases such as, "The Meta Model doesn't really matter, just as long as you get the general idea", or, "You don't have to know what any of it is called, the labels just get in the way".

Do you remember the other day, what happened with that thing? In that place? You know... where was it? Those people were there. Come on, you must remember.

You could teach apprentice mechanics to fix engines without labels. You know what a screw looks like without having to use the word. You know what kind of wrench you need. You know when a bolt is tight because you can feel it. You could teach mechanics to tighten the thing with the whats-it, and keep on turning the other thing until the thing is tight enough.

Who needs torque wrenches? We all know whether a bolt is tight or not. Would you be happy to drive your car out of the garage if the mechanic did everything by hand and couldn't actually explain what he'd done?

The labels are rather important if you want to communicate effectively, and the Meta Model labels are important if you want to use this, the most fundamental, powerful and flexible NLP tool, purposefully, effectively and consistently.

Before looking at the different elements or 'patterns' of the Meta Model, listen to someone giving an interview, on TV or on the radio. When you listen critically, what deletions, distortions and generalisations can you hear? What do they mean?

Deletions, Distortions and Generalisations

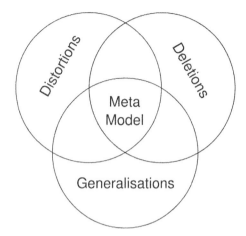

The Meta Model deals with Deletions, Distortions and Generalisations, as follows:

Deletions

Something has been removed and can be recovered.

Distortions

Something has been changed and can be changed back to its original form.

Generalisations

Something has been simplified and can be specified.

Meta Model patterns might fit into these three groups, bearing in mind that all three "filters" are operating on all information flowing in and out. Therefore, a Meta Model pattern may be a Deletion, but it can also Distort and Generalise. The Meta Model categories are therefore a matter of focus, not of strict categorisation. You'll see that the practice examples might contain multiple patterns.

Meta Model Patterns

Meta Model Structures in Detail

The Meta Model deals with Deletions, Distortions and Generalisations, as follows:

Deletions

Something has been removed and must be recovered.

Distortions

Something has been changed and must be changed back to its original form.

Generalisations

Something has been simplified and must be specified. Some generalisations also generalise time, so that a single event becomes projected into the future.

Unspecified Nouns

An unspecified noun deletes either the subject or the object of a verb, forcing the listener to insert their own expectation. The noun might be missing altogether, or it might be replaced with a word like "it" or "thing".

Unspecified Verbs

Either the verb is deleted or its adverb is unspecified, putting the speaker's focus on the end result rather than the way in which it was achieved.

Simple Deletion

A simple deletion is also known as a "sentence fragment", which may or may not be grammatically correct.

Comparative Deletions

A hidden comparison is implied by words such as 'better' or 'faster'. The deletion hides both the reference point and the criteria for making the comparison.

A threshold also hides a comparative deletion. 'So that', 'just', 'until' and 'when' imply comparisons because they represent points on a scale of values.

Universal Quantifiers

A type of generalisation, the universal quantifier takes a single example and makes it apply to all cases or at all times, e.g. always, everyone, all, never, nowhere, nothing.

Presuppositions

A presupposition is what we must hold true for a person's language to be grammatically correct. For example, "The cat is in the tree again" presupposes that you know which cat, which tree and that you had an earlier experience of that cat being in that tree.

Mind Reading

With a mind read, we act as if we know what someone else is thinking or more likely project our own thoughts and attribute them to someone else.

Lost Referential Index

This deletion misses out the person or thing that the statement is attributed to, so we cannot test the validity of the statement.

Distorted Referential Index

A common distortion is to say "you" when I mean "I", which implies a dissociation where the speaker sees themselves as if they are looking at a film or in a mirror. The speaker's sense of self becomes detached from the visual representation of themselves.

Lost Performative

A performative verb is a statement which is itself an action, such as "I'm telling you to tidy your room". The action in the statement is the telling, not the tidying. A child's response might be, "I'm doing it now", when it would be more accurate to say, "I'm telling you that I'm doing it now". The response is a distortion because the child isn't doing it now, they're only saying so because what they really mean is, "I know you've told me to do it, and I'll do it later", with 'later' meaning 'never'.

A passive form of a verb also loses the person performing the action. A meeting was held, a decision was made. By whom? About what?

Negation

We can negate events in language which cannot logically be negated in the 'real world'. But don't worry about that right now.

Modal Operators

A modal operator is a rule which influences the future performance of an action. Any statement which is not a real time commentary will be phrased either in the future tense or the past tense. If the action took place in the past, it's a certainty, and there won't be a modal operator, just a commentary of what happened. However, for future actions, there is no certainty. Who knows what you may or may not do in the future?

There are broadly two possibilities for future actions; either you'll do something because you choose to, or because you are reacting to something or someone else. Your behaviour is being driven either from your internal desire map or the external reality map.

For a future action, you might say, "I want to read later", or, "I have to read later". Do you notice the difference between those two statements?

Modal Operator of Necessity

MONs are rules based on external triggers.

Model Operator of Possibility

MOPs are rules based on internal desires and options.

Nominalisation

A nominalisation is a verb that has been turned into a noun, indicating a "stopped" mental process. The object of the verb is also hidden.

Subordinate Clause

When, while, as or during are words which tell us that two or more events are taking place at the same time, and are therefore connected through time.

Complex Equivalence

The speaker takes two unrelated concepts and holds them as equivalent and therefore both true at the same time.

Cause and Effect

The cause and effect implies a relationship in time, so that when one event takes place, a second event will automatically follow. Words such as 'because', 'so' and 'until' are indications of cause and effect.

Selectional Restriction Violation

The class that something belongs to defines the qualities that it may have; a room may be cold but not sad. A person may be sad but not blue. We resolve these incongruences by transferring the qualities to ourselves, so sitting in a comfortable chair means that you are comfortable while sitting in a chair.

Unspecified Noun

Example: "I need a lift"

Response: "What kind of lift?"

A simple deletion omits and therefore implies part of the statement's meaning, either the subject or object, relying on the listener to insert their own assumption.

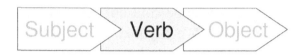

The missing information can be deleted entirely, or it can be replaced with an unspecified pronoun such as "it".

We derive meaning within a frame of reference. For example, what is the opposite of black? What is the opposite of red? With no frame of reference it's harder to answer the question.

When a conversation is taking place within a context of rapport, vague communication is processed as if it is specific. When someone asks you for "the thing", they expect you to know what they mean.

Practice examples

I need it now
It's good, isn't it?
It's all on top of me
I'm going

I wish I hadn't started
That's the way things are
It's for the best
Who wrote that?

Unspecified Verb

Example: "She ignored me"

Response: "How exactly did she ignore you?"

An unspecified verb is a simple deletion in which the verb is missing or replaced with something else.

As with the unspecified noun, we accept the validity of the action by interpreting the language within our own frame of reference. We need to check the action or behaviour in order to understand the speaker's frame of reference and recover the meaning that they intended.

The deletion may imply that the client's interpretation of some event is very different to someone else's.

Practice examples

Now you've done it

It's all over

I gave him the message

Let's get going

Let's go

She's gone

I calmed him

We're going places

He flew in

It's all getting too much

I built this up from nothing

I've lost it

Simple Deletion

Example: "I'm unhappy"

Response: "Unhappy about what?"

An even simpler deletion than the unspecified noun or verb, the simple deletion is also known as a "sentence fragment" and is unusual in the Meta Model in that it's not grammatically correct. With the other examples, the fact that the grammar is complete and correct tends to make the listener accept what is said automatically. At least the simple deletion alerts most people to its presence by providing insufficient information to the listener.

We tend to process simple deletions by filling in whatever is necessary to complete the grammatical structure. When you are strongly in rapport with someone, you can almost finish each others' sentences. We finish each others' sentences anyway, and with simple deletions, we sometimes insert a meaning which was not intended by the speaker.

Practice examples

You can't

If only

You're wrong

I'm lost

Never again

I'm falling

I know

I'll go

I'm stuck

That's it

Comparative Deletion

Example: "Our new product is more effective"

Response: "More effective than what [when, who etc.]?"

The speaker is creating a statement based on an implicit comparison criteria. The criteria itself is hidden, and so the listener learns the "rule" by absorbing the language. Often, the object of the comparison is missing too, so the listener learns to equate "better" with "best".

A comparison reveals a higher level category. For example, a car is better than a cow. Why? Because a cow's horns don't work. The joke reveals the higher category of 'transportation'.

Challenging comparative deletions is useful, not because it's important what is "best" but because we can learn a great deal about the speaker's perceptions and criteria.

Practice examples

This is far more efficient
Everything is better now
She's much brighter
He's more tolerant
Now we're getting somewhere

This is more like it
They're too slow
Blue is better
It's easier when you know how
It's better this way

Universal Quantifier

Example: "He never listens to me"

Response: "Never?"

Response: "Was there ever a time when he did?"

A type of generalisation, the universal quantifier takes a single example and makes it apply to all cases or at all times.

Think of someone who says, "I always fail". There are two problems here; firstly, the person is only noticing times in the past when they failed and is filtering out times when they succeeded, because success would disprove the rule. The second problem is that "always" means every time in the past and every time in the future, so by saying, "I always fail", the person is setting their perceptual filters to notice failure in the future, and they are then generating behaviour that is likely to lead to failure.

In short, by creating a universal rule, the person will create a self fulfilling prophecy. This is a very useful ability if you apply it to a belief like "I am always successful".

Practice examples

Nobody likes me
It's always the good people who lose
Nothing's the same any more
All our competitors are doing this
I've tried everything, nothing works
None of these examples make sense

Nothing works here
Everyone knows that
We all need to do this
You never do what I want
I've been everywhere
My boss never listens

Presupposition

Example: "I'll do that after I win this contract"

Response: "How do you know you'll win that contract?"

A presupposition is knowledge shared two or more people for the purpose of simplifying communication. For example, if you're attending my Master Practitioner training and I say, "Take a look at page 37 in the book" then we both know that we're talking about this book. At a more basic level, we both understand English, can count, can recognise numbers, can see, and so on.

Presuppositions cause problems when the speaker does not know for certain if the listener shares their knowledge, but acts as if they do, because, surely, everybody knows that, and you would be stupid if you didn't know it.

A presupposition is not an assumption. A presupposition comes before the message, an assumption comes afterwards.

In general, we would challenge the validity of the facts that are presupposed in the statement.

Practice examples

Why are you doing that again?   When are you coming back?
She's just left   Pass me your book
Here we go again   It's easy once you know how
Don't worry, this won't hurt   When are you leaving?
I'll never learn this   I wish I found it as easy as you

Mind Reading

Example: "You don't like me"

Response: "How do know that I don't like you?"

Response: "What leads you to believe that?"

Response: "What makes you think that?"

With a mind read, we act as if we know what someone else is thinking. Of course, you may be right so the point is that you do not know for certain and it may not be useful to respond as if you do.

You might do something, or not do something, because you know how someone would react. You may know that person very well, but the only way to know what they are thinking is to ask them, as uncomfortable as that may be.

Practice examples

I know you don't believe me   He'll hate you if you do that
He doesn't want to help me   He's in a bad mood today
You just don't care   She's much happier now
He wouldn't want me to   They won't buy that
She'll never believe me   People don't want that now
My boss thinks I'm lazy   I know what you're thinking

Lost Referential Index

Example: "They don't care"

Response: "Who doesn't care?"

This deletion misses out the person or thing that the statement is attributed to, so we cannot test the validity of the statement. The statement becomes a belief, merely as a result of it having been attributed to someone.

Practice examples

The writing's on the wall
They should know better
People make mistakes
No-one does that any more
People drink too much
Everybody knows that
It's such a pity

That's too expensive
This happens every day
People shouldn't do that
It's vital to be on time
Cars are dangerous
Sales is difficult
Global warming is bad

Distorted Referential Index

Example: "You don't care"

Response: "Who doesn't care?"

Often you will hear people distorting a referential index, saying "you" when they really mean "I". This is a sign of dissociation; the person says "you" because, in their minds, they are addressing themselves as a separate person.

However, there is a deeper and more significant meaning. When you hear "you" where "I" would be correct, what you might be hearing is an instruction, where the speaker is attempting to normalise their experience by getting you to feel the same way.

Practice examples

We don't like this

You can't have what you want

You're on your own

You know what it's like

You shouldn't eat fatty foods

It makes you want to scream!

You know how it is

My team doesn't agree

They don't listen

You'll live to regret this

You must be on time

What you want to do is...

You feel trapped

When you feel bad, you cry

Lost Performative

Example: "These new prices are a bit high"

Response: "Who said that the new prices are high?"

A performative verb is a statement that is itself the action that it represents. "I'm telling you to be quiet" is an example, whereas, "I'm going mad at the kids" isn't a literal action. You might see a person running, but to say they are rushing is a distortion. A lost performative could be either the missing action of hearing someone tell you, or the missing action that has been distorted by a judgement.

This is a tricky one to get your head round. Every statement contains both a part which represents an action, and a part which literally is the action itself. *I'm telling you about lost performatives* so that you can learn the Meta Model, for example. However, in most of our everyday conversations, the performative part is missing. Instead of saying, "The boss told me to get this finished today", we say, "I need to get this finished today". By deleting the performative, the statement becomes automatically true, which makes it hard to challenge.

Consider that a passive verb is also a Lost Performative – a meeting was held, actions were taken, people were spoken to. By whom? About what?

Practice examples

A good day was had by all
Books are wonderful
I need to get home early
There's nothing good on TV
Time flies like an arrow
I was just about to say...
The boss is going crazy

Learning is easy
The Meta Model can't be used
Computers have been changed
These new glasses don't suit me
Fruit flies like a banana
There's no better way to learn
I'm working on a report right now

Negation

Example: "I can't do that"

Response: "Can you remember when you did do it?"

Response: "What would happen if you did do it?"

With language, we can create conceptual models which cannot exist in the 'real world'.

What was in this box?

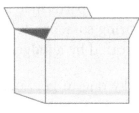

How about this box?

A negation provides a frame of reference for an event occurring in the past or the future. "There is no elephant in this room". Was there one here yesterday? A negation can also hide a simple deletion. "There is no elephant in this room (which I am prepared to talk about)".

A negation therefore tells us that the thing or event being negated actually does exist, somewhere, sometime. Otherwise, why would the person mention it?

Practice examples

I wouldn't do that
No-one listens to me
I can't decide what to do

Honestly, I'm not lying
We never go out
Don't tell me

Modal Operator of Necessity

Example: "I must learn this"

Response: "What happens if you don't?"

Modal operators modify the verb and are often an indication that the speaker is basing their behaviour or thoughts on rules, beliefs about their behaviour.

The important question to explore here is "how did they learn those rules?"

People are very good at learning rules and will continue to follow them, or break them, long after the need for the rule has gone away.

MONs are an indicator of external rules, and often appear together with a Lost Performative. For many external rules, this is often a parent or teacher from childhood, and hearing a MON tells you that the person is projecting control onto someone else. When you hear a MON you'll often also hear a Distorted Referential Index (you) – a sign of dissociation.

Notice that some words which we often categorise as modal operators are actually not. They serve a similar role in relation to future actions, but they do not contain rules. Can you see which words these are?

Practice examples

We shouldn't do that
You ought to get a good appraisal
I mustn't let this get me down
I have to finish before I go home
You should always be dressed smartly
You shall get that work done to day

You must arrive on time
You can't leave yet
You've got to laugh
You'll need your coat
I have to get this right
You ought to listen more

Model Operator of Possibility

Example: "I can't get the hang of this"

Response: "What stops you?"

Response: "What would happen if you did?"

Where the modal operator of necessity indicated the presence of a rule, this language pattern indicates the presence of a choice, and that an exclusion has been applied to that choice.

"I can't tell her everything" indicates that the speaker has imagined telling everything, imagined something undesirable happening and has chosen not to.

MOPs are an indicator of internal rules, also known as decisions and choices. Hearing a MOP tells you that the person has control. When you hear a MOP you'll often also hear a first person Referential Index (I) – a sign of an associated kinaesthetic experience.

As with MONs, there are some words which we often treat as modal operators which are actually not, they are examples of something else. Can you see which these are?

Practice examples

I can't call that customer	You can't do that
He wants to go home	You can finish that report
I can just imagine!	You could if you wanted to
I can't imagine that	I can't tell him that
I will stop	You might succeed if you try
I'll never to able to learn this	I can't apply for that job
I would go to the party	You could at least try

Conditional Rules

Modal operators are much more interesting than simple modifiers on verbs – they tell us how rules execute. A modal operator tells us under what conditions an action will take place in the future.

What you'll often hear is the first part of the rule, with the second part deleted, for example someone might say, "I would go to the party". By deleting the 'if' and the 'else', we don't know what conditions are or are not being met in the speaker's experience.

Must	External rule, mandatory, also cause and effect
Have to	External, future possession - a lost performative
Shall	External rule, command or instruction
Need	External rule, essential or important
Ought	External rule, obligation, derived from 'owe'
Should	External rule, obligation, derived from 'shall'
Might	If, derived from 'may' (past tense)
Could	If, Then, But/Except/Else (past tense of 'can')
Would	If, Then, But/Except/Else (past tense of 'will')
Want to	Future possession of something currently lacking
May	Future, possibility or permission
Can	Future, capability
Will	Future, intention or desire

Not Actually Modal Operators

As I've mentioned, there are some words which we often treat as modal operators but which are not.

- Have to, Have, Had

- Got to, Got, Get

- Want

- Need

What are they, then, if they are not modal operators. Let's first consider what a modal operator is; a rule which determines a future action. The words listed above are not rules.

Have, got and get are statements of possession. I have cheese, I got cheese, I get cheese. I will get cheese. I am getting tired of cheese. Have you got any cheese?

Let's refer to the ever-useful Online Etymology Dictionary.

Have: Old English habban to own, possess; be subject to, experience". To have to for "must" (1570s) is from sense of "possess as a duty or thing to be done" (Old English).

Get: c. 1200, from Old Norse "o obtain, reach; to be able to; to beget; to learn; to be pleased with".

These definitions make have, got and get unspecified verbs or lost performatives. In the infinitive or future tense, they indicate that the speaker expects to possess something in the future which they do not possess now. In their perception of time, they can skip from the present to the future with no indication or idea about what actions they will take.

How about want and need? The word 'want' defines the entire self-help industry. What do you want? Have whatever you want.

Want means 'lack'. It is not a modal operator, we could say that it is closer to a comparative deletion. How do you know that you want something? Because you can see that someone else has it. Advertising is designed to show you all the things that you don't have - yet.

Need also means 'lack' but in terms of a necessity, something which you depend on. So you will need things which you had and depended on such as air, water, love and a new phone.

We could treat these words as modal operators in that they represent future expectations and therefore drive current behaviour, however we have to be careful with the time gap of the lost performative or unspecified verb, and the external comparison of want and need.

With get or have, we might question the time gap or the actions to be taken, as for an unspecified verb or lost performative.

With want and need, we might question the reference, as for a comparative deletion.

Practice examples

Got to get you into my life	Get it done
I have to leave right away	I want it all
I need you tonight	He say what he wants
We had a great meeting	You can't have what you want
I've got to be on time	We need to get better at this
You don't want to miss out	Get lost

Nominalisation

Example: "I want recognition"

Response: "How do you want to be recognised?"

Response: "Who do you want to recognise?"

A nominalisation is a verb that has been turned into a noun, indicating a "stopped" mental process. Imagine yourself at a meeting, making a decision. Now imagine yourself meeting with people, deciding about something. Different? In the first example, did you imagine a still image whereas in the second example, you imagined a moving image?

You'll often hear dissociations too, as if the person is looking at a photograph of an event.

When people are "stuck" you will hear nominalisations. You can then ask questions which turn the nominalisation back into an active verb, for example turning 'a meeting' back into 'to meet'.

Turning the verb into a noun can put it in either the subject or object position. As subject, the action now makes the speaker passive.

Practice examples

We made a decision	They've got no patience
It's love	He makes a bad impression
I want more direction	This needs more attention
There's no relationship	We need better management
We had a great meeting	It's a tricky situation
The argument made me angry	Omissions are unacceptable

Exception

I've seen many trainers over the years talk about the word 'but' as a negation. "I'd like to go to the party but I'm so busy" means that you're not going to the party, therefore 'but' is a negation.

BUT IS NOT A NEGATION

But is an EXCEPTION to a rule.

How could so many NLP trainers have missed the most obvious clue? The phrase, "All but one", as in, "All but one of us went to the party".

Computer programs are built upon rules, and those rules cannot satisfy every possible configuration of a system, so rules must have exceptions otherwise the computer will crash. Therefore, a programming rule might look like this:

1. If the sun is shining

2. Then open the window

3. Else the window is open

In other words, if it's sunny, open the window unless the window is already open.

When you hear the word 'but', what you're hearing is an exception to a rule, and that is a very important thing to hear because it tells you what the speaker does when they can't do what they intended to do. The exception prevents the person from 'crashing' or becoming stuck and unable to move forwards.

Conflict

I've seen many trainers over the years talk about the word 'try' as a negation. "I'll try to go to the party but I'm so busy" means that you're not going to the party, therefore 'try' is a negation.

TRY IS NOT A NEGATION

'Try' tells you that two or more rules are operating, at the same time, in conflict.

Have a go at this experiment. First, imagine yourself opening a door. Next, imagine yourself trying to open a door. What difference did you notice?

When you imagined trying, I predict that you visualised a short movie that looped over and over, where you attempted to open a door and failed. Trying is neither opening nor not opening, it is both at the same time.

Another word that you'll often see in combination with 'try' is 'just'. Again, imagine yourself just opening a door.

Let's imagine that 'try' is a loop joining two states which cannot coexist, forwards from 'now', and 'just' is a loop joining two states which cannot coexist, backwards from 'now'. 'Just' can also mean 'recent past'.

"I'll try to finish this chapter" (Finish/not finish loop)

"I'll just finish this chapter" (Will/just loop)

"I just finished this chapter" (Recent past)

"I was just about to finish this chapter" (Past/future loop)

Negation and Contraction

Modal operators can change slightly when negated and contracted. For example, 'need' can negate to either 'not need' or 'need not', with different meanings. 'not need' negates the needing, whereas 'need not' negates the action that is needed.

Here are some more variations.

Must	Must not		Mustn't
Have to	Have to not	Not have to	
Need	Need not	Not need	Needn't
Ought	Ought not		Oughtn't
Should	Should not		Shouldn't
Might	Might not		Mightn't
Could	Could not		Couldn't
Would	Would not		Wouldn't
Want to		Have?	
May	May not		May not
Can	Can not	Cannot	Can't
Will	Will not		Won't
Am	Am not		Aren't

Subordinate Clause of Time

A subordinate clause adds additional information to the main statement and varies in detail depending on the prior knowledge of the listener.

"My cat is ill"

"My cat, which I only got last week, is ill"

"My cat, when I say my cat of course I really mean next door neighbour's cat but it spends more time at my house, is ill"

When a subordinate clause relates to time, it can indicate two or more events happening at the same time. While you're reading this, you're breathing, for example.

As	Yet	When	Since	Before	After
During	While	As	Yet	Already	As soon as

You'll notice that these words are similar to either Cause and Effect or Complex Equivalence.

In a Cause and Effect, one event precedes another.

In a Complex Equivalence, two events or 'facts' coincide.

Practice examples

I'll be happy when I leave
I can't speak to her about it until things calm down
I'll be free as soon as I get a new job
I've already made my mind up
I have to make sure everything is perfect before I go away
After this weekend everything will be different
Since Friday things have been a bit better

Quote

A very interesting form of subordinate clause comes when a person writes a phrase in parentheses (), quotation marks "", or separated by hyphens - -. For example:

"My boss (who is not happy) cancelled my appraisal"

"My boss, who is "not happy", cancelled my appraisal"

"My boss, who is 'not happy', cancelled my appraisal"

"My boss - who is not happy - cancelled my appraisal"

In spoken language, quotes can be marked out using a change in voice tone. "My boss keeps telling me that I have to *take responsibility* and I've had enough."

Here are some real examples:

"I will also know more "stuff" and feel more confident about utilising "it" at a beyond technique level."

This student wanted to use NLP techniques easily in coaching without thinking about it. If we regard the words in quotes as another voice, trying to interrupt and say something, it's actually an instruction to himself to "stuff it", to relax, let go and trust his instincts.

"Greater understanding, tools, techniques for how to work with clients (and myself) to achieve behavioural changes"

This student's statement was interrupted by another speaker, (myself), wanting to make sure she didn't get left out.

When a person quotes themselves, who is really speaking?

Complex Equivalence

Example: "When she's quiet I know she's angry"

Response: "How do you know that quiet means angry?"

The speaker takes two unrelated concepts and holds them as equivalent. If one is true then the other must also be true. If I equate my personal worth with 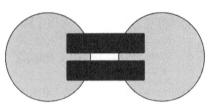 promotion, and I miss out on a promotion then I feel worthless. If I equate love with being listened to and someone doesn't appear to be listening to me then they don't love me.

The complex equivalence and the cause and effect reflect our ability to generalise rules about the physical world and are vital for our survival. Rules such as "red sky at night, shepherd's delight" would have ensured our survival as a species, but the same ability now creates rules such as "Boss's door closed, he is in a bad mood" which may not be useful. When you challenge a Complex Equivalence, look for the sensory experience that the generalisation is based on.

Practice examples

Tall people are scary
Loud music is bad for you
He's late... he'll get fired
It's raining... another bad day
I failed, I might as well give up

When she smiles she's happy
Food is a comfort
I'm in trouble, I messed up
Carrots are good for you
This is the only way to learn

Cause and Effect

Example: "I was late, the whole day is going to go wrong"

Response: "How do you know the day will go wrong?"

Response: "How are you going to make the day go wrong?"

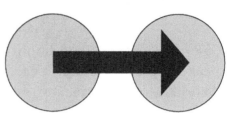

The cause and effect implies a relationship in time, so that when one event takes place, a second event will automatically follow. This is useful in the physical world, so that if I step off a cliff, I will at some point in the future hit the ground with a "splat".

When we apply the cause and effect rule to people, we often get into problems because people do not follow the same physical rules as inanimate objects, and they do not always behave in predictable ways.

Practice examples

My boss makes me angry
I've started so I'll finish
Once you pop you just can't stop
If I go to the meeting, I'll just get angry
I won't apply because they'll never give me the job
Things always go wrong when she walks in here

If you do that I'll leave
I'll do it after I finish this

Selectional Restriction Violation

A SRV is the attribution of qualities or behaviours to something which logically cannot have those qualities, because an object cannot act, it can only be acted upon. For example, 'relaxing' cannot be a quality of a chair, because relaxing is an action that a chair cannot perform, therefore the verb must apply to the person in the chair.

A SRV is a form of dissociation. "It was a tense moment." The speaker recalls feeling tense, doesn't like feeling tense, dissociates from the feeling, logically attributes the feeling to something else in the sentence, and the moment, or the situation, or the meeting becomes tense.

When we hear a SRV, it's like hearing a Distorted Referential Index, where the speaker is dissociating in order to avoid a primary experience of a kinaesthetic response. We might choose to challenge that directly by inviting them to associate with the response and discuss it, or we might make a note of it and park it for later. Whatever the SRV verb or adjective is, it cannot logically apply to the noun that it is applied to, therefore it must only apply to the actor in the statement, either the speaker or the person they are speaking about.

Practice examples

It was a tense moment	This book is fascinating
The bath is running	It's such a happy song
I don't like uncomfortable silences	Say, that's a nice bike
What a big smile you have	Where's my big coat?

I can't bear to be in an empty room, the silence is deafening
I'm not happy with my partner's undesirable hobbies
That was a wonderful experience

Passive Verb

The final structure that I'll mention is the passive verb, where the speaker becomes the recipient of an action and another person or even an object becomes the actor.

I'm sure you've heard a child say, "He made me do it". As an adult, no-one can make you do anything. They can present you with compelling reasons, and you might feel obligated to do what they are asking, however you are still making a free choice. When you say that someone else 'made you', what you're actually doing is trying to maintain control by avoiding responsibility.

Like the child who tries to shift blame onto the big boy who did it and ran away, adults often don't want to face an imagined punishment, and the internal conflict which arises from them doing something which they know is wrong will surface in their language and behaviour.

Sentences containing passive verbs are easy to miss because they appear to be grammatically correct. "I made him" and "He made me" are both well formed, so we have to step back from the detailed structure to the logical sequence which is being described.

There are certain actions which a person cannot perform upon themselves. Tickling, holding, carrying, pushing, driving and catching are physical actions which cannot logically be performed on yourself. You also cannot ask, love or see yourself. When you find that the speaker is the object of these verbs, a dissociation is taking place which you can investigate further.

Why?

You may or may not have noticed that the one apparent omission from the Meta Model is the question, "Why?"

That's because a NLP Practitioner would *never* ask why.

Are you thinking, "What, *never*?"

If so, then you are learning the Meta Model. Well done.

If not, then you a very good student. Well done.

Either way, I bet you're itching to ask, "Why?"

Consider this example:

"I can't get that done today"

"Why?"

"Well, because I have to get this done, and that done, and everyone's demanding this and that, and I'm going to be working late anyway, and..."

"Sorry I asked..."

Essentially, what the person gives you in response to "why" is not causes but reasons or justifications. However, the grammar of the answer implies that these are all causal events which pre-dated your request and mean that they really cannot get that done today.

We ask 'why?' when we want to understand the reasons behind something, but only an authority or creator can answer that. Children ask 'why?', for example 'why is the sky blue?' or 'why can't I have ice cream for breakfast?', and common answers from short-tempered parents include 'because it is' and 'because I said so'. The child whose 'why?' questions go unanswered may develop a tendency to look outside of themselves for answers in life, because they never learn to internalise the process of figuring things out. For example, a client recently brought a list of 7 questions to a coaching session. I asked what the invisible 8th question was, and she replied, "Why does this keep happening to me?"

The obvious answer is, "Because it does". A more challenging answer might be, "Because it's what you want".

An authority figure would ask 'why?' which leads to justifications, and this is the problem with the question 'why?'.

When your client or colleague answers the question, they are giving you a series of events that are all happening now, but their answer implies that these events happened in the past. The question presupposes a causal connection between the question and the answer, even though there usually is none. In other words, causes are in the past, justifications are created in the present.

Here's an illustration.

"Why aren't we in Birmingham?"

1. "Because you wanted to stop for a break and then we hit traffic and it's been raining and then we got talking about work."

2. "Because we're on the road to London."

Both of these answers are grammatically correct, both are phrased as a series of events which pre-date the question, yet only one can really stand up to any scrutiny as a valid response to the question.

Human beings have a need to structure time, as explained very nicely by Eric Berne in his work on Transactional Analysis. From TA's point of view, humans structure time in a number of ways, such as engaging in rituals or playing interpersonal games.

From NLP's point of view, we are more interested, not in what we do in structuring time, but in how we code and represent these structures of time.

In practice, this means that human beings have an interesting ability to imagine the future, place goals in it and then take action towards those goals.

On the downside, this also means that we can imagine barriers to achieving those goals and then act as if those barriers are real now, thereby blocking or diverting any efforts made towards achieving the goal.

Another view of goal setting is that we each have many goals, and some of them are in conflict.

Let's say that someone at work is afraid of public speaking, but they also feel driven to please their boss. Pleasing your boss by being conscientious and hard working is a typical TA 'script'. Fear of public speaking is a typical NLP 'fear'.

What happens when this person thinks about presenting? Do they think of it as if they're saying, "I need to get some milk on the way home?"

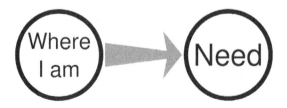

No. They don't. Their fear sits in the background, as if someone is holding a magnet under a table while you try to roll a steel ball across it. They know that they need to present, and they know that they need to please their boss.

However, the fear is an opposing force, created by an imaginary goal. The person's desire to deliver the presentation is one goal, their expectation to fail is another. Your brain does not differentiate between what you want as being good or bad, it just delivers what you think about through a cycle of selective attention, action and reinforcement.

Let's ask this poor person why they don't want to deliver the presentation.

"Because it's going to go horribly wrong and I'll let everyone down"

The grammatical structure is identical to that of the previous examples, but this time there is a curious difference; the reason is expressed as a past event when in fact it is a future event, and if there is only one thing that we can say for certain about the future, it is that it hasn't happened yet.

The person has constructed a sequence of imaginary events, where one, the problem, precludes the other, the goal. But since both are imaginary, there is no causal connection between them. The only thing that makes these events plausible is that, when the person talks about them, their language is grammatically correct.

Instead of asking, "Why", let's try some alternatives.

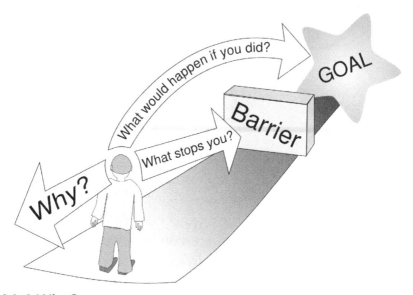

14.1 Why?

Have a partner think of a statement that begins with "I can't...", for example, "I can't think of a statement"

Have them say the statement in exactly the same way, then ask them these three questions, like so:

(Statement)

"Why?"

(Statement)

"What stops you?"

(Statement)

"What would happen if you did?"

Notice how the three answers are structurally different.

Meta Model – Worked Examples

Let's put all of that together with some worked examples.

"It's easier when you don't think about it"

The normal response would be, "Mmm, yes", however the statement is actually quite a complex hypnotic instruction. Let's pull it apart.

It's   Simple deletion; what is 'it'?

       Simple deletion; contraction hides the 'is'

       Complex equivalence; 'is'

easier Comparative deletion; easier than what or when?

       Kinaesthetic, therefore first position

when Subordinate clause of time

you   Shifted referential index

don't Simple deletion; contraction hides the command 'do'

       Negation; contraction hides the 'not'

think Direct command

       Auditory digital

about Dissociation to second position, possibly visual

it   Simple deletion; is this the same 'it' as before?

Goodness. All of that in one, throwaway phrase. What seems like an innocent expression, a hint for how to make a technique easier, becomes a covert command. The subordinate clause of time in the middle is the focal point for the two halves of the statement. It is an instruction for the listener to hold the first part in memory, thereby making "it's easier" a presupposition for the second part.

It's easier	Presupposition
when you	Forces the presupposition and command to coexist in time
don't think about it	Direct command to think about it

Consider this request, "When you go to the shop, could you fetch me a drink please?"

To make sense of the question, the listener must hold both halves of the statement in their mind and overlay them so that they coexist at the same time. There would be no point in getting you a drink before or after going to the shop.

The first part presupposes that you are indeed going to the shop; let's say that this is a true reflection of your intention.

You can picture yourself going to the shop, and at the same time, add a picture of you getting me a drink.

The subordinate clause of time is a very important linguistic tool, because in forcing two statements to coexist in time, it forces two mental representations to coexist in time, and if one is already true, it makes the second true too.

We haven't even come to the simple deletion yet. What is 'it'? Well, whatever you want to be easy, obviously.

I was walking in the park earlier and I met a flasher. "Nice out, isn't it?" he said. The 'it' is ambiguous. Does 'it' mean the weather, or does 'it' mean 'it'? You know what I mean.

So the whole phrase presupposes that you want something to be easier, and that whatever it is will be easier when you think about it. The "don't think about it" part is like saying, "don't think about a dog" or "don't worry".

Superficially, the instruction is to not think about 'it', when unconsciously, the instruction is to think about 'it'.

The result is a very effective trance induction.

"I have a difficult situation at work"

Is there a nominalisation in this statement?

Yes, there is. The nominalisation is the word "situation".

To counteract a nominalisation, you must turn it into an active verb. It seems an awkward thing to ask, however, the grammatically appropriate response is:

"Where do you situate yourself with respect to the people you work with?". And while it might not appear to make any sense, the way we would normally ask this is, "Where do you sit at work?" Asking the question, even the most odd-sounding question, reveals new information.

Remember, to find a nominalisation, just look for the noun that you can't put in a wheelbarrow.

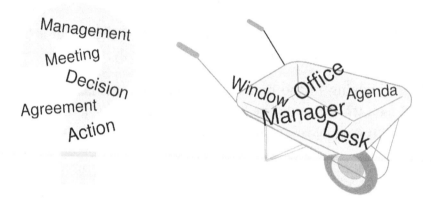

A nominalisation is a sign of a "stuck" mental process, although in reality, our thoughts don't stop. Think about other things in the world around you that use a still image to represent an action or event. What do you notice about them?

15 Presuppositions

Presuppositions and the Meta Model

Presuppositions are important in NLP because they give hints about a person's inner experience and therefore the 'reality' that they have created for themselves. When you ask your colleague to pass you a pen, your reality probably excludes the possibility that they will say, "You can take this pen and stick it up your nose, loser", on the grounds that if you thought that this would happen, you wouldn't ask them.

If you get a response like that, you have two options. Since their response doesn't match your reality, you can either discount their response and hold your reality true, or you can take their response to heart and discount your reality. In practice, the latter is very, very difficult for some people.

A reality based reaction to this would be to think, "Oh my goodness, what did I do to upset them? I must find out and put things right". A subjective or self-centred reaction would be, "What's eating them? All I did was ask for a pen. If something's wrong with them, they shouldn't take it out on me".

As you can see, a reality based, objective reaction is based on the belief that the world does exist out there, it does contain people with their own free will, and it is liable to change from one minute to the next.

A subjective, self centred reaction is based on the belief that the world is how it is and that any disparities are down to the peculiar behaviour of other people.

In Transactional Analysis, these world views are described in terms of whether a person believes themselves and other people to be 'OK' or not.

Any statement contains multiple presuppositions, however some are more valuable than others in terms of understanding the speaker's inner experience.

Let's have a simple definition of what a presupposition is; it's the collective set of observations that must be true in order for a statement to be grammatically correct.

In the Meta Model section of this book, there are many examples of statements that you can use to practice the Meta Model. We could say that they are all forms of presupposition, and what the Meta Model does is to give you different ways to recognise and clarify them.

Just take a moment to review the previous paragraph and notice the presuppositions that it contains. For a start, it presupposes that you can read, that you understand written English, that you are reading the book, that you have read the Meta Model section, that you know what the Meta Model is and so on.

Here are some ideas for approaching the practice examples that were given in the Meta Model section:

When this plan fails I'll say "told you so"

- How do you know the plan will fail?

- Are you saying that you are going to make it fail?

I don't know how to manage such a difficult project

- How do you know it will be difficult (casual listeners will accept the presupposition and focus on the speaker's ability or confidence)

- Are you setting out to make it difficult?

Don't worry, this won't hurt

- What makes you think I'm worried? (casual listeners will accept the presupposition and focus on the speaker's anticipation of pain)

- Do you want it to hurt?

It will be easier when he leaves

- What makes you think he's leaving?

- How do you know it will be easier?

- What will be easier?

- What makes you think that easier is better?

What will the next reorganisation bring?

- What makes you expect a reorganisation?

When are you leaving?

- What makes you think I'm leaving?

- How do you know I'm still here? (My little joke...)

You'd find Meta Model easier to learn if you'd slow down

- What makes you think I'm finding it difficult?

- How would slowing down be be better?

Verbal language conveys only a small part of communication, the rest being made up of voice tone and physiology. In practice, this means that verbal language is a shortened, condensed version of a rich mental representation. Whenever you communicate, you're passing only a tiny part of the information required, so the listener has to insert part of their own experience in order to derive meaning. This all happens unconsciously and instantly, making presuppositions so powerful.

However, a typical adult is estimated to have a vocabulary of around 50,000 words, compared to 616,500 entries in the Oxford English Dictionary.

With 50,000 words to draw upon, we are able to make surprisingly fine distinctions in meaning, especially when we add facial expressions and voice tone into the mix.

15.1 Presuppositions

Take a moment to consider these questions, paying careful attention to your response, including what images come to mind as you hear or read each question.

Are you thinking about NLP training?

When are you thinking about NLP training?

Why are you thinking about NLP training?

Are you thinking about your career?

What plans are you making for your career?

What plans have you made for your career?

What plans will you make for your career?

What is important about your career plans?

Remember, every single sentence you speak is full of presuppositions, they're a necessary part of the syntax of natural language. They help us to keep our language short and relevant so that we can reduce the number of words we need to convey a simple concept or instruction.

Our common frame of reference generates presuppositions, without which we would have difficulty communicating verbally. We could say that, usually, we communicate from our own frame of reference, whilst rapport creates a shared frame of reference.

It's always worth noticing the presuppositions that people use naturally, as they give away a great deal of information about their own frame of reference, their values, their beliefs and their needs.

In other words, presuppositions are a clue to a person's reality. If they want to change that reality, the first thing that needs to happen is for them to 'wake up' to an objective reality that is different to what they have created in their minds.

One step towards this is to reflect back and unpick presuppositions, comparing them to objective reality.

My mother once said, "No-one comes to visit me". I should add that I did not seek to change her world view, because she didn't ask me to. When I am a 'son', I am not a 'coach'.

First, we have a generalisation that we know cannot hold true, because at the time she said this, I was visiting her. So we know that there is a generalisation because we can hear it, we know that there is a distortion because I'm sitting there as counter-evidence, and we know that there is a deletion because something must have been deleted in order for the statement to accurately reflect her world view.

Later in the conversation, she commented on something that my sister said to her. "When did you see her?", I asked. "When she came over on Friday", replied my mother.

Shortly afterwards, she commented on something that my brother said to her. "When did you see him?", I asked. "When he came up last weekend", replied my mother.

And the same thing happened with my Uncle Ron. He visited my mother just a few days previously, too.

How much counter-evidence does she need to prove that people do in fact come to visit her?

None. If that amount of counter-evidence doesn't make any difference, it's because it is excluded from her world view. Although statisticians argue otherwise, as far as human logic is concerned, the existence of white swans does not have any impact on our belief that there are no black swans. This gives us an important clue as to what my mother is deleting.

What she actually communicated was this:

"No-one [deleted] comes to visit me."

It's still grammatically correct, and if we try out a few different candidate words, we'll see that the statement also works as a comment on her reality.

"No-one nice comes to visit me."

"No-one new comes to visit me."

"No-one who cares about me comes to visit me."

"No-one important comes to visit me."

"No-one I care about comes to visit me."

"No-one who isn't visiting through obligation comes to visit me."

The last one is the closest match. She believes that people only visit elderly relatives through a sense of obligation, and she believes this because that was her view when she was younger. Therefore, people do visit her, but they don't count because they're only visiting because they have to. She wants people to visit through choice.

The illogical and hurtful truth for her visitors is that they are visiting through choice. They all have many other ways to spend their time. But the longer she holds this view, the more likely she is to lose their company, leaving only the people who do feel obliged, such as my sister or someone from Age Concern. Her statement becomes true in reality, over time.

My mother's statement contains a second, and far more important generalisation. Have you spotted it? Here's the statement again:

"No-one comes to visit me."

'No-one' is an obvious generalisation, but it is simply a rule for excluding people who "don't count". There is a far more important presupposition in there, maintaining her world view over time so that it cannot be changed.

That presupposition is the word "comes".

She is taking a past perception and projecting it forwards into the future by maintaining it in the present. We can conceive the concept of time, and we can imagine events in time. We can even write in diaries and put future plans on 'to do' lists, just to prove that there is a past and future. However, as far as our minds and bodies are concerned, there is no past or future. I feel hungry now because I skipped breakfast this morning. I feel tired now because I was up early this morning. I have to wash the car today because I drove through some mud last week. All of these present conditions serve to remind us of past events, however those events can no longer change the present reality.

What I intend to do tomorrow or in five minutes' time is irrelevant. What I am doing now will shape tomorrow. When I know that I need to do something and I put it off, I just create a situation where that need is heightened and I put myself under more pressure to do what I need to do.

"No-one came to visit me last week" has one obvious generalisation and is easily challenged.

"No-one is coming to visit me next week" is unverifiable.

Fortune tellers use such statements to influence their clients; "I sense that you are reading a book at the moment, and I feel that it will bring many new opportunities into your life in the coming months and years".

So the specific phrasing of "comes" means that this world view is true now, and "now" means "always".

There are subtleties within language that can take a very long time to learn and master, and NLP Practitioner training really scratches the surface. This is why I said in the introduction that it doesn't matter how long you spend in NLP training, it's never long enough.

16 Milton Model

Broadly, speaking, the Milton Model is the converse of the Meta Model, and can they serve opposite purposes, depending on the current goals of the client and Practitioner.

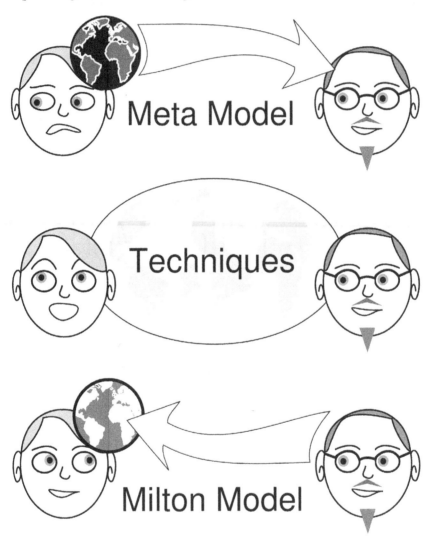

I'm going to explore Milton Model at this point because the Milton Model should be something that you work to incorporate into every step of your coaching process.

As with the Meta Model, the Milton Model is based upon fundamental grammatical rules but instead of using them to recover lost information, it uses them to deliberately lose information, allowing the listener to add their own experience or expectations in order to create a complete meaning.

For a NLP Practitioner, this means that you can shape a context within which your client can play out their goals and desired behaviours.

However, you can probably see why Milton Model is so popular with marketers and sales people.

Let's face it, as soon as someone comes along with a new model of influence, someone else will seize on it as an opportunity to get what they want at others' expense.

Before NLP came subliminal messaging and body language. After NLP came Cialdini's principles of persuasion. Even Dale Carnegie's "How to win friends and influence people" can be said to shroud influencing tips within an overall message of being charitable to others.

I can't dictate how you employ NLP. I can only share what I have learned.

Let's look at the various Milton Model 'patterns' in detail.

Milton Model Patterns

Presupposition

I've already discussed presuppositions in some depth. There is a story that Milton Erickson once agreed to see a young boy with behavioural problems. Other counsellors and therapists had declared that nothing could be done with him.

Allegedly, the boy sat in Erickson's office. Erickson said something like, "How surprised will you be when you discover that your attitude has completely changed?"

"I'll be very surprised!", said the boy.

According to the story, the boys behaviour did then change. What we don't know is what really happened next. Let's believe that the boy became a model of good citizenship following Erickson's intervention. It's a nicer end to the story, isn't it? If you're screaming, "Nicer than what??" then "well done".

The story serves to illustrate an important aspect of presuppositions, which is that one statement can presuppose another, and in order to make sense of one, the other has to be true, even momentarily, and if it is possible for that statement to be true, just for a moment, then it is possible that it can remain true, if that is useful.

The question therefore remains; how pleased will you be when you find yourself mastering presuppositions?

- What's the *most* important thing you've achieved in your life so far?

- When do you want to begin coaching?

- How do you know that this is the best book on NLP?

Awareness Predicates

An objective model of reality presupposes that things exist, whether or not you were aware of them. If a tree falls in the forest and no-one is there, does it make a sound? Yes, the sound of a squirrel going "splat".

For example, have you noticed the weight of the book yet? Nice, isn't it? What about your feet? Have you noticed how warm they are? And the air! What about that air! There's so much to breathe!

All of these things existed before you noticed them, which gives them a realism that doesn't exist when you create ideas in your mind out of nowhere.

Of course, since awareness predicates are a form of presupposition, they don't necessarily have to relate to objects or events that actually existed prior to the moment of awareness.

- Have you noticed that you're reading this book?

- When did you first realise that you could really master the Milton Model?

- I just realised – you must be wondering how to sign up for a coaching program, how negligent of me[1]

- What was that? Did you hear it?

---

1 Remember, this book isn't only about the technology of NLP, it's about how to be a good NLP Practitioner, and for that, you need clients

Conversational Postulates

Sometimes, people ask questions that hide a command. What they are essentially asking is, "Can I tell you what to do please?"

You're probably familiar with the more socially acceptable version, "Can you do me a big favour?"

Or the version that is acceptable within personal relationships, "How much do you love me?"

This Milton pattern has the effect of gaining compliance to a command.

- Can you tell me the time?

- Can you imagine making a decision soon?

- Would you let me know tomorrow?

- Can you think about how you want the future to be?

- Would you consider a possibility?

- Do you think you can imagine being successful?

- Could you consider how your life will be different?

Utilisation

Utilisation is the art of taking what happens or what is said and using it as if you had planned for it. If you start a presentation with, "none of this is true", then if someone disagrees, you can say, "that's OK, because it's not true!"

A good way to start a business meeting is by saying, Thank you all for coming, I know that you made time for this, and that you have made an effort to be here, so I want to make sure that we all get real value for that time by keeping to the agenda and staying focused. How do you feel about that?"

If you're training or coaching, you can use utilisation as a way of pre-emptively dealing with interruptions.

- If you hear a mobile ring, it's a sign that you're paying attention

- If you need to deal with an important message, go and take care of it so that, inside this room, we are all free to focus

- In this exercise, you might find yourself wanting to close your eyes, and if you do, that's fine because it means that you can really concentrate

- You can read these words now, yet when you put the book down, you may find some of the ideas still running around in your mind which is a sign that you're really making sense of it all and learning

Commentary Adjective

You can easily understand how to use the Milton Model when you confidently realise how elegantly simple it is to practically apply.

A commentary adjective is a word that describes another phrase, like a person commenting on what they're saying, while they're saying it. Luckily, it's something that you'll hear in natural language if you listen out for it.

Fortunately, happily, sadly, interestingly, unluckily, boldly, confidently, tentatively, narrowly, broadly, generally, specifically, joyfully. These words frame what comes next and superficially instruct the listener in how to react to the phrase which the adjectives comment on.

At a deeper level, they are anchors to elicit emotional states.

- Fortunately, we have an hour to work together

- Sadly, we only have 6 sessions remaining

- Interestingly, you already know the answers

- Boldly, we go

- Confidently, your ideas and beliefs can evolve

Commentary adjectives can also have the effect of shifting the listener's attention so that what follows can contain an embedded command. Luckily, you are not susceptible to any embedded commands to enjoy this book, or you could only begin to imagine what might happen.

Comparative Deletion

It is usually better to use a comparative deletion when you want to imply that someone will be happier and that life will be easier as a result of them taking action to achieve more.

I think you get the point; this is a simple converse of the Meta Model pattern, so by deleting the reference for the comparison, the listener has to create one.

This is a form of pace. If someone tells you that they are unhappy, and you suggest a course of action that results in them being happier, they will infer that you mean happier than they are now, not happier than a cat stuck up a tree.

I've seen a cat stuck up a tree. It was not happy.

- Now that you're feeling more positive

- We can move on to the next step that I know you're more eager for

- And as you work harder to achieve your plans

- I feel that you'll end up wiser

- And, more than likely, stronger

- Until the right time comes

- So that you'll know exactly what to do

Universal Quantifiers

We speak in generalities but apply them specifically. Everyone knows that, don't they?

What we're talking about is classes or sets. If we take the class defined by "everyone", then you have to know whether you're a member of that class in order to apply the above statement to yourself. If you strongly disagree with the statement, then the word "everyone" sticks out like a sore thumb. If you don't strongly disagree, it's easier to apply the class to yourself.

Remember also that generalisations in time roughly translate into "now".

- You'll always be able to enjoy more

- Everyone can relax

- There are opportunities everywhere for good people

- These feelings can stay with you forever

- Every cloud has a silver lining

- You'll never need to worry ever again

- We all like to feel in control

- You'll always discover new ideas

- Nothing is certain

Tag Questions

A tag question is a question that is tagged onto the end of a statement, which typically asks the listener to verify their understanding of or agreement with the statement. You do understand, don't you?

"It's warm today, isn't it?"

"We could stop for lunch now, couldn't we?"

"Let's go ahead and get the paperwork completed, shall we?"

A tag question is an odd grammatical construction, because it's neither a statement nor a question, but somewhere in between. It's as if someone is voicing a desire or a tentative statement and is looking for the other person's agreement or compliance. It's as if you're saying, "If I knew for sure that you wanted to sign the contract, I'd ask you".

For our purposes, a tag question does have one very important feature. In answering the tag question, the listener must momentarily accept the preceding statement as true. And even accepting the statement momentarily leads to a greater chance that it will become "true" permanently.

In order to answer a question, the listener must hold the question's presupposition true in order for the question to make sense. "How did the cat get in the tree" presupposes that the cat is indeed in the tree, and in order to answer the question, "How?", you must hold true that fact.

A presupposition is not an assumption, which is a cognitive process, made after information becomes available. I might assume your social status from your clothes or your accent. A presupposition precedes facts that must be true in order for a statement to be grammatically correct.

A question such as, "When did you first realise how valuable this book is for you?" makes grammatical sense, and in answering the question, you must accept certain facts as true. You might disagree later when you stop and think about it, yet on some level, you can see that there is some value in the book, even though, "not at all", is a perfectly acceptable answer to the question, "How valuable?"

So instead of thinking of tag questions as a peculiar linguistic quirk that some people use necessarily, think of them as a powerful tool for directing a listener, or reader, to at least consider a statement as true and evaluate it thoroughly rather than reject it out of hand.

That all makes sense, isn't it?

- Doesn't it?
- Isn't it?
- Aren't they?
- Have you?
- Is it not?
- Could it?
- Will you?
- Can't you?
- Don't you?
- Does he?
- Couldn't I?
- Won't you?
- Do they?
- Can it?

Double Bind

Two options are presented which amount to the same outcome. The listener focuses on making a choice without critically assessing the choices offered.

- Will you decide now or later'?

- You can listen to me or not, it makes no difference to what happens

- Whether you keep your eyes open or closed, you can relax easily

- You can relax quickly or slowly, whichever is right for you to enjoy it

- Are you going to take the next step by yourself, or will you talk it over with your partner first?

- Do you think it's better to be happy with who you are or comfortable in your own skin?

- Whether you choose to change or not makes no difference to the fact that the clock is ticking

- Change is the only constant

- Whether you feel ready to change now, or you prefer to sleep on it first, you know that it's there for you

Mind Reading

A mind read can be a form of pacing. Rather than 'mind reading' a random instruction that you want to 'implant', the mind read should be used to tentatively offer an insight into the client's thought processes.

For example, as you're reading about mind reading, you might be wondering how it relates to the Meta Model pattern of the same name, and you know, that's a good question because it is the same pattern, just reversed. Instead of presuming that you know what someone's thinking, you are offering a suggestion about what they might be thinking, if they turned their mind to it.

- You might think that

- You know, people often ask me

- I know what you're thinking

- You may be wondering how you can use this

- I know that you can read these words

- I know you can hear me

- You're probably thinking that this is good advice, but it won't work

- You're wondering what to make of all this

- If I were in your shoes, I'd be wondering, right now, if it's really true, if I can open up and talk to this person

Lost Referential Index and Lost Performative

By dropping either the person doing something or the person saying that someone is doing something, the listener will often insert a generic speaker or performer into the statement, thereby accepting it as true simply because someone else said it was.

- They say that

- I've heard that

- It's good to feel relaxed

- Relaxation is good

Consider these two examples, and pay attention to what questions come to mind as you read each of them.

"Sharks live for a hundred years"

"The kid next door asked if sharks live for a hundred years"

"My teacher says that sharks live for a hundred years"

My guess is that for the first example, you questioned the statement. For the second two, you questioned the speaker.

Which is more likely to influence you? Having to figure out how you know that sharks don't live for a hundred years, or dismissing the words of the kid next door?

And are you now wondering how long sharks *do* live for?

Quotes

The other day, someone said to me, "You can achieve whatever you want when you can put your mind to it".

A quote is a short form of a story. By attributing a statement to someone else, you are presupposing that it is true, because someone said it.

Compare these two examples, and take a moment to become aware of what comes to mind for each:

1. You must learn Milton Model to master NLP.

2. I was talking to a student on a Practitioner course recently, who said, "You must learn the Milton Model if you are to master NLP", and I must admit, I was impressed by her dedication.

What did you notice?

Perhaps you felt a sense of challenge towards the first example, a desire to prove the statement as true or false.

The second example is more interesting[2]. I'm going to guess that first, you imagined a student. Then, you imagined her speaking those quoted words. Then you put yourself in my shoes and imagined why I would be impressed. Overall, you reacted, not by asking "Is it true?", but by wondering, "How can it be true?", a subtle yet important difference.

You can use quotes from films, books, repeat back what someone says, and even embed a suggestion in quotes.

---

2 More interesting than a camping weekend in Birmingham, that is.

Negation

Language is itself a model of reality, and in reality things can't not exist. A void exists. A hole exists. The number zero exists. Nothing exists. However, in language, we have a way of coding things that don't exist, much like numbers can make an object appear, even though it isn't there.

Let's use an example of a teacher in a school lesson.

"If you have five apples, and you give three to Sarah and two to Tom, what do you have left?"

"A teddy bear, miss"

It's a fair answer to the question. If instead the teacher asks, "If you have five apples, and you give three to Sarah and two to Tom, how many apples do you have left?" then the answer can be, "none, miss", as the teacher expected.

If the child doesn't know about the concept of zero then he doesn't have the same frame of reference for answering the question as the teacher had for asking it.

You may have heard the expression, "Don't think of an elephant" which, in linguistic terms, is known as a "negative command". It makes perfect sense to say, but in reality it's impossible.

What about a TV detective drama, where the detective asks the suspect, "What's that in your pocket?", and the suspect replies, "It's not a gun!"

Who mentioned guns?

The fact that nothing exists is a quirk of our perception. Neuroscientists believe that we construct the majority of our perceptual world from memory, which certainly fits with the concept of sensory filtering that we discussed earlier.

Therefore, by speaking about something that does not exist, we make it exist within that statement's frame of reference. Not only can we create real objects, such as five apples, we can create concepts, such as a desire to make a decision.

"I'm not saying that you need to make a decision now, because you'll do that in your own time and when you're ready, you'll let me know, won't you?"

"I can't tell you to feel comfortable because only you know that this is the right decision for you."

"Now, this is the contract paperwork, but don't think about signing that yet, let's make sure we both understand the facts of the situation first."

"Now, I'm not asking you to make a decision to hire me right now, because I know that you've already waited two months since this first became a problem, so maybe you're not in any rush to solve it, so think about what I've said, talk over the recommendations I've made and don't take action too quickly because I want to know that you have thought this through properly, haven't you?"

- I'm not going to tell you that

- I can't make you relax, no-one can

- You couldn't lend me some money, could you?

Modal Operators

Modal operators modify a verb and reveal information about how a person feels about the activity; whether they are motivated, obligated and so on. This in turn tells you the conditions under which they will take action.

For example, if you say, "I will read this section and get my head round modal operators", then that is quite different to saying, "I would read this section and get my head round modal operators".

The latter implies a conditional "but", and "but" is a very interesting word to hear because it implies a hidden exception – essentially a 'get out clause' for any goal or commitment.

In 'Genius at Work' and 'The NLP Master Practitioner Manual', I explore this in more detail because it is very relevant to modelling behaviours at Master Practitioner level. For now, we'll look at modal operators at a more fundamental level.

A state has its own vocabulary. The words you use, your voice tone and the things you talk about are influenced by, and can influence, your state.

People talk about being "motivated" to do something, when even a cursory observation will tell you that they are not actually doing it. "I'm really motivated to make some sales calls", says the call centre operator, doing pretty much anything he can to avoid picking the phone up.

Think back to Meta Model; what is interesting about the word "motivated" in this context?

It is a bit like a nominalisation, isn't it? Frozen in time. I am happy. I am sitting. I am reading. I am motivated. And, by omission, I am not making sales calls.

Think about something that you do easily, something that you can always find time for or that you only have to think about in order to do it.

What do you say to yourself as you think about it?

- Can
- Will
- Am
- Now
- Want
- May

Now think about something that you're really good at almost getting round to. Something that is your job, or that needs doing, but you really don't want to do it, so you always find a way to avoid it.

What do you say to yourself as you think about it?

- Ought
- Must
- Should
- Need
- Try
- Later
- If
- Might

Do you notice a pattern here? And is it possible to swap the words we use round in order to change the states?

Take something that you need to do, let's call it "X". Pay attention to how you talk to yourself about it. If you say, "I really ought to do X today" then actively change the words. Say out loud, "I am going to do X today".

Of course, you haven't done it yet, it is in the future and is therefore still an uncertainty. We can make the language even more powerful by shifting it into the past:

"By the end of the day I will have done X"

Now we have the problem that, "the end of the day" is not very specific. Which day? And when exactly does it end? We can go one better:

"By the time I walk out of the door to go home today, I will have done X"

We can still make the language even more powerful still:

Stand up. Look up. Take a deep breath. Smile. Think about something you really love doing and really enjoy. Now say in a confident, musical voice:

"By the time I walk out of the door to go home today, I will have done X"

But be careful with this, you'll find yourself whizzing through all your outstanding chores like a whirlwind. We need to even the balance up.

Take something that you always end up doing, even though you think someone else should do it.

Sit down. Look down. Think about something you would rather not do, such as a bad habit. Say in a flat voice:

"I really ought to try to do [bad habit] soon"

If you're wondering how this fits with our broad definition of how you would apply the Milton Model[3] then listen carefully to the words that someone uses when they talk about something they really enjoy doing. Then make sure you use those exact words back to them when you talk about what you want them to do.

For example, when someone talks about something they had to finish off at work they might say, "I kept telling myself that I really should do it, I finally ran out of time and had to finish it off before coming here tonight". When they talk about going shopping at the weekend they might say, "so I said to myself ooh! I've just got time to pop into town". Now you have everything you need.

"You should stay at home instead of going to the gym, but you might get home and think "ooh! I've just got time to pop down to the gym", and imagine how great you'll feel for having done that!"

Therapeutically, you might use Milton phrases such as:

"You really should have another cigarette, or you can take a deep breath and notice how good the air tastes, doesn't it?"

This combines the client's own avoidance modal operator with utilisation, an awareness predicate, a complex equivalence and a tag question.

And if we keep on looking at that sentence, we'll add more Milton patterns too. We've added three already! Can you see any more?

3 Would? If what condition were satisfied?

Nominalisations

A nominalisation is a verb that has been distorted into a noun.

Consider these two statements:

- I met with my boss who made a decision about my presentation to the board

- I had a meeting with my boss and he decided that I'll be presenting to the board

How about these two:

- I'm afraid of what will happen if I stand up for myself

- Fear stops me from making a stand

By turning a verb into a noun, it is stopped in time. Did you notice that in each pair of statements, you visualised a still image for one, and a moving image for the other?

If your client is having difficulty putting an unpleasant memory or thought out of the mind, you can turn the active verbs into nominalisations and freeze those memories in time.

Ambiguities

Ambiguities are a source of great confusion amongst students of NLP.

Cast your mind back to the point in the book where I said that your brain's linguistic centres have the difficult job of picking out vocal sounds from the fog of background noise and then decoding that into some kind of relevant meaning. In doing so, your brain has to hold all possible meanings of a sound as valid until a most likely candidate arises from the overall context.

You can easily demonstrate this way in which your brain parses language with a passage like this.

My aunt, who always sat quite upright as she smoothed her apron out and delicately enquired if any of us would like tea, knowing full well that my brother and I could not stand the treacly potion that you could stand your spoon up in and would sooner have had a glass of that Corona Orangeade that we knew was lurking in the cupboard under the stairs, except if the Corona delivery man had offered cream soda, another favourite, or, worst of all, cherryade, which was really most sickly and unpleasant, said "Hasn't it been cold lately?"

Without looking, who asked if we thought it had been cold?

What just happened is that I took the normal structure of Subject Verb Object and separated it. In order to understand the meaning of the sentence, your brain had to hold part of it and make sense of some more before hearing the conclusion and sticking it all back together.

I used the word 'parse' earlier on this page, so in case you haven't heard that before, here's what Wikipedia has to say about it. "Parsing ... is the process of analysing a string of symbols, either in natural language or in computer languages, according to the rules of a formal grammar.

The term is also used in psycholinguistics when describing language comprehension. In this context, parsing refers to the way that human beings analyze a sentence or phrase ... in terms of grammatical constituents, identifying the parts of speech, syntactic relations, etc."

Whenever you're trying hard to make sense of something that a friend is telling you as you think, "Why are they telling me this?", or, "Who did what to who?", you can be sure that they are unwittingly trying to cram too much into one sentence.

Business writers have an unfortunate habit of using 'passive voice' which strips language of its sense of movement and attribution. Mistakes were made. Lessons were learned. People have been reprimanded. Customers have been informed. The situation is under control.

Eh? Who made mistakes? What mistakes? What lessons? Who learned them?

Oh, I give up, which is exactly the effect of passive voice. In order for the listener or reader to make sense of it, they have to be able to convert the words back into mental representations. They need to be able to create a mental movie of someone doing something to someone and something happening as a result. With passive voice, so much is deleted that it's very tiring to keep up with what's going on. If a book is written in this style, the reader will tend to give up on it. A business report? Well, you might have to read it in the course of your job, but it's no joy, is it?

Right, let's get back to ambiguities. There are four different types; Syntactic, Semantic, Scope and Phonological.

Syntactic

Syntactic ambiguities are sequences of words in which the overall meaning can change depending on where the punctuation marks are.

For example, it would be unethical of me to advertise this book by saying that, in NLP Practitioner training, it will really help you to get by. The book should sell itself, if people like it enough. People will like it to buy it, and that would make me very happy that people like the book. Peter Freeth for your next conference or corporate event would be a good idea. You just can't dictate what your colleagues will like. This book, as a gift, perhaps for a birthday or competition prize, would be an excellent choice.

Here's that passage again with the ambiguities marked out. Ignore the punctuation. One of the words is also a 'phonological ambiguity' which I'll come to shortly.

For example, it would be unethical of me to advertise this book by saying that, in NLP Practitioner training, it will really help you to get **by. The book** should sell itself, if people like it **enough. People will like it** to buy it, and that would make me very happy that people like the **book. Peter Freeth for your next conference or corporate event** would be a good idea. You just can't dictate what **your colleagues will like. This book, as a gift**, perhaps for a birthday or competition prize, would be an excellent choice.

Semantic

Words that have two meanings, usually as a result of an action that can be applied to the subject or object with different results, or a root word which can be either a noun or a verb. While there may be one generally accepted meaning, the word is, in itself, ambiguous.

- Book; this manual or to make a reservation

- A part/apart; together or separate

- Light; verb or noun

- Clear; verb or noun

Scope

An adverb or adjective could apply to more than one clause of a sentence, so its qualities can be attributed in multiple ways.

- They were eating apples

- They are cooking apples

- Are you running water? (No, I'm Sitting Bull)

- Look at all the small business owners

Phonological

Phonological ambiguities are 'homophones'; words or phrases that sound alike or similar.

Personally, I can't stand people who are always using words that sound like other words. I'm homophonic.

Annoys	=	A noise	See = Sea	
Write	=	Right	Wait = Weight	
Caught	=	Court	Sitting here = Sit in here	
Eye	=	I	Here = Hear	
Soften	=	So often	Buy = By	
Bean	=	Been	Ate = Eight	
Nose	=	Knows	Weak = Week	
One two	=	Want to	Allowed = Aloud	
Won	=	One	Bored = Board	
Sun	=	Son	Innocence = In a sense	
Fourth	=	Forth	Letters = Let us	
Apart	=	A part	Four candles = Fork handles	

In shops, there's a growing trend for the shop assistants to apologise for time spent queueing, when in fact there's nothing to apologise for. I saw the queue, I chose to join it. However, upon reaching the till, the assistants seem compelled to say to me, "I'm sorry about your wait." I'm always tempted to say, "And I'm sorry about your face. At least I can lose weight. You're stuck with that monstrosity."

And finally... let's not forget the contestant on Channel 4's program 'Four Rooms' who was introduced as a Flora storer. Presumably he works in a margarine warehouse. Or did they mean a floor restorer?

And finally finally... the master of all ambiguous linguists, Ronnie Barker, who gave us such gems as fork handles and the phonetic menu:

"FUNEX?"

"S, VFX"

"FUNEM?"

"S, VFM"

"MNX"

> Write some of your own ambiguities.

Using Ambiguities

You may recall that at the start of this chapter I talked about the experiences that are called to mind when we're processing language. And you may be wondering how ambiguities can possibly be useful, because surely no-one would ever want to talk so confusingly?

An ambiguity creates a moment of confusion into which a suggestion can flow. Have you ever found yourself, momentarily distracted, saying "yes" to someone before you had even heard the question?

We structure time around our attention, and if you have ever lost track of time when deep in thought or put on the spot, you'll know that your 'inside' time can be very different to what other people are observing.

Milton Erickson was a hypnotherapist, and hypnosis is an aspect of many NLP Practitioner courses, and Milton language can feature heavily in a trance induction.

For example, here is a short passage with a few Milton patterns and ambiguities in it. If you want to try it out, read it to a friend or colleague and, afterwards, ask them to comment on how it affected them. Read it quite slowly, remembering that the objective is not to bore them to sleep.

As a rough guide, it should take you one minute to read this, slowing down towards the middle and picking up pace, pitch and energy at the end.

You know when you're feeling really comfortable, relaxing, like when you're snuggling up in a really cosy, soft, drifting, down duvet, and you feel almost as if the outside world is drifting away, and it can be so quiet, isn't it, that you can begin, slowly, to turn your mind to your own thoughts, the feeling of down, that duvet, warmth, comfort, relaxing and close your eyes are the window to the soul searching for an answer that you know is in there somewhere, and like something you're trying as hard as you can to remember and the harder you try, the further away it drifts, and the further away it drifts, like a distant, soothing voice, saying your name and letting you know that you are absolutely safe and sounds fading and softer now, and in a moment, beginning to feel a sparkle of energy, revitalising and stronger, growing and lifting you up to a feeling alive, wonderful, invigorated and refreshed and wide awake.

Embedded Commands

And now we reach what is probably the most controversial aspect of the Milton Model; the assertion that a direct command can be covertly embedded within some other statement, compelling the listener to carry out your instructions, such as "Someone asked me today if they could **buy this book** and I said, yes, of course you can."

Let's revisit an example passage that I shared earlier on, and use it as a 'carrier' for a command.

If you feel like experimenting, read this to a friend or colleague and ask them what their immediate thoughts are.

> My aunt, who always sat quite upright as she smoothed her apron out and delicately enquired if any of us would like tea, knowing full well that my brother and I could not stand the treacly potion that you could stand your spoon up in and would sooner have had a glass of that Corona Orangeade that we knew was lurking in the cupboard under the stairs, except if the Corona delivery man had realised that *you are thirsty* and offered cream soda, another favourite, or, worst of all, cherryade, which was really most sickly and unpleasant, said "Hasn't it been cold lately?"

In fact, read the passage to as many people as you can and keep a note of what percentage report that they feel thirsty afterwards.

Ordinals

First, you picked up this book and started reading. Then you came across this page. Finally, you might wonder why you would use ordinals in Milton Model. People make verbal bullet points in natural conversation. They say, for example, "Right, two things I'm not happy about. 1, you keep leaving dirty plates on the worktop. Put them in the dishwasher!! And b, when the dishwasher has finished, take the plates out!! Don't just leave them in there! And another thing..."

Ordinals tell the listener to expect more. Generally, we keep ordinals together, like this:

"I'd like you to do three things for me, one, just relax, two, aim to keep an open mind and three, be honest with me and challenge anything that you don't agree with."

However, if we're using Milton language within hypnosis, we might do something different:

"I'd like you to do three things for me, one, just relax, two, and when I ask you to relax, I mean both physically and mentally, if you can imagine how that's possible for you right now and two, aim to keen an open mind as we explore the issues that are really important for you, together because I want you to feel free to challenge anything, and free to be honest about what you really want, and three, just be honest and challenge anything that you don't agree with because when we're honest with each other, we'll make wonderful progress, aren't we?

Subordinate Clause of Time

"As the sun rises, the world wakes up. Yet when the alarm clock rings, you wonder why the nights are so short. Since you're in such a rush in the morning, you eat breakfast at your desk. But before you get a chance, your manager calls you. After you put the phone down, you have to rush to another meeting and breakfast is forgotten. During the meeting, your stomach reminds you and while you try to pay attention, your mind wanders. As you try to put your hunger pangs out of your mind, you notice every word that reminds you of food. The meeting hasn't finished yet, and you're already checking the clock and working out how you can get out to the café as soon as possible."

What did you notice as you read through that paragraph? Did you notice lots of mental images? And how did the whole story move through time? Look back again and find the following words:

As   Yet   When   Since   Before   After

During   While   As   Yet   Already   As soon as

These words join statements together, either at the same time (as, during, while) or in sequence (before, after, when). By linking an external event to an imagined event, you can connect outcomes or desired states to natural, external triggers.

- As you sit, you might notice how relaxed you can be

- As you leave, don't forget to be successful today

- While you listen, you can easily learn

Complex Equivalence

Once again, this is the exact converse of the Meta Model pattern of the same name. It allows the Practitioner to connect together two beliefs, one which is currently accepted as true and one which can come to be accepted as true.

- Reading these words means you're learning

- Breathing is a sign that you can relax

- Seeing these words means that you can focus

- You're reading these words and you can begin to imagine how to put this into practice

- Being able to look at your hands means that you can become more self aware

- Seeing yourself in the mirror means that you can see what others see in you

A simple form of complex equivalence is the word "is". Read some advertising slogans, what do you notice?

Cause and Effect

As with the Meta Model pattern, we can join together two events with a causal link. The causal link doesn't have to make any logical sense whatsoever. For example, many people find learning the Milton Model to be a little tricky at first, then they take a break, get a drink and maybe watch TV or listen to music, then they find that they pick up the book again and everything just seems so much clearer to them.

This is no causal connection between music and learning, in this context, it is merely a sequence of events in time.

- Once you've read this page, you'll be ready for more

- After you have started to learn NLP you'll find more and more people asking for your advice

- The next time you travel, you can reflect on what you have discovered along the way

- By the time you walk out of the door, I wonder how much better you'll already be feeling?

- By the time you put this book down, you'll surprise yourself at how much you can learn

- By the time you reach the end of this sentence, you'll already have thought of even more examples of cause and effect patterns

Selectional Restriction Violation

Attributing qualities or behaviours to something which logically cannot exhibit them means that the listener has to insert themselves into the grammar. Since 'relaxing' cannot be a quality of a chair, because a chair has no ability to relax, the verb must apply to the person in the chair.

Superficially, the statement is not disputed because it is grammatically correct, but at a deeper level, the quality is applied to the listener.

- It's a relaxing chair

- We've got a happy office

- It's a bold decision

- It was a tense moment

- This is the productive desk

- That's a fascinating thought

- Do you think this is a curious idea?

- What a confident tie you're wearing

- Do you want the comfortable chair?

- Let's take a refreshing break

- Let's go to the learning room

- Here's a knowledgeable book

- What a nice story

Milton Model Tips

When I worked in a large British telecommunications company, a colleague of mine was assigned a mentor as part of a HR mentoring initiative. In the period of time he was supposed to work with her, he never actually got to meet her once and therefore felt very frustrated when he read an interview with her in the internal magazine, espousing the virtues of the mentoring program.

He told me that the quote from her said how wonderful mentoring was, and how important a mentor had been to her, which made her hypocritical as she had never made the time to meet with him. I asked him to read the quote, and this is what it said:

"I cannot put into words the impact that having a mentor has had on my career. Certainly, if I had not had a mentor, I would be in a very different place today"

He repeated his assertion that this proved her guilt, and I asked him to read it again and tell me what it really said. As he read it a couple more times, the penny dropped. "It says absolutely nothing at all!" he exclaimed.

It was a perfect example of Milton Model language in action.

So, a hypnotherapist or an excellent public speaker may use ambiguities to induce "trance" states. And a comedian may use ambiguities to create tension that is released through laughter (in other words, because they're funny). Can you think of times when those peoples' skills would come in handy for you?

"Make sure you have a pen, because in a moment I'm going to ask you to right now fill in an order form"

"You can feel the weight in your hands, and you can feel the weight in your feet, and you can feel the wait for the moment that you can let go and relax"

With written ambiguities it helps if you read the words out loud. You should form your own opinion about using this kind of thing in written communication such as sales letters or websites.

In NLP, we would use this form of language again to bypass the client's critical filter, with their full permission and participation. For example, a direct command such as, "be more confident" or "you are more confident" is easily rejected because it doesn't fit the client's map of the world. If we put that into Milton language, we might get something like, "you can be more confident", "I wonder how you'll find yourself working even more confidently?" or "I wonder how much confidence it takes to ask for help with being more confident"

In reality, you wouldn't actually do this, because confidence isn't an end in itself. Confidence to do what? By focusing on the outcome, the confidence takes care of itself – often by becoming irrelevant in the achievement of a goal. I don't like ironing, but I still do it. Does it matter whether I like it or not?

In Milton language, we can reframe beliefs, introduce useful suggestions, direct attention to more useful behaviours and outcomes, introduce possibilities, influence state and do many other things without every having to resort to trance, and it also means that we can influence people's state and behaviour very quickly and covertly where necessary.

Milton Model in Practice

During a client session, you'll be using Milton Model patterns to reinforce the process of change. This could mean building rapport, or creating the possibility for change, or adding more detail to the client's imagined future.

Here's a typical way in which you might do this:

"As you notice the comfortable chair and the bright sunshine and the open conversation, you might begin to notice that as you have become more aware of your dreams and desires, and you can more easily realise the power within, supporting you, now."

The structure of this statement is:

Pace + Lead

If we use Meta Model to further break down the structure of this statement, we get:

Subordinate clause of time + referential index + awareness predicate + selectional restriction violation + selectional restriction violation + selectional restriction violation + referential index + modal operator of possibility + subordinate clause of time + referential index + awareness predicate + subordinate clause of time + referential index + awareness predicate + comparative deletion + awareness predicate + nominalisation + nominalisation + referential index + modal operator of possibility + comparative deletion + commentary adjective + awareness predicate + nominalisation + presupposition + association + presupposition + dissociation + association.

That's a lot to remember! It's certainly a lot to think about when you're first practising how to apply Milton Model.

16.1 Milton Structure

In groups of 3, take it in turns to think of a modal operator, an awareness predicate and a selectional restriction violation. Here's the structure together with some examples to get you started. Rotate around the group, with a different person taking turns to start as Practitioner 1. Continue for a few minutes and notice the effect on your group.

Practitioner 1	Practitioner 2	Practitioner 3
MO	AP	SRV
You can	notice	the easy chair
We might	discover	interesting ideas
I could	see	the clear light

Come up with your own sequence and structure and repeat the exercise. What happens?

Practitioner 1	Practitioner 2	Practitioner 3

16.2 Random Milton Game

In groups of any size, take it in turns to choose patterns at random and see what mysterious language emerges, and how even random words and phrases can take on deeper meaning.

Practitioner: Pick a Milton Model pattern at random from the list below and show it to the next Practitioner.

Next Practitioner: Say a word or phrase which fits the pattern you have been shown. Then pick a Milton Model pattern at random and show it to the next Practitioner.

See how quickly you can keep the flow moving around your group.

Presupposition

Awareness Predicates

Conversational Postulates

Utilisation

Commentary Adjective

Comparative Deletion

Universal Quantifiers

Tag Questions

Double Bind

Mind Reading

Lost Referential Index

Lost Performative

Quotes

Negation

Modal Operators

Nominalisations

Ambiguities

Embedded Commands

Ordinals

Subordinate Clause of Time

Complex Equivalence

Cause and Effect

Selectional Restriction Violation

16.3 Milton Opening

When we start a coaching session, we have to bridge the client gently from the outside world, with all of its noise and distractions, into the cosy environment of the coaching session. We can achieve this very quickly with Milton language. Let's practice a simple structure for this.

Component	Example
Subordinate clause of time	As we begin
Awareness predicate	And you notice
Utilisation	The chair supporting you
Modal operator	You might
Awareness predicate	Discover
Comparative deletion	Even more
Instruction	New ideas and insights
Future pace	Supporting you now and in the future
Tag question	Do you see?

Now put together your own structure and come up with a variety of statements. Test them with your colleagues and clients.

16.4 Milton Closing

When we end a coaching session, we have to bridge the client gently back into the outside world, with all of its noise and distractions, leaving behind the cosy environment of the coaching session. We can achieve this very quickly with Milton language. Let's practice a simple structure for this.

Component	Example
Subordinate clause of time	As you move on from our time here today
Awareness predicate	And notice
Utilisation	The air outside, all around you
Modal operator	You might
Awareness predicate	Remember
Comparative deletion	Even more
Instruction	Opportunities to practice what you have discovered here today
Tag question	Can't you?

Now put together your own structure and come up with a variety of statements. Test them with your colleagues and clients.

If you want me to make this even easier for you, you can use the random Milton Model generator at:

www.geniusnlp.com/milton/

You might also write out some simple Milton patterns and try them out at every opportunity.

Imagine saying to a shop assistant, "And as you give me my change, you can begin to imagine the change that you can bring, so easily, into your life as soon as want, now." The blank look on the assistant's face is a sign that you are developing your wonderful skills, easily, and not a sign that they are about to call security.

Meta and Milton Comparison

Let's compare Meta and Milton patterns and see how they are relevant in each of the models.

Meta Model		Milton Model
	Presupposition	
	Awareness Predicate	
	Conversational Postulates	
	Commentary Adjective	
	Utilisation	
	Deleted Comparison	
	Universal Quantifier	
	Tag Questions	
	Double Bind	
	Mind Reading	
	Lost/Distorted	

	Referential Index	
	Lost Performative	
	Quotes	
	Negation	
	Modal operator – Necessity	
	Modal operator – Possibility	
	Nominalisation	
	Embedded Commands	
	Ordinals	
	Subordinate Clause of Time	
	Complex Equivalence	
	Cause and Effect	
	Selectional Restriction Violation	

17 Values and Beliefs

A lot of what you'll read about NLP on the Internet and in other books centres around the notion of "belief change"; that by using some magical technique to change your beliefs, you won't have to think about your behaviour, it will all just fall into place by itself.

For example, let's say that someone believes that they are a poor manager at work. They have to struggle to get things done, to enforce boundaries, to manage performance and to hold disciplinary meetings. They don't push their careers, and feel 'left behind' by other managers.

After one session with a NLP Practitioner – whoosh! - by changing this one belief with a magical technique, their whole life falls into place. They have the confidence to lead and the assertiveness to manage their team's performance, and now that they believe that they are a good manager, they aggressively pursue the promotion opportunities that they had missed out on.

Sadly, this is a very optimistic set of expectations; of the client, of you as a Practitioner and of NLP itself.

Being able to uncover a belief and offer the client evidence to support the formation of new beliefs is valuable, and it will influence the client's behaviour. However, wholesale belief change is not what NLP is about.

Imagine the owner of a conference and events company who is a nervous presenter. When he introduces a conference and welcomes the guests, he nervously shuffles, fumbles, sweats and can't wait to get off stage.

How would you approach this?

Would you perhaps anchor confidence? Or maybe set a Well Formed Outcome for a successful presentation? Or you might use some of the techniques that you'll find later in this book to 'reframe' his nervousness as a useful and valid choice; one of many.

I can't tell you what 'would' work in a hypothetical situation. I can, however, tell you what I did in this real life situation. What I looked for was the underlying rule that drove his behaviour. I figured that any techniques to address only his anxiety would just give him more to worry about.

In exploring his role in the conference and how he saw himself in relation to the audience, I was able to reveal a belief; that his role in the conference was not important.

We can then draw a line between the belief that his role was not important, therefore he was not important, and all of his anxious behaviours.

First, I did a 'conversational reframe', which is simply a way to offer up alternative points of view. If you were to pick apart what I said to him, you could see a number of NLP techniques within it. I appeared to ramble, which is something I do well, on a number of subjects; going to the cinema, seeing a play or pantomime, going to a conference and so on. All of these examples contained a similarity; that what happens at the very beginning determines how you feel about the whole event. He then realised that his role in the conference was potentially the most important. His role determined how the guests answered, in their own minds, the question, "Did I make a good decision to come here?"

So, now he was open to other possibilities, but he still needs hard evidence, so I used a little trick that is one of my personal favourites. I got him to focus on something that was such a minor detail, in this case his use of 'cue cards' rather than trying to remember everything. He had watched other conference speakers working without any notes, and assumed that their confident appearance meant that they were much 'better' than he was. In fact, there are other explanations. They have probably delivered the same lecture or speech hundreds of times and they know it like a child knows a nursery rhyme. That doesn't make it good. Their confidence might actually be arrogance, a sign that they have disconnected from the audience, which is not good.

I asked him if he thought that these confident presenters were any good, in his opinion. He said no, but the audiences always applauded.

That's what audiences do.

Nightingales sing, rain falls, audiences applaud politely.

To be fair, he had done what we all do; taken snippets of reality and put them into a collage, the result of which was a belief that he wasn't as good as these other presenters, and his role wasn't important. He had made them the stars of the show and whilst they may have been what the audience were paying to see, my client was unwittingly the 'warm up man', and if the warm up man doesn't warm up the audience, the main act falls flat on his or her face.

At this point he had a number of different options, which meant that he was receptive to new information to support a change in belief. And now we get to my favourite trick.

Remembering everything that he had to say was a problem too. He had tried cue cards, but found that they didn't help. I suggested that writing words on cue cards was the problem for him, because he had to stop speaking in order to read the words, and that interrupted his natural flow and allowed the self doubt and anxiety to creep in. I gave him some slips of paper to use as practice cue cards and got him to think up symbols instead of words. A "   " for start and finish times, a "⊙" for breaks, a " ♀ ♂ " for where the toilets are, a "👤" to introduce the speakers, a "💬" to let the audience know when they could ask questions, and so on. Part of his problem was that he couldn't remember everything that he needed to say, and he had created an unrealistic expectation based on what he'd seen other presenters do.

Another perspective is that when the conference speakers deliver their habitual lectures, they are telling a story, like walking a well worn path. It all connects together, and they're using slides and other prompts to keep themselves on track.

My client's introduction was quite disjointed, the things he needed to say were all important, but they didn't have a flow or story. The ancient Greeks had a way of giving such disjointed items a story of their own, called the Method of Locus. This would involve an imaginary journey that begins with looking at your watch and noticing the time, stopping for a cup of coffee, going to the toilet, meeting someone and talking to them, meeting someone else and asking them questions, and so on.

I didn't get him to try this, I just stuck to the cards because they were easier. The thing I like about simple tricks or props is that they serve many purposes.

For example, the symbolic cue cards gave my client:

- A reason for his past difficulty (reading words)

- Something to do with his hands

- A reminder of what to say

- Something new to try (the symbols)

- A magic token, like Dumbo's magic feather, Popeye's spinach or any other 'placebo' (an anchor)

- Something to focus on

- Something to take his mind off the problem

- An activity that presupposes change

- A rehearsal activity

I had him practice his introduction a few times, during which he relied less and less on his cue cards.

Did this "work"?

If you mean, "Was the client able to present at conferences more comfortably, without anxiety?", then the answer is yes. But a technique, or a whole coaching process, is only the beginning, and you must never underestimate the amount of work that your client must still do in order to achieve what they want. In many cases, you are asking them to break the habits of a lifetime, and accept a different possibility for the most difficult belief of all; that things will always be the same.

Limiting Beliefs

You may have heard coaches and NLP trainers talking about their clients' "limiting beliefs".

A belief in limiting beliefs is, in itself, a limiting belief.

To ascribe the power of limitation to a belief is to make the client powerless, and therefore dependent on their beliefs, or more likely, a kind-hearted NLP Practitioner to magic them away.

People's beliefs do not *limit* them. They *protect* them.

Your beliefs are one way in which you map the world. You might believe that your bed is comfortable, or you might believe that you need to buy a new mattress. When you carry around this knowledge in your mind, you have a belief which persists outside of the situation that it applies to. When you collect enough evidence that you can pile other beliefs on top, the original belief gets pushed beneath the surface. It still shows up in your behaviour at certain times, you're just not generally aware of it to the extent that you would put it into words.

Some beliefs give rise to behaviour that you would rather change, and now you're not only allowing a belief to float beneath the surface, you're actively pushing it to the bottom of the pile, because no-one in their right mind would think that they were inherently worthless or unwanted.

Yet even beliefs like these do not *limit* someone, they merely influence the course of their lives by influencing their daily interactions with others.

An entrepreneur may be driven to success by a belief that he is "not good enough", because his life is devoted to proving someone wrong, and that 'someone' becomes anyone who he unknowingly projects that belief onto.

It's impossible to predict how a person is shaped by their beliefs, you can only look at their beliefs as a context for their behaviour. If they are dissatisfied with their behaviour because their environment has changed, you can bring that difference into their awareness so that they can gather the evidence necessary to form new beliefs.

Beliefs are just rules. There are no deeper or higher beliefs. As for values, everyone wants love, respect, freedom, safety, belonging. Values tell you nothing about what someone will do. You only need to think about behaviour, and to change your behaviour, you only have to change your focus.

The Johari Window

In 1955, Joseph Luft and Harry Ingham created a self awareness tool called the Johari Window. It comprised a list of 56 words and a 2x2 grid in which to place them:

The four squares, or "rooms", represent a different aspect of your personality. Room 1, the Arena, is where you are completely open.

Room 2, the Blind Spot is where you think you are hiding something but you are in fact broadcasting it through your actions. Your friends accept you in spite of it, your enemies exploit it.

Luft and Ingham describe your 'Unknown' Room 3 as mysterious, containing things which no-one else knows about you, and which you don't even know yourself. This room may contain your hidden depths which only rise to the surface in times of threat or danger. For example, people can achieve physical feats beyond their beliefs when saving the life of a child.

Room 4, the Façade, is where your 'brave face' or your 'front' exist. You know that, secretly, you lack confidence, but your colleagues are always pushing you up to deliver presentations because you seem to be confident. You engage in behaviours to hide what you perceive as a weakness, although I suspect that the truth is that everyone can see right through you, should they care to look.

Perhaps the difference between the Blind Spot and the Façade is in your intention to conceal. Do you genuinely not know something about yourself, or do you try to hide it?

You can try the exercise for yourself.

17.1 Johari Window

From the following list, pick 6 words that describe your personality and place them on the grid.

Ask your friends or colleagues to do the same, picking words that apply to you.

What does the result tell you?

How do you feel about the words that are in your Blind Spot?

How do you feel about the words that are in your Façade?

How do your hidden qualities 'leak out'?

The 56 words are quite 'likeable' qualities. What would happen if you tried the exercise with a list of less likeable qualities, or words which are the opposite of these ones?

'Fortune tellers' use a technique whereby they attribute qualities to you which seem very personal but which actually apply to anyone. Could you apply all of the 56 words to yourself if you wanted to? Or do some definitely not fit your personality?

Able	Idealistic	Relaxed
Accepting	Independent	Religious
Adaptable	Ingenious	Responsive
Bold	Intelligent	Searching
Brave	Introverted	Self-assertive
Calm	Kind	Self-conscious
Caring	Knowledgeable	Sensible
Cheerful	Logical	Sentimental
Clever	Loving	Shy
Complex	Mature	Silly
Confident	Modest	Smart
Dependable	Nervous	Spontaneous
Dignified	Observant	Sympathetic
Energetic	Organized	Tense
Extroverted	Patient	Trustworthy
Friendly	Powerful	Warm
Giving	Proud	Wise
Happy	Quiet	Witty
Helpful	Reflective	

Values

Values could be thought of as a type of belief which is generalised across more contexts in a person's life. Your beliefs don't change depending on circumstances, but you do access different beliefs depending on the situation.

For example, you might believe that it is important to drive safely, except when you're at the fun fair, chasing your opponents round in the bumper cars. However, your values are not as easily adapted, they tend to guide you regardless of where you are or what you're doing.

We're often unaware of our values, this gentle guiding hand, until they are threatened. You may not be aware right now of your need for security, but you might become aware of it if you are approached by a suspicious stranger. And let's face it, a stranger would have every right to be suspicious in these circumstances.

It can be useful to map out a person's values, for a number of reasons.

Firstly, it enables your client to have a clearer idea of what guides them. They can take a look at their values and think about whether they are still useful or appropriate for them.

Secondly, if you do elicit values as group exercise, perhaps in a conflict resolution meeting, you will often find that peoples' values are very similar, even if they feel that their opinions are poles apart. This can provide valuable 'common ground' for a negotiation, and it can focus their attention on choices and experiences rather than personalities.

17.2 Values Elicitation

Ask your client to think of a situation where they feel that they are 'being themselves'. Ask them, "In that situation, what is important to you?"

Take that answer and ask,

"And what does that give you?"

Work your way up their hierarchy of values until you get to the top, indicated by their inability to answer any further questions.

This exercise is generally easier when you add a bit of variety to the questions. Here are some suggestions:

What is important about [value]?

What does [value] give you?

What does [value] get you?

What is important about having [value]?

What does [value] do for you?

These questions all direct your client's attention upwards. The question, "Why is that important?" will direct their attention downwards, and they will give you reasons or causes, which is not the purpose of the exercise.

Be careful with values. Some trainers make a big fuss out of eliciting values, and even talk about a hierarchy of values. Values are context-dependent, meaning that what is important to you depends on what's going on around you in that moment. If you feel stuck in a dead-end job, freedom will perhaps be a value. If you are self-employed then security might become more important. Values are not constant over time, therefore, if you think you know what is important to someone just because you have 'done a values elicitation', think again.

18 Logical Levels

Robert Dilts developed the idea of Neurological Levels, often abbreviated to Logical Levels, from Gregory Bateson's work on systems thinking. Whilst some people protest that this isn't NLP and shouldn't be part of NLP training, it is very useful in many ways, and we can't overlook the huge contribution to NLP made by Robert Dilts.

The Logical Levels framework has six levels, and they describe the hierarchical levels of organisation that you will hear within language, particularly language that a person uses to relate to themselves.

System	The bigger system that I am within
Identity	Who I am, the role that I play
Belief	What is true about my world
Capability	The choices that are available to me
Behaviour	What I am doing
Environment	Where I am, what is around me

Using the logical levels format, we can guide someone through a thought process which allows us to explore a problem in a structured way which tends to create alignment between the levels, leading to a higher degree of congruence which means that the person's natural motivation and energy is transferred more efficiently to the goal or outcome.

You may find Logical Levels useful, particularly as a tool for influencing the level of someone's thinking. Just remember that they are another filter, not an absolute truth. They cannot be directly modelled with Meta Model, and that's why they are not, strictly, NLP.

18.1 Logical Levels Coaching

Explore an issue by "walking through" the logical levels.

You can write the names of the labels onto pieces of paper and place them on the floor to make it easier to mark out the levels.

Begin at Environment, and at each level ask your client to describe their experience. Make sure that they stay at the level you're currently working on, which you'll be able to hear in their language.

18.2 Logical Levels Reframing

Listen to your client's description of a problem or decision.

Pick out the logical level statements, then shift all the levels up one as you reflect back the problem or decision.

For example:

"I can't work here" → "You can't do this work?"

"It's not working" → "You can't get it to work?"

And so on. Keep on conversationally reflecting back any statements that sit in the logical levels structure as questions, phrased one level above the statement.

19 Stories

Listen to any conversation and you will hear a combination of:

- Belief statements, which sometimes sounds like facts

- Questions, for many different reasons

- Narrative, which gives characters and sequence

Human beings communicate with each other in a narrative. We don't communicate using factual statements; they are linked by a narrative, which includes characters, who did what to whom, and a sequence in time, so that the listener can recreate the situation mentally.

If you think about it, this implies that spoken language evolved at least in part for the purpose of coding events through time.

"You get this spear and go and poke the brontosaurus with it and the rest of us will ambush it"

"Mrs Ug, I'm afraid Mr Ug has had an accident. You see, he had this spear, and there was this brontosaurus..."

"Have you had an accident which wasn't your fault? Then call bronto-claims direct."

Things change. People, as a sub-class of things, can cause things to change. Things can cause things to change through the unseen forces of nature.

Change is a difference over time, and every action, every verb, describes a difference over time. We "make sense of" grammatically correct language by trying to recreate the original events being described, partly from what we hear and partly from what we previously knew.

If someone tells me that their cat is stuck up a tree, I already know what a tree looks like, and I know what a cat looks like, so I can easily imagine the scenario and start calculating options.

If someone tells me that I'm having sandwiches for dinner, I can picture them and understand what to do with them.

But if someone tells me I'm having Brioche, Biscotti and Bobotie for dinner, I'm wondering if they're ingredients or a visiting delegation from the local multi-cultural centre. I don't know what those labels mean so I don't know what to do with them.

The more narrative you use, the easier you are to listen to. The richer your narrative, the more accurate are the pictures you create in your listener's mind. And when I ask people on workshops what qualities they associate with excellent presenters, one which always comes out is that the presenter knew a lot about their subject. And when I ask how they knew that the presenter knew a lot, they told stories.

Just within the past hour you will have heard many stories, so start to listen out for them. As a NLP Practitioner, you can tell stories with greater purpose, to communicate valuable information and to influence your listeners. You can also pay more attention to the stories that other people tell. Your clients' stories have the power to draw you into their reality, and you have to be able to resist that.

19.1 State Story

You can use a story to help lead someone out of a particular state, towards a target state through an event which may or may not be related to either state.

Present state → event → desired state

Begin with someone in a state that the listener will identify with personally. Then move through some kind of transition to a desirable end state.

"I remember a client who was confused once, and the more they thought about it, the more they went round in circles, so they just decided one day to stop and talk through the problem and, while they didn't understand it at first, it began to get much clearer and they felt a real sense of relief and peace."

The story will be very short, it will pace the client's current state, it will provide some kind of bridge and it will define a new state.

Importantly, the transitional event doesn't need to have anything to do with the present or desired states at all. There isn't a logical connection between them, only a sequence of time which our pattern matching minds turn into a causal sequence.

For example., there was a world war, then I was born, then the Berlin Wall fell and Europe was reunited. There is no logical sequence there, and none implied, yet our minds create a causal relationship wherever there is a sequence of time.

Storytelling is one of the most powerful communication techniques you can employ. It directly affects the listener's emotional state and it bypasses their critical filters. Stories can be used to change, to influence or even just to enjoy.

19.2 Teaching Story

> Tell a short story, perhaps something that happened at work, maybe a story about change, maybe a story about someone you know who has achieved something remarkable.
>
> This isn't just a random story though, it is specifically chosen to achieve a desired purpose and to introduce a new idea or possibility.

We have, hard wired into our brains, a remarkable ability to build simulations, not just static maps of the world, but living models that, loaded with rules and starting data, will run by themselves and simulate the world and the people within it.

Read Gallese and Goldman's work on Mirror Neurons, which you can easily find with an Internet search, for more on this.

This ability ideally builds simulations of live role models, but in their absence, a story will serve a similar purpose.

A story will follow a sequence in time which a list of direct rules probably does not, so we can see how relationships between parts of the story connect over time.

If we strip a sequence down to simplified steps then we can't form a simulation using that information. We could form a mental image of the checklist, or hear the sounds of the words, but to form a simulation it needs people.

If you've ever followed a recipe from a TV chef only to find it didn't turn out the way it looked on the TV, you've experienced this directly. The recipe isn't enough to reproduce the original, because that required a whole lifetime of experiences that you don't have. Even making a simple omelette that requires you to beat the eggs, how? For how long? With what? Does it make a difference? It does, if you want to reproduce the original exactly[4].

When you watch a TV chef, they show you their insider tips for how to beat the eggs, to get air into the mixture, or they might fold the eggs gently. Recipes in cookery books generally only give you the ingredients and the order in which to combine them. No wonder nothing ever turns out like the pictures.

Nothing. Ever. Get over it.

Those insider secrets that we need to reproduce excellence are what we seek to learn with NLP modelling.

> What stories have you already heard today?

---

4 This could explain why it's possible to buy kitchen utensils endorsed by TV chefs. Maybe if I bought his signature wok, I too could be a master of the masher, an emperor of the egg, king of king prawns.

20 Hypnosis

For many people, hypnosis and trance summon up images of swinging watches, covert influence and people acting against their wills.

Pick up any serious book on hypnosis, or go to any serious hypnotherapy course, and you'll learn that there are many myths surrounding hypnosis and trance which are based on fear rather than reality. Here are a few ideas about hypnosis that you may wish to confirm for yourself.

Anyone can be hypnotised. People who think quickly tend not to respond to the slow paced, traditional trance induction as they get bored half way through. They respond better to fast inductions using pattern interrupts and suggestions. We can say that anyone can be hypnotised because everyone spends some time in a trance, every day. And by 'trance'. I simply mean a 'heightened focus of attention'.

It's even possible to say that we live in a trance. Typically, our days comprise both attention to the outside world and the daydreaming, thinking and remembering that are all trance states. Essentially, a trance state is where one or more of your senses are directed inwards. Every time you remember a telephone number, think about what happened yesterday or worry, your senses are directed inwards and you partially disconnect from the outside world. A deep trance is where all of your senses are directed inwards, although even in a deep hypnotic trance you will still hear the hypnotist's voice or a fire alarm. At worst, it will be like being woken from a deep sleep.

The magicians and witches of the middle ages were probably hypnotists. Magical spells and enchantments were most likely trances, exaggerated by fear and mass hysteria. In a modern world where science and television have banished the myths and legends of our ancestors, the reality of hypnosis is much different, although the fears and doubts are much the same for some people. In some parts of the world, witchcraft is still a very powerful social motivator.

So, the use of trance is natural and ethical, when you have your client's full participation.

> When were you most recently in a trance today?

> When did you most recently put someone else into a trance, accidentally?

Cycling Representational Systems

If you rotate your focus of attention through your senses, you will find that your attention will become directed inwards.

20.1 Cycling Representational Systems

You can see these words, hear sounds, feel the temperature of the air, see your hands, hear noises in the distance, feel the weight of your feet, see the colour of the book, hear the words, feel that feeling inside and so on.

It's important to pace your client's current reality, using examples that your client is most likely to be aware of.

If you feel that you are running out of things to comment on, either repeat yourself, or comment on your inability to think of new things to comment on.

If you do find yourself 'mind reading', at least soften your comments with, "you may be able to..." or "you might notice..." etc.

With corporate visioning being so popular, it's not uncommon to hear managers ask what people will see, hear and feel when they achieve a certain objective. You can imagine how easily you can build this pattern into a presentation or business report.

Utilisation Pattern

This pattern cycles your awareness from outside, to inside, to outside, and so on. Suggestions relating to states work very well with this pattern, so it's a good way to become more focused, energised or relaxed. Point out three things that are in your client's direct sensory awareness, make a suggestion and then ask where their attention is focussed. Here's how it goes:

You can see the paper, you can hear the words, you can feel the weight of the book, you can realise how pleased you are that you bought it, and what are you aware of now?

20.2 Utilisation pattern

The Practitioner alternates pacing and leading as follows:

1. True

2. True

3. True

4. Suggestion

5. "And what are you aware of now?"

The client signals any time the Practitioner says something that "jars" and is therefore not properly calibrated or paced.

If you do find yourself 'mind reading', at least soften your comments with, "you may be able to..." or "you might notice..." or "you can become aware" etc.

An important aspect of this type of induction is the utilisation of events and sensations in the room to pace and lead the client. This means that if you view hypnosis as something which must happen in a quiet room with no distractions, you're going to run out of things to comment on very, very quickly.

The busier the environment, the more you have to work with, so this is an excellent exercise to use in practising your general communication skills.

Excellent public speakers have the ability to take anything in their stride and to act as if interruptions were planned by them, this is utilisation.

Can you think of a presentation or speech where you have heard a utilisation pattern being used? If not, watch the major news programs for the next few days and you're sure to see some.

Pattern Interrupt

Whenever you do something automatically, you are running a behavioural program that enables you to complete complex tasks without having to devote too much conscious brain power. Whenever you are lost in a pattern and someone or something interrupts you, your brain is stuck for a moment, unsure of how to complete the program. At this moment, you are open to suggestion.

How many times have you been in the middle of something, or lost in a daydream, when a colleague has asked you a question and you've found yourself complying as if it were a command? Perhaps you have been interrupted while deep in though, only to find that you can't remember what you were doing beforehand?

Perhaps you have also seen TV magicians using various pattern interrupts as a way of putting someone into a trance, or getting them to act upon a suggestion. This is certainly possible, but what you see on TV is a carefully controlled situation, usually involving a great deal of set-up which may not always be obvious to either participant or the viewer.

No one is truly immune to pattern interrupts because we would be unable to function without our habitual behavioural patterns. When your computer gets interrupted, it crashes, so just be grateful that it only takes your brain half a second to reboot and continue. Imagine what it would be like if you had to run the disk repair program every time someone interrupted you, or you went to sleep without finishing what you were doing!

Hypnosis Scripts

There are many sources on the Internet of good scripts that you can use in hypnosis. Here's one that you can use for general relaxation, and to deliver a specific suggestion.

Before you see the script, a word on suggestions. Firstly, the suggestion must conform to the criteria used for Well Formed Outcomes, in that it must be stated positively and have no unwanted side effects. So, a suggestion that someone will give up smoking is very badly formed and will not have any effect. On the other hand, a suggestion such as "you will surprise yourself with how easily you forget to smoke" is much better, because it is well formed, and also because it's phrased indirectly.

A suggestion such as "you will be more confident" can be quite jarring, especially if the person believes they lack confidence. Rather than accepting the suggestion, they could reject it, breaking rapport. A better way to phrase this would be to choose a specific example when the person would like more confidence, for example "you can find yourself breathing more confidently". You see the subtle difference? You're taking the emphasis off the suggestion, so that the person can integrate it more easily rather than questioning it. If you think back to the Milton and Meta Models, you're embedding the suggestion within a presupposition.

Does this mean that you can command people to do things against their will? Opinion is divided on this, and I stress the word opinion. In my experience, a state of hypnosis is just a state. It does not render the person vulnerable to instructions, nor place them at your mercy. As you will find out for yourself if you try this script, the person in the trance feels alert and in control the whole time, yet very relaxed and at ease. If anything interrupts them such as an unwelcome suggestion or a feeling of unease, they will open their eyes and be fully attentive. Whether people are in a trance or not, they can still tell what's good for them.

You move into suggestible states naturally throughout the day. Imagine a time when you're daydreaming and someone asks you a question. Often, you answer before you even heard the question, wondering what you just agreed to!

Now for the script, which is an "Elman induction". Before you start to read this, prepare a suggestion and write it down so that you can weave it into the script seamlessly. Your voice tone, pitch and rate of speech are as important as the words, so that's something you can practice and play with.

Read everything that follows, even what seems to be a general instruction at the beginning. Read through the script in advance, because there are some points marked in [square brackets] that you need to prepare for.

Remember that you are reading this to a living, thinking person, so do remember to pay attention to your client. Notice the speed at which they follow your instructions and adjust your pace accordingly. When they do something to follow your instructions, give them gentle feedback by saying, "good", or, "that's right". If something interrupts you, refer to it like you did with the utilisation pattern as a sign that they are present, safe and able to relax even more easily.

20.3 Elman Induction

In this exercise you must be happy to learn about how to develop your relaxation skills and follow instructions exactly as asked, neither taking too long to follow instructions nor anticipating what will be asked.

Now take a long deep breath and hold it for a few seconds. As you exhale this breath, allow your eyes to close, and let go of the surface tension in your body. Just let your body relax as much as possible right now.

Now place your awareness on your eye muscles and relax the muscles around your eyes to the point they just won't work. When you're sure they're so relaxed that, as long as you hold on to this relaxation they just won't work, hold on to that relaxation and test them to make sure they won't work.

Now, this relaxation you have in your eyes is the same quality of relaxation that I want you to have throughout your whole body. So, just let this quality of relaxation flow through your whole body from the top of your head, to the tip of your toes.

Now we can deepen this relaxation much more. In a moment I'm going to have you open and close your eyes. When you close your eyes that's your signal to let this feeling of relaxation become 10 times deeper.

All you have to do is want this to happen and you can make it happen very easily. OK, now, open your eyes.

Now close your eyes and feel that relaxation flowing through your whole body, taking you much, much deeper. Use your wonderful imagination and imagine your whole body is covered and warmed up in a warm blanket of relaxation.

Now, let every muscle in your body become so relaxed that as long as you hold on to this quality of relaxation, every muscle in your body is totally relaxed.

In a moment I'm going to have you open and close your eyes one more time. Again when you close your eyes, double the relaxation you now have. Make it become twice as deep. OK, now once more, open your eyes.

And close your eyes, and double your relaxation. Good.

Let every muscle in your body hold on to this quality of relaxation. In a moment I'm going to lift your [right or left] hand by the wrist, just a few inches and drop it. If you have followed my instructions up to this point, that hand will be so relaxed it will be just as loose and limp as a damp dish cloth, and will simply plop down.

Now don't try to help me. Let me do all the lifting so that when I release it, it just plops down and you allow yourself to go deeper still.

[Gently lift their hand by the wrist and drop it onto their leg]

Take a long, deep breath as you let yourself go deeper still. Now relax the muscles around your eyes to the point where they won't work and pretend you can't open them even though you know full well that you can.

As long as you hold on to this relaxation, you can pretend that they just won't work. When you're sure they're so relaxed that they just won't work, continue to pretend that they won't work and test them to make sure they won't work. Test them hard. That's right.

We want your mind to be as relaxed as your body is, so I want you to start counting from 100 backwards when I tell you to. Each time you say a number, double your mental relaxation. With each number you say, let your mind become twice as relaxed. By the time the numbers get down to 98, you'll be so relaxed the numbers won't be there.

Now, you have to do this, I can't do it for you. Those numbers will leave if you will them away.

Now say out loud, the first number and double your mental relaxation. Say 100.

Now double that mental relaxation, say 99.

Now double that mental relaxation, let those numbers already start to fade. They'll go if you will them to. Say 98.

Deeper relaxed, now they'll be gone. Dispel them. Banish them. Make it happen, you can do it; I can't do it for you. Put them out, make it happen! Are they all gone? Now really enjoy the skills and relaxation until I say something important to you, which I want you to take in at an even deeper level, easily and honestly if it's what you need.

[Insert client's suggestion]

Now come back to this room when I've counted from 3 up to 1 and you've realised that you've learnt something important to you.

3...   2...   1

21 Reframing

Now that we have explored some of the building blocks of NLP, we can move onto some more complex techniques.

There are techniques for changing processes, for splitting problems, for combining problems, for using your creativity in problem solving, for neutralising the impact of an experience, all kinds of things.

The important thing to remember is that at Practitioner level, NLP training is essentially giving you a big bunch of keys. When you get to a locked door, you can go through all the keys, one by one, or you can take some time to understand the lock so that you've got a much better chance of choosing the right key. At Master Practitioner level, I'll teach you how to pick locks, speaking metaphorically.

All of the techniques are based upon simple principles that relate to the way that we experience the world, and the way that we organise those experiences. Some people get stuck trying to explain all this in terms of neurology and connections in the brain. This, for me, is analogous to explaining how to use some software on your computer by explaining how the magnetic data is stored in memory. Thinking in terms of the electro-chemical brain function tells us absolutely nothing about the user interface.

Reframing is the process of changing meaning by changing perception. Have you ever changed an opinion of a person or event after seeing things a different way? And have you ever changed your behaviour as a result of that?

The important thing to remember is that our behaviour is a response to what we make an experience mean, it is not a response to the event itself, because our sensory filters and perceptions get in the way.

21.1 Direct Reframing

Your client offers you a description of an experience that they would be happy to have an alternative meaning for, or a different feeling about.

You reframe it by thinking of an alternative interpretation and saying "No you're wrong, it didn't mean x it meant y".

21.2 Context Reframing

Your client offers you a description of an experience that they would be happy to have an alternative meaning for, or a different feeling about.

You reframe it by asking them about background details for the experience, such as colours, other people, textures, anything in the experience which they did not notice at first.

21.3 Rapport Reframing

Your client offers you a description of an experience that they would be happy to have an alternative meaning for, or a different feeling about.

You reframe it by getting them to talk about the experience while you occasionally break rapport.

21.4 Meta Model Reframing

Your client offers you a description of an experience that they would be happy to have an alternative meaning for, or a different feeling about.

You reframe it by asking a variety of meta model questions.

21.5 State Reframing

Your client offers you a description of an experience that they would be happy to have an alternative meaning, you do anything you can think of to change their state and ask them to think of the experience again and notice what seems different in its meaning.

You might:

- Get them to stand up and walk around
- Ask them about a random subject
- Surprise them
- Walk off and ignore them
- Be extremely enthusiastic
- Talk about something you love doing
- Push them

Discuss how that works out.

Imagine that you have an oil painting, a family heirloom. You keep it in your spare bedroom because, although you think it's important to your family and probably valuable, you think it's hideous. One day, while looking for something else, you notice the frame rather than the painting itself. The frame is an ornate, gaudy and battered thing, only just big enough for the painting. You pause for a moment, then take the painting down off the wall and remove it from the frame. You begin to see colours you hadn't noticed before. Convincing yourself that it's purely out of respect for your ancestors, you take the painting to a frame shop, and they make some recommendations. A week later, you pick up the painting in its new frame and you can't believe the transformation. Yes, they've cleaned the canvass too, but the main difference is that the frame now shows the painting in a totally different light, and you proudly hang the painting above your fireplace. This is "reframing".

Perceptual Positions

This reframing technique works well with experiences of personal interactions such as presentations or conversations.

21.6 Perceptual Positions

Ask your client to recall an interaction that they would like to have a different perspective on.

Ask your client to recall that memory and run through it, recalling every detail as if it were happening right now. This is 1st position.

Now ask your client to walk over to where the other person was, and step into their position. In this 2nd position, your client watches the whole sequence again, watching and hearing themselves through the other person's senses.

Now have your client walk over to a 3rd position on the other side of the room. If they have difficulty dissociating from the emotional content of the memory, you can ask them to imagine stepping outside of the room and watching through a window, as a casual onlooker.

Ask them to watch the whole sequence again, paying attention to the interaction between positions 1 and 2. Ask them for any new information or insight they have in this position. Ask how they feel watching and listening to the interaction between the two people in the room, and to note how the other person seems to be responding.

Now have your client move back to the 1st position, in their own shoes, and run through the whole scene again, taking with them any insights gained during the exercise.

What has changed for them?

Meta Mirror

Meta Mirror adds a fourth, 'meta position' to the Perceptual Positions exercise. Essentially, the client is commenting on how they judge themselves.

This is a self image exercise, because how you judge yourself is something that you learned from how someone else judged you, often a parent or other influential person from your childhood.

21.7 Meta Mirror

Follow the basic procedure for perceptual positions, then at position 3 the client then moves to position 4, the meta position, and comments on 3's feelings towards and relationship with position 1, such as supportive, judgemental, critical, lenient etc.

The client takes this new information back to position 3 and comments on their new perspective on the experience before returning to position 1 and integrating the different perspectives.

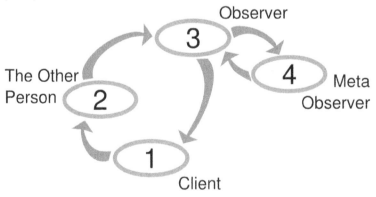

How would you adapt these techniques to help someone prepare for a presentation or other important event?

Six Step Reframe

This is a more complex technique than the ones we've explored up until now. You could say that the Six Step Reframe is an entire coaching process, all in itself, as it can take up to an hour to work through. It doesn't help that the language of the original is so impenetrable and relies on setting up unconscious finger signals, where the client's fingers wiggle unconsciously to indicate yes/no answers. Our experience is that this is an unnecessary level of complexity for what is a straightforward, if intricate, technique that you can use in a wide variety of situations, including a team problem solving and creativity exercise.

It also doesn't help that the original Six Step Reframe has seven steps in it. Really.

The six step reframe is a good technique for generating alternative ways of achieving complex outcomes, when the current behaviour has become a habit and is not getting the end result. The client may feel stuck, or like they are banging their head against a brick wall, yet they don't know what else they can do.

The most important step in the Six Step Reframe is the first, because if you don't pin the behaviour down, you'll spend the remaining steps going round in circles. Problem behaviours are quite often avoidances, distracting from some other need or behaviour which is in conflict with the client's present values or environment.

The nice thing about the Six Step Reframe is that you can easily adapt it as a team creativity tool, as you will see later.

21.8 Six Step Reframe

Step 1 Identify the pattern of behaviour to change. You have to be very specific about what it is that is to be changed. It is rarely as simple as the issue the client first presents, and the behaviour that the client thinks is a problem may in itself be a distraction for something else.

This is especially true in the case of "negative" behaviours i.e. the person *doesn't* do something. In this case, you have to look at what the person *does* do as a substitute for what they don't do.

Step 2 Communicate with the part that generates the behaviour. Every behaviour has a useful purpose and must be generated from somewhere, by a part that is responsible for achieving that outcome.

"Part" is a metaphor, you could think of it as a software program, or a member of staff with a particular job to perform.

Step 3 Separate the intention from the behaviour. What is the part aiming to achieve through the behaviour? The intention may not be desirable given the client's current values or environment, but it is positive, in that it is designed to achieve something. The intention is what you need to focus on.

Step 4 Create alternatives. Find the creative part, everyone has one even if they don't think they are creative. They don't have to accept they are an artistic person for this, just that they have a creative part. When they first start generating alternatives, you'll probably notice that they are thinly disguised variants of the problem behaviour, in that they are constrained by the the belief that the behaviour is a problem. Keep pushing your client for more and more alternatives and you'll almost see them throw a switch, where they move outside of the problem's boundaries and get into a real creative flow.

Step 5 Accept responsibility for change. The original part needs to take responsibility for its outcome, and therefore for achieving its outcome more effectively. If you get stuck at this stage, it's probably because you have not clearly established the positive intention.

The NLP Practitioner Manual

There are two tips that I have found useful at this step of the process.

Firstly, you can reduce the perceived size of the change, so you're not saying that the part has to change its behaviour immediately and for ever, you can say to the part, "I know that [purpose] is important to you, so to help you achieve [purpose] even better than you already have, would you be willing to try some of these new behaviours, just for the next 24 hours (or ten minutes, or whatever is relevant) and see for yourself how it works out? And if you don't like the result, you can just go right back to the old way of doing things."

Secondly, you can turn the part in on itself. Let's say that the positive intention of the part is to maintain self control. Well, in that case, wouldn't you think that a part that maintains self control would have the self control to try new and different ways of maintaining self control?

Step 6 Check for ecology. Make sure there are no other parts that are dependent on or benefit from the behaviour. The behaviour will be part of a complex system, and when you change one part of a system, you change the entire system. You need to make sure that there are no unmet needs that are likely to sabotage the changes.

Step 7 Future pace the change by talking though a number of future scenarios where the old behaviour would have occurred and testing for the new response, or ideally, a moment of confusion where the client evaluates new choices rather than responding out of habit.

Earlier, I said that the Six Step Reframe is easily adapted to other uses. Let's find out how, by looking at how the technique works.

Identifying the specific behaviour to address is an obvious first step in any technique, so that part is not unique.

In step 2, you identify and isolate an imaginary 'part' of a person that is responsible for the behaviour. This presupposes a number of very important and valuable things about the behaviour that they are seeking to change:

- It is not random

- It serves a purpose

- It does not define the whole person

- It is one of a number of possible behaviours

- It is somehow under the client's control

The identification of the part responsible for the behaviour therefore sets up the scenario that the behaviour is not the problem; the client's choice of behaviour is the problem.

Remember, as the NLP presupposition says, "Every behaviour has a positive intention, and a context within which it is useful".

No matter how dissatisfied the client is with their behaviour, it serves a purpose for them. It may have served a purpose once, and now they don't seem able to shake it, or it may serve a useful purpose which is now redundant.

A very common problem is that the person learned a particular behaviour at a time when their lives were a certain way. Now they are older, their environment has changed and they have different relationships. However, they still engage in behaviours which are fine in themselves but are no longer effective in their new environment.

The role of the 'creative part' is to separate ideas generation from the problem. It is vital that the new possibilities are not constrained by the original problem. If someone's stated problem is that their boss never listens, it is not much use if their creative part generates the following alternatives:

- Talk louder

- Talk faster

- Stand closer

None of these changes the underlying dynamic of the relationship, namely that getting their boss to listen presupposes that the fault lies with their boss and not with their own communication.

The ecology check is important because a person is not, in fact, made up of separate parts, each with a neatly defined purpose. A person is a whole, and the metaphor of parts only serves to isolate and dissociate the behaviour in order to presuppose that it is under the person's control and serves a useful purpose. If that behaviour is not serving its purpose then that is not because of a fault; it is because the behaviour is now being taken out of context.

Remember the presupposition; "The positive worth of the individual is held constant, while the value and appropriateness of internal and/or external behaviour is questioned."

So what we have is a technique for isolating a problem, reframing it as a useful behaviour taken out of context, generating alternatives that fit the current context, checking for systemic acceptance and then testing the end result.

The Six Step Reframe is, in my experience, one of NLP's most intricate, comprehensive and powerful techniques. It shows NLP at its best; not as a quick fix set of parlour tricks but as a systemic approach to change.

A person is only one complex system that the Six Step Reframe works with. Others? A company, a team, a family.

I'm not going to spell out how you would adapt this technique to those systems, partly because I want you to do some of the working out for yourself and partly because it's covered in one of my earlier books Change Magic, which I am planning to rewrite at some point. But if you're desperate, drop me an email and I'll ask my creative part to give you some ideas.

> List some other situations where you could use an
> adapted Six Step Reframe

Association and Dissociation

Our emotional experience of an event depends on the point of view that we observe it from. How do people naturally associate and dissociate? e.g. "feeling present" or "detaching themselves from the situation"

You are self aware. You have a self concept that you can place into a map of the world. You can imagine yourself doing certain things in the future, going places, meeting people. And as a side effect of this self awareness, you are self conscious. That doesn't make you nervous, it makes you consciously aware of yourself.

Where does this self image come from? Well, here's the strange thing. It doesn't come from your memory of seeing yourself, because you've never seen yourself. You might have seen a reflection of yourself, or a photo of yourself, but these are distortions. You have never seen yourself the way others do.

What you do have first hand experience of, though, is how you feel. You have direct experience of your sensations and emotions. And you take these sensations and from them create a self image.

You have a physical self concept that enables you to navigate, to locate your body in space. That's called proprioception. And the self image enables you to judge how others see you.

You know how you feel but not how you look. You know how other people look but not how they feel, and you connect the two together.

What we all do is to imagine that because we know how we feel, we know how we look. Similarly, because we know how other people look, we imagine we know how they feel.

One of the most striking ways that you can see this in action is when people are presenting. Someone who has an image of themselves as a poor presenter imagines that they look as nervous as they feel, when in fact they look perfectly relaxed. They then see a colleague present who looks relaxed and say, "Oh, you're really good, you're really confident. I'm rubbish because I'm so nervous."

Then their colleague says, "No, I'm nervous inside even though I don't show it!"

You'll also see this when people are tying on clothes. They'll ask you, "how do I look?", and no matter what you say about how nice they look, they pull that face that indicates they know you're only saying that to be nice, because they have already decided how they look, based on how they feel.

The only evidence I have for how I look to you is how you feel about me which I mind read from how you look at me.

If your observation and spoken judgements of me are helpful and encouraging, I might tend to create a self image that elicits good feelings, pride, happiness, high self esteem and so on. On the other hand, if what I get from you is frowns, and tuts, and criticism, and "you're not going out wearing THAT are you?" then I'm more likely to create a self image which elicits guilt, embarrassment, low self esteem and resentment.

So the problem isn't the self image in itself, it's the way that we can create a self image that is so different from what others really see. Because of course, for someone to judge you in a critical way, what they're really responding to is their own feelings, not you.

Here are some examples of situations where we can see this mismatched or disconnected self image:

- Someone who believes themselves to be overweight or unattractive in some way and feels bad about the way they look.

- Someone who believes themselves to be a poor or nervous public speaker

- Someone who socialises with people much younger than themselves, the common expression being "mutton dressed as lamb"

- Someone who believes that they aren't well regarded by colleagues

- Someone who sees themselves in an unusually positive way given the "reality"

- Someone who tries on clothes in a shop and is disappointed that they don't look they way they had imagined

What I have found is that people create a self image based on their feelings and project it out into the world so that over time they begin to look more like their self image.

What do we do with this information? How do we change a self image?

I've found it's possible, and the key is in understanding that the self image is dissociated, it's disconnected emotionally from you. So all you have to do is identify where it is and go and stand in it. Many people find they can simply imagine doing that, others find it helps to physically stand in it. Either way, you step into and become your own self image, and the moment you do that, you can become aware of the physical sensations associated with it.

At this moment, you can connect with the physical sensations that would be associated with the self image as it has been created, and in these situations it tends to feel uncomfortable in some way. So the next step is that I asked them to give themselves a shake and a stretch, as if they're trying on a new suit and checking if it fits properly. As they become more aware of the sensations, they can adjust them, because whilst they have only been looking at the visual appearance of the self image, they haven't had access to the detailed sensations.

Next, I ask them to step out and have another look. This time, as they become more aware still, they can make some changes to the outward appearance, and this will change the feelings and sensations again, so they step back in to check. I'll ask them to step in, adjust, step out, adjust and so on until they can step in and feel really good. What's important is that the feeling is guiding this, the appearance is following.

Finally, they step out and put the self image in a useful place. The physical change in the person can be dramatic. I've seen people physically grow taller, look younger and more relaxed, tangibly gain confidence and just generally look like they're more comfortable in their own skin.

You might be wanting to give this a go for yourself now, in which case you might be about to go back over the last few paragraphs to pick out the process. Don't worry, I'll summarise it for you.

21.9 Self Image Association

Identify the location of the self image, where you see it in the room.

Either mentally or physically step into the image and associate with it, looking out through your own eyes.

Become aware of the sensations associated with the image as you stretch and settle into it.

Don't like how it feels? Stretch it a bit more.

Step out and have a look, making some adjustments to the appearance.

Step back in and notice how it feels, continuing to stretch and make it comfortable, always being guided by the feeling.

Continue to step in and out until it feels right, whatever that means for you.

Finally, step out and put the image where you would like to see it and enjoy feeling good about yourself.

Fast Phobia Cure (Progressive Dissociation)

A phobia is an extreme, uncontrollable, incapacitating response to a stimulus, often learned during a traumatic event. A phobia triggers the freeze/flight/fight response which is hard wired into all of us thanks to our evolved survival instinct.

True phobias are extremely rare. You are much more likely to encounter a fear rather than a phobia; a strong desire to avoid something. What I have found very interesting is that the fears which seem most common are of events which a person has never actually experienced, for example a fear of drowning, or of being in an air accident. I find that the fears that we inherit from others are much more powerful than the scary things we experience first hand.

A nurse told me that many people are afraid of the dentist and as a result, their children grow up with poor oral health. New parents are encouraged to take their children to the dentist, even before their teeth emerge, so that they can get used to the experience. One young mother was so determined that her daughter would not inherit her fear that she pushed herself to take her daughter to see a dentist. The little girl was curious. As the girl sat in the chair, her mother said, "Don't worry, it won't hurt". What image does that statement create in your mind? Is we analyse the language with Meta Model, it is an instruction to be afraid of something unspecific, so [insert your worst fear here].

The Fast Phobia Cure is very effective for inherited fears like this, and also another common type of fear; the fear of what might happen. Well Formed Outcomes is a model of a process that you naturally use to focus on goals. What if you focused on something that you didn't want, or even something that is scary? Your brain doesn't judge, it just gets you more of what you focus on.

This Fast Phobia Cure is a dissociation technique that is very useful for reducing the intensity of an emotional response so that you can work on the cause without getting lost in the emotional response that follows. If you remember Meta Mirror, the Fast Phobia Cure uses a similar progressive dissociation.

As with the Six Step Reframe, this could be an entire session in itself and can take perhaps half an hour to complete for a very emotive subject. Equally, it can take five minutes if you carefully test the dissociation at each stage.

No doubt you have heard the expression about trying to change a tyre while you're driving along. It's sometimes difficult to change a thought process when there is a strong emotional reaction to it, because the strength of that reaction will often kick in long before you have a chance to discuss the underlying triggers.

The Fast Phobia Cure allows you to, metaphorically, stop the car and jack up the wheel. It allows you to temporarily detach the emotional response from the triggering event. However, as far as a phobia is concerned, the response *is* the problem. Mice, or spiders, or dogs, or heights are not in themselves a problem. The problem is that the way someone feels about those things is uncontrollable.

The existence of mice is not a problem. Feeling fear is not a problem. Put the two together and you have what people often describe as an "irrational fear". It makes no sense, but they can't help it.

Depending on how strong the emotional response is, and how good you are at managing the stages of dissociation, you may need fewer or more dissociations than the example script below. Therefore, don't read the script verbatim, pay attention to your client and modify it accordingly. The clue you're looking for is that your client's physical response has completely diminished compared to your first test. At that point, you can start working on the submodalities. Play with different coloured filters, distortions, soundtracks, whatever comes to mind.

At each stage of the dissociation, your client is looking at themselves in the previous stage. They are not looking at the screen so after the first seat, don't mention the image on the screen again.

21.10 Fast Phobia Cure

Imagine yourself in a cinema, seated in the middle of the front row. See the screen in front of you and notice the colour of the seats, the size of the auditorium, the lighting. Be aware of the sensation of the seat comfortably supporting you. Notice the texture of the seat. Up on the screen, see a black and white snapshot of yourself in a situation just before an experience in which you would have had that feeling.

Imagine that you can step out of your own body, see yourself sitting in the front row looking up at the screen.

Now imagine that you can stand up out of your own body, turn and see yourself sitting in the front row and imagine yourself walking to the middle row and sitting over to the far side of the room, looking at yourself in the front row, with the glow from the screen gently lighting what you can see.

Once again, stand up out of your body and walk to the back row on the other side of the cinema. Sit down and look at yourself sitting over on the opposite side. Notice the pale gentle light on your face.

Stand up out of your body again and walk out of the door at the back of the cinema, and look back in through the window, so that as you stand in the corridor and look through the little window, you can see yourself at the back of the cinema looking at yourself in the middle of the cinema looking at yourself in the front row.

You can even step out of your body in the corridor and walk up to the projection room and see the projector and all of the controls and equipment.

Walk over to the projector, and noticing yourself standing in the corridor, start the projector.

Let the black and white movie run all the way through to the end and stop.

Now run the film backwards. Run the film backwards quickly, so all the people are moving backwards, all the sounds are backwards, all the way back to the start.

Run the movie forwards at double speed, hear all the high pitched sounds. Rewind it to the start.

Add a coloured filter to the lens, play the movie forwards at double speed. Rewind it.

Choose some cartoon music as a soundtrack to the movie.

Turn the movie upside down and play it forwards and backwards.

Keep running the movie backwards and forwards. When you're ready you can add in some colour and gently slow the movie down until it is running forwards and backwards at normal speed.

Allow the movie to slowly come back to the start. Walk back to the corridor where you are looking through the window, and then through the door to the back row, and then to the middle on the opposite side, and then to the front row.

Imagine you can stand up from the front row and walk to the screen. Touch the screen and see the light on your hand. Push the screen and notice it feels springy and soft. Push your hand through the screen and step through the screen into the picture.

Allow the whole movie to play forwards at normal speed, in colour, with sound, and notice what has changed.

As a reminder, the steps of the Fast Phobia Cure are:

1. Dissociated, still image of the moment before the event which the emotional response is linked to, or an example of it

2. Multiple, progressive dissociations, calibrating the client's physical responses in order to know how many dissociations you need

3. Change submodalities while dissociated

4. Progressively re-associate, paying attention the client's physical responses to make sure they are comfortable

5. Final association into the memory of the event and test

What's interesting about the Fast Phobia Cure, which for some reason I abbreviate to "FFC", is that it does nothing to change either the stimulus or the reaction, it merely breaks the connection between the two.

Firstly, the progressive dissociation allows the Practitioner to test the point at which the reaction is small enough to be able to work with the imagery. However, the relief of the dissociation itself is temporary. If you step back and progressively re-associate at this point, the reaction will still be there, as strong as ever.

Think back to the section on submodalities. Do you see a connection between dark, distant and small and the emotional detachment of dissociation? It's as if we instinctively know how to minimise the pain of certain memories, but holding them in the shadows requires effort.

Secondly, the jumbling up of the images prevents the mental movie from automatically running.

Many years ago, I had a head-on car crash and for weeks afterwards, a two second movie of the event played over in my mind with slowly decreasing regularity.

Scientists have conducted experiments with mice that may explain how the FFC works. Perhaps a scientist from the past was scared of mice and decided to experiment on them in order to deal with his phobia.

Scientists simulated two traumatic events; being in a falling elevator, and being in an earthquake[5].

They achieved this by putting mice in boxes and either dropping the boxes or shaking them, while monitoring the brain activity of the subject mouse.

5   Scientific American, 'The Memory Code', June 17, 2007

They found that a part of the brain that processes incoming sensory data activated at the time of the original event, and it then reactivated, in exactly the same way, at decreasing intervals until it eventually stopped. The mouse was having flashbacks! The scientists theorised that the mice were 'reliving' the traumatic event in order to become desensitised to it, so that a similar event in the future would be less stressful.

Their work was designed to demonstrate how memories are formed, and the role that part of the brain called the hippocampus plays. From their experiments, they were able to observe the formation of memories within the physical structures of the brain.

For our purposes, the research provides some insight into the way in which we 'relive' and neutralise traumatic memories. Whilst we may mentally push a memory away and put it in a dark corner or at the back of a mental cupboard, it is still there, and if something causes that memory to come into the open, the memory can be as difficult to deal with as the original event was.

By jumbling up the connections between the event and the emotional response, the Fast Phobia Cure gives the client a new way to observe and analyse events objectively and choose more resourceful ways to respond to them.

> How can you tell when a client has a genuine phobia, as opposed to an intense dislike, or even a display of attention seeking behaviour?

22 Time

In NLP, time is usually related to the set of techniques known as "timelines". I'll explore two areas of time here; firstly understanding how your internal perception of time relates to your external behaviour and secondly, how you can use timeline techniques to change past and future events.

Our subjective perception of time is a very powerful and valuable resource that can be used to create change or to plan effectively.

When we talk about time, we use words that also apply to space[6], saying things like:

- Put it behind you

- Your future is in front of you

- Let's look ahead

- It's a long way off yet, don't worry about it

- Don't look back

- I can see a time when this will be different

As you might expect by now, these kinds of words can be taken literally. If someone says that they have put an experience behind them, it's literally what they have done.

The way in which we interact with time also causes a few problems, in particular:

- We imagine a future problem and act as if it is real

- We relive a past problem as if it is still happening

6 lera.ucsd.edu/papers/language-time.pdf

Rationally, you know that those reactions are unhelpful. You know that if something hasn't happened yet, you can choose or at least influence the way it turns out. You also know that if something has already happened, there's nothing you can do to change it. Of course, people do get stuck in patterns of behaviour that we can get them out of.

Essentially, you can use past timelines to change a person's perceptions of past events, or future timelines to plan more effectively for the future.

As with the rest of NLP, timelines haven't been invented, they're just patterns that people like you and I already have within our natural though processes. We already have an internal representation of the flow of time that we interact with, and we already have both individual and generalised ways of interacting with time. Most people imagine their future being in front of them and their past behind them. If you ask someone to imagine a line that connects past, present and future, they will be able to point to it, even though they had never consciously considered it before.

Think of a timeline as a graphical user interface for your perception of events in time, just like your computer's operating software. If you look inside your computer, you won't really find folders and notepaper in there. The interface is just designed that way so that it's easier to use.

Where do you imagine the future and past to be? As I said, many people imagine that the future is in front of them, and the past is behind them. Consequently, your parents tell you that you have your whole life ahead of you, and friends tell you that particular experiences are all behind them. They might even say, "it's all in the past now" as they point behind them, or wave over their shoulders. This is all extremely valuable information, as you are no doubt becoming aware.

Imagine you have several applications open on your computer, and you have the windows stacked on top of each other. You can only see the window at the front and to get to other applications you have to stop what you're doing and switch programs. This is what some people experience when they think about future goals, so they tend to focus on the thing that is immediately in front of them and not see goals that lie further away.

Other people have everything laid out in front of them like photographs across a desk. They can only realistically focus in one area at any time, and it is difficult for them to know what is most important at any particular time.

We can see a relationship between a person's representation of time and their behaviour towards time coded events such as appointments and deadlines. The person who experiences time in the "now" with a series of goals rushing towards them is generally very good at panicking but not so good at long term planning. They tend to be on time for events but tend not to see how experiences relate to each other through time. They see time like this:

It's often hard for people who are used to seeing time in one way to see it in the other way. After all, you have spent your whole life knowing what time is and being frustrated at other people for not seeing things the way you do. After all, isn't it obvious that if you have to be at a meeting at 9:00 that you leave home at 7:00? And isn't it obvious that you shouldn't just focus on the next thing you have to do, you should think and prioritise and look at everything you need to get done?

Take a few moments to fully pay attention to what is going on around you. Literally stop reading and pay attention to the sights, sounds and events around you.

Assuming that you did pause and look around you, during that time you were living "through time".

Often, we summarise events as snapshots. We think back to past events, particularly unpleasant ones, and instead of seeing a movie, we see a still image. Of course, events are never stationary in real life, so in order to take a snapshot, you have to distort reality. A snapshot like this is an "in time" representation and is a highly deleted, distorted and generalised form of the original event.

Consider someone who smokes and wants to give up. Or someone who stays late at the office, or always does all the housework. What they are acutely aware of, because it's what they focus on, are the times when they are doing the thing they want to stop doing. They create a mental movie of those instances, connected together, and ignore the time in between. So the person who wants to give up smoking focuses on the times when they are actively smoking and, from that, deduces that they are always smoking. Certainly, if you watched a movie of someone, and in every scene they were smoking, you would say they were always smoking.

In the films "Seven", "Meet Joe Black" and "Ocean's 11", Brad Pitt's character is eating in many of the scenes. Most people would say he was "always eating". It's probably fair to say that Brad Pitt himself was eating, we just didn't want to confuse him with characters he played in films.

If you say that he was "always eating", what you have created is a series of "in time representations in a between time structure". "Between time" is the space between the times you are not doing the thing that you are always doing, and your deletion of the times in between is what makes this a generalisation.

We often collapse a sequence of events into a moment in time. For example, I think it will take me no time at all to fill my car up at the petrol station, so I don't allow any journey time for it. Unfortunately, it does appear to impact on my journey time. You'll hear people say things like, "It will take no time", "It will only take five minutes" or "I'll be back in a minute/flash/jiffy". Logically, these activities take time. Subjectively, we collapse them into no time.

Many time management training sessions get people to un-collapse time. I remember one from the 1990s which gave you a "time planner" into which you had to mark time for yourself. The idea was that you set aside some time each day for planning, writing to do lists etc. rather than just reacting to whatever came your way.

Imagine you go to the cinema to watch a film. The poster outside is an "in time" representation. It is one snapshot that contains everything you need to know.

Or you could think of it as the cover on the DVD case. The film "Funny Bones" has a cover designed to make the British comedy appealing to am American audience. It actually has nothing at all to do with the film and has a picture of two of the characters that was not in the film. The original publicity material features a still from a scene which actually summed the film up perfectly, although it wasn't visually exciting.

The trailer for the film is a series of "in time representations in a between time structure", a series of snapshots assembled to give a certain meaning. The trailer will comprise clips taken out of sequence, and even clips which aren't in the film itself. This, together with the voice-over, is designed to create an impression of the film, a meaning.

And the film? That's the "through time" representation.

So you can only really understand what the film is about by watching the film.

By the way, if you read NLP discussion forums or websites, you will find differences of opinion on these definitions. This is partly because some people find this a difficult subject to understand and partly because second and third generation licensing bodies sometimes change the terminology, based on the misunderstandings of their founding trainers. The definitions here come 'from the horse's mouth' and have been checked with Christina Hall, owner of the Society of NLP.

Here's another way to think about it. When you are "in time", you are standing in a river with the water flowing around you. When you are "through time", you are moving through the events around you as if time is standing still. It's as if you're browsing through the items in a shop or a photo album. When you are "between time", you are in the gaps between these representations, just like there is 'nothing' in between the rows of shelves in a shop, or between the photos in an album.

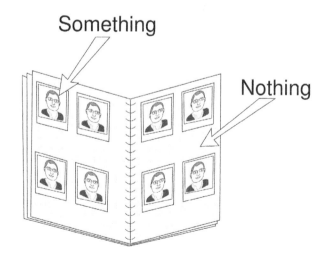

You'll no doubt recognise "nothing" as a universal quantifier, a generalisation that requires a distortion, bringing the 'somethings' together, and a deletion of the 'other things' between the 'somethings'.

How is this relevant? Listen to anyone describe an emotional problem to you and they'll give you something analogous to the movie trailer. It will have clips out of sequence, and it will have a voice over – internal dialogue - to explain what's happening and how you are supposed to feel about it.

Listen to anyone in your business describe a complex issue and you'll get a trailer. You'll get a series of "relevant" events, collapsed together into one. And the meaning of that is derived exactly from that sequence, so if a little editing is required to really underline the intended meaning then so be it.

And if you ask for a brief summary? You get the poster. And, of course, that contains exactly the information in exactly the sequence needed for the other person to convey the meaning they want to convey.

Sequence gives an experience meaning. It sounds almost ridiculous to say that, because it seems so obvious. You can only get a new job after you have applied for it. You can only feel bad about a meeting after you have been to it. Unless, of course, you can imagine it going badly beforehand.

Here's the more interesting idea though; if you change the sequence, you change the meaning. And if you only imagine changing the sequence, you change the meaning too. Remember that the difference between imagination and reality is highly subjective and tenuous, assuming that there is any reality of course.

It seems odd at best, and a philosophical discussion at worst, to say that these words aren't "out there". They are in your head. The feeling of the book is in your head. The voice reading these words is in your head. The voice writing these words is in my head. And from your point of view, those positions are reversed. You can read intention into my words just as you read intention into emails and newspaper articles.

Thinking back to sensory filters; we delete, distort and generalise as a function of perception, they are not conscious processes. The meaning we end up with, the conclusion we jump to, is based on a small amount of data.

The more we can recover the original "through time" experience, the closer we'll be to understanding it and, if necessary, changing it. Of course, we can't change what actually happened, but we can edit a new trailer that changes the meaning. Take any film and edit it down and you can create a comedy, tragedy, documentary, anything you like. If you have ever been lulled into seeing "this summer's hit comedy" only to realise that the trailer was funnier than the film, then you'll understand the power of editing.

The word 'now' has a special meaning. Each of us has a very different, unique and subjective concept of time. For some of us it passes quickly, for others, more slowly. Some of us see time as a series of impending deadlines, others see it as a range of possible paths ahead of us. And each of us has a different interpretation of the duration of "now".

22.1 Where is Now?

Imagine that you can see the flow of time as a visible line, like a project plan for your whole life, showing past, present and future.

Where is the past? Behind you, to the side or somewhere else?

Where is the future? Is it in front of you, to the side of you or somewhere else?

Where is now?

How big is now? (Indicate with your hands)

How long is now? (As in seconds, minutes, hours etc.)

Ask your friends, colleagues and family to answer these questions and note how they 'see' time.

Think about the differences between you and other people.

Do these differences explain any confusion or conflict that you have ever experienced relating to time, such as deadlines, priorities or a sense of urgency?

When you get to know your clients, you might notice that they too have different subjective experiences of time. This makes a huge difference when you are trying to keep control of the sales process and move things along at the right pace. If you feel that the client is taking too long to respond, they might be putting you off, or they might just have a very different understanding of what "soon" means.

Time is not a real entity, it is something that is only implied through movement and change in the world. We cannot sense time directly, we can only infer its passage indirectly with tools such as clocks and egg timers. Constants such as the force of gravity and the size of the grains of sand mean that the egg timer fills in around five minutes, every time.

Similarly, constants such as your client's business environment and their own sense of priority create a 'pace' for any project that you deliver with them.

Years ago, a business process required the manual typing of order forms, the distribution of internal memos, paperwork going backwards and forwards in the mail for signature, manual filing in filing rooms and it required all the people involved to be in the same place, every day.

Today, the majority of business processes are entirely automated. A manager types his or her emails, they arrive almost instantly and the sender expects an instant reply. Copies are made automatically, electronic signatures are acceptable and all of this can happen when the people involved are in the office, at home, or, sadly, on holiday.

We generally want things done 'as soon as possible', whether that means two weeks or two seconds. Technology simply raises our expectations.

22.2 How Soon is Soon?

In small groups, discuss what period of time these words imply to you.

Now	Soon	A moment
Currently	Recently	Right away
Imminent	ASAP	Immediate
Not long	A minute	Eventually
Not long ago	Ages	A while
A bit	Forever	A tick
Five minutes	A second	Back then

How do other people answer differently? What differences do you notice? How is that interesting?

What will you do differently when someone says they'll call you back "in five minutes" or when a client says they will review your proposal, "soon"?

Project managers often 'sand bag' or pad their timescales and deadlines. In turn, the people who are working on their projects do the same. Everyone builds in a little leeway in case everyone else fails to deliver on time. The result is that the project is delivered late, because no-one is working to an accurate expectation.

The timeline concept in NLP is based on the exploration of a person's sense of time as a means of changing the impact of past events or planning effectively for future events. Here are a few exercises that you can use yourself in exploring timelines.

22.3 Basic Timeline – Exploring a Goal

Make sure that you have plenty of floor space for this exercise, and then guide your client through the process as follows.

Imagine a line on the floor that represents time, with the future in front of you, and the past behind you. The point where you are standing is "now".

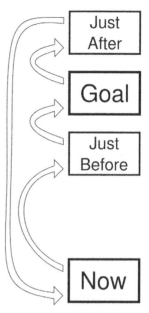

Think about something you want to achieve and notice where it lies on the line, how far into the future it lies. It might be something quite ambitious, so you would like to achieve it but don't yet know how to, or how difficult it might be.

Walk forwards until just before the goal. Notice how that feels.

Now step onto the goal itself, and notice how that feels. Finally, take one more step so that the goal is completely achieved and notice how that feels.

Turn round and look back to the present moment, noticing all the milestones you passed on the way.

Walk back to the present, taking with you everything useful you learned on the way so that the experience and knowledge can help you in the present.

When you get back to "now", look towards the goal again.

Has anything changed? Is it in the same place?

Of course, you didn't really travel through time, your brain just thinks you did. This is the same thing, in terms of your sensory experience, and what else do you have to go on?

This is a very powerful technique for exploring future possibilities and overcoming perceived obstacles more easily. Here are a few more ways that you can use this technique.

22.4 Resource Timeline

However the current situation seems, there have been times in your past when you have achieved more than you thought possible, and those experiences serve as resources for the future.

> Start in the present and ask your client to consider a situation where they would like to have more resources, perhaps more knowledge, or more skills, or a greater sense of understanding, or more creativity, or whatever they might find useful.
>
> Have your client turn round and walk backwards in time, noticing any past experiences where those resources may be found. When they feel that they have reached such a time, pause for a moment and absorb that resource.
>
> Continue back in time collecting as many resources as your client wants.
>
> Walk a little further, then turn and look forwards to the present. Walk forwards, collecting and holding on to those resources and bring them fully into the present.
>
> How does the client now feel able to handle the situation?

22.5 Overcoming Obstacles

This variation is useful when there is something that your client wants to achieve, and they feel that there are many obstacles or barriers to overcome.

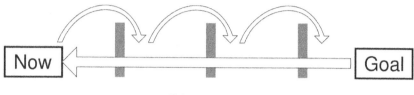

Obstacles

Start with the basic technique, this time asking your client to stop briefly each time they encounter a barrier or obstacle.

Pause, and then step over, or around each obstacle. Continue until there are no more obstacles and you have reached your goal.

Turn round and look back through the obstacles you overcame or problems you solved.

Walk back to the present, walking through each barrier, being aware of anything you learn or notice.

When you arrive back at the present, turn and look towards the goal again.

What has changed?

22.6 The Undo Button

This version is useful for when there is a decision that your client made in the past that they're not happy with.

> Turn round and face the past, looking back to that decision and noticing everything that has happened since then.
>
> Walk slowly back to the decision point, collecting up everything that you have learned since then.
>
> When you reach the decision point, take one more step. Turn and face the future.
>
> With all of the experience you have brought back with you, what decision will you make?
>
> Move forward to the present, exploring the consequences of that decision.
>
> How does your client feel about the decision now?

22.7 Motivation

You can use this version when your client is finding it difficult to motivate themselves to take action on something. For example, going to the gym now to be fit for a holiday, or working hard now to pass an exam in the future. Ultimately, you have to make time now for preparation, but when there are more pressing demands on your time, it's often easier to put it off until tomorrow.

> Picture, in the future, your goal in the way that you would achieve it if you put the effort in now. Walk up to the goal and stop just beyond it.
>
> Enjoy the feeling of having achieved that in the way that you wanted to. Return to the present.
>
> Next, picture yourself in the future when you haven't put the effort in, perhaps at the exam without having revised, at the presentation without having prepared etc.
>
> Walk forwards again. There's a good chance you will feel resistance, and a feeling of impending doom as you walk forwards.
>
> Stop at the goal and take plenty of time to fully experience your sense of disappointment in yourself. Really regret not having made the effort!
>
> Now, literally grab hold of this feeling as you walk back to the present and stretch that awful feeling of regret all the way back to the present so that you can experience it now in relation to your daily planning and time management.
>
> Walk forward slowly, thinking about your daily routine and finding time to do the work you need to do. Continue doing this all the way up to the goal and notice how good it feels, both to have achieved the goal and to know that you made the effort and commitment necessary.
>
> Take this feeling and stretch it back to the present, pulling back that good motivating feeling and bringing it back with you so that you have it now.

22.8 What If?

You can use multiple timelines, in slightly different directions, to explore the future consequences of different options.

22.9 Destiny

You will need plenty of room for this. Start with a basic timeline and, when your client reaches the goal, ask them to pause for a moment and reflect.

Walk forwards for as far as you practically can given the constraints of where you are.

You may find that your client feels a growing sense of unease, a sense that they are 'going the wrong way', which is an excellent observation about the congruence of their original goal. If this happens, return to the start, adjust the goal based on that new information and start again.

As they reach the furthest point, have them turn back and look all the way back to their starting point.

Ask your client the following:

"When is this?"

"Where are you now?"

"Where has your goal brought you to?"

"If you could sum up, in one word, who you have become as a result of the path you have chosen, what would that word be?"

Have them create a strong mental image of what that word represents that they can keep with them.

Creativity

Timeline is an excellent creative and problem solving technique, because you can use it in a variety of ways to make a creative problem solving process more effective.

One of the biggest challenges in problem solving in a corporate environment is the current situation, which defines the rules by which new ideas are judged. I'm sure you've been in a situation where comments such as, "We've already tried that" and "That wouldn't work" only serve to make the solution more elusive.

I once coached a technical manager in an engineering company. I'll call him Fred. One of the things that this company did was manufacture hydraulic cylinders, which have to be cut from solid metal with absolute precision, otherwise the hydraulic fluid leaks out and they don't work. After cutting, the next step was to paint them, however, small flakes of paint were getting inside the cylinders, causing leaks and ultimately, failure.

The various engineers and managers got together for an emergency meeting. One of them would say, "What if we...", and Fred would interrupt and say, "That won't work because". Then another would say, "What if we...", and Fred would interrupt and say, "That won't work because".

The production of new ideas slowed, until solving the problem became a laborious process that no-one took any pleasure from.

Fred was forming a mental picture of the suggested solution and instantly seeing the flaw in the idea. He thought that he was doing a marvellous job of cutting out the 'wrong' ideas, but the consequence was that he was suppressing the group's creativity. In fact, he was crushing it.

I suggested that, instead of jumping in, he wrote down the suggestion and then asked the person questions about it.

Superficially, writing the suggestions down was good practice. Secretly, it was to slow down his thought process. He could still see the flaw in the suggestions, but he was no longer 'shooting them down'.

Next, I suggested that, instead of saying, "That won't work", he asked, "How do you see that working?"

The other person would start to talk it through, get halfway through and then stop, realising that their idea wouldn't work. Fred was right all along, but at least he was no longer rubbing his colleagues up the wrong way.

However, something very interesting happened. Well, it was interesting for Fred. Someone else would jump in and say, "Well, no, you're right, that wouldn't work, but what if we took your basic idea and did this instead of that?"

The result was that the generation of new ideas accelerated, and new ideas built upon each other.

Rather than each person being under pressure to come up with the 'right' idea, they could each now contribute part of an idea, and together they created a whole solution.

The result? They solved complex production problems in half the time, with a better atmosphere and better relationships.

Crucially for Fred, he didn't miss out on the credit for finding the solution either, because everyone could see how he had learned to apply his expertise more skilfully.

In this instance, Fred constrained the group's creativity, yet in every organisation, new ideas will be constrained by current 'facts' such as technical or financial limitations.

Timelines enable a project manager to shift the group's mindset into a future state when the current limiting conditions no longer apply. Ideas don't have to 'work', they just have to be plentiful, and changing the group's state will ensure that this is the case.

Once again, my book 'Change Magic' describes this process in detail, and explains how you can use timelines in many different and even conversational ways to unlock creativity.

> What other creativity techniques can you think of? How do they relate to the principles discussed here?

23 Future Pacing

Future pacing is an important way of reinforcing new behaviours, and also checking to make sure that they are congruent over time and in different situations. It's a very simple technique where you give a commentary of a situation that is in the future and you talk about it as if it's happening now, whilst checking for any signs of incongruence.

For example, at some point you might put this book down for a while and ponder on some of the ideas you've read about. You might go back to previous chapters, or you might carry on through, as the ideas begin to work their way into your unconscious, helping you to apply NLP easily in whatever business situations you find yourself in.

Future pacing is simply the process of getting your client to mentally walk through the changes that you have made together.

There are a number of important reasons for future pacing:

- To check for congruence

- To 'dry run' new skills in challenging situations

- To reinforce new skills through repetition

Every technique and every coaching session should end with future pacing, and you should also future pace throughout a session as a way of testing your progress.

23.1 Future Pacing – Visualisation

Guide your client through three instances of future scenarios where they can test out their new skills or perspectives.

Explore each scenario in great deal, paying close attention to submodalities. If you find incongruence, back up and approach the scenario in a different way, helping your client to resolve the incongruence.

Question your client on what they see, how they feel, what reactions they can get from other people. Play devil's advocate and offer "What if?" suggestions.

23.2 Future Pacing – Movement

Find somewhere that you will have plenty of space to move around.

Ask your client to stand in a location that they call "now" and see the future in front of them.

Invite your client to walk slowly forwards, talking through their progress one step at a time. Each step could be a minute, a day, a year, whatever your client feels is a useful pace.

Pay attention to your client's language and physical movement. For example, if you notice them pause, or sway, or 'jump over' something, point this out and ask what it means.

Guide your client through three instances of future scenarios where they can test out their new skills or perspectives.

24 Meta Programs

Thinking Preferences

We've discussed the different ways that people organize and exhibit their sensory preferences, and there are other communication and thinking preferences that are worth exploring too.

Think for a moment about the amount of information available on the Internet. When the Internet was a relatively small academic network, there were no search engines and only very basic text browsers. As the Internet evolved, the major problem wasn't the storage or transmission of all of this data, it was providing a means for people to find what they need.

Search engines have evolved into incredibly complex systems for categorizing and organizing data, and the ease with which you can 'Google' your chosen subject gives no indication of the amount of data that is being sorted and organized.

As of 18th August, 2014, if you search for the phrase 'persuasion skills', Google returns "About 1,510,000 results".

And now consider the amount of information that is all around you at this moment, the sights, sounds, smells, sensations, words, music and voices that serve as the background to your everyday life. How do you even begin to sort through this mass of data to pick out and focus on what you need?

The answer is that our sensory experience is organized through a set of filters that we have been building and adjusting since before we were born.

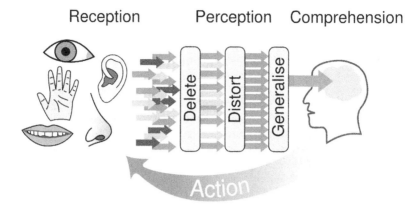

Reception   Perception   Comprehension

Delete   Distort   Generalise

Action

These filters; Delete, Distort and Generalize, do not work randomly, they work according to patterns that we have learned throughout our lifetimes. Just like an Internet search engine, they sort through the available data, discard what is irrelevant and organize the remainder into categories.

The way that this filtering process manifests itself is that we each tend to see and hear what we want to, and our experience of the world reinforces what we already 'know'.

NLP Meta Programs have been the subject of work by a number of people including Robert Dilts, Rodger Bailey and Shelle Rose Charvet. The selection described here seem to be the most relevant, useful and easy to identify, especially in a business context such as a sales meeting or interview.

Our experience is that NLP trainers teach meta-programs as NLP's very own psychometric profile, but this is very dangerous, and couldn't be further from the truth.

It would be analogous to saying that, because you once painted your bedroom, you are a decorator, or because you say, "C'est la vie!", you are French.

A metaprogram is a real time configuration of sensory filters, hence you must be careful not to generalise someone's personality for how they see the world in any given moment.

Of course, how someone sees the world determines how they face the world, and how they face the world is what we call their attitude, and their attitude is what comes across to most people as their personality.

The key advantage of using Meta Programs as a profiling method is that it is based on listening to language structures in normal conversation. It is important to note that a person's behavioural profile will change in different contexts and this will be reflected in their choice of language.

For example, you may behave differently in a library to at a football match and your repertoire of language will change too. This is not a conscious decision, it is the process by which you adapt to different environments. A state has a vocabulary, and therefore the unconscious structure of language gives us clues about the underlying unconscious processes.

These thinking preferences or Meta Programs aren't fixed; they are very context specific, so rather than using these preferences to pigeon-hole people, use them to understand a person within the current context, situation or conversation.

Let's explore these thinking preferences in more detail, see how they fit together and discuss ways to use them.

Sensory Preference

Visual, Auditory, Kinaesthetic, Olfactory, Gustatory

Does everyone see images of memories inside their heads? Does everyone feel an emotion in the same way, with the same intensity? Does everyone hear a voice inside their head, reading out loud, giving instructions and feedback?

The answer, or course, is no. As you might expect, everyone is different. Not only that, but everyone uses all of their senses to differing degrees.

You might think that it's impossible to know if someone is seeing a picture or hearing a voice inside their head but it's actually the easiest of all of the Meta Programs to determine.

Listen carefully to what someone says - there will be words in their sentences which aren't part of the content which are called predicates. These predicates are biased toward the person's sensory preference. For example, if we're talking about having a conversation with someone:

- We saw eye to eye (Visual)

- We clicked (Kinaesthetic)

- We spoke the same language (Auditory)

This is important when communicating with people. As you can guess, visual people can easily understand pictures, auditory people like to read about or listen to a description and kinaesthetic people like to physically experience something new.

In order to make sense of information, people with a visual preference will construct imagines in their heads, whereas people with a kinaesthetic preference will check their feelings to make sure an idea "feels right".

Here are some more examples of words to watch and listen out for:

	See	Vision	Sharp
	Picture	Outlook	Background
	Look	Bright	Shine
	Watch	Clear	Reflect
	Magnify	Near	Far
	Perspective	Focus	Eye catching
	Notice	Dark	Distant
	Listen	Quiet	Whistle
	Hear	Amplify	Whine
	Sound	Tell	Roar
	Noise	Resonate	Silent
	Replay	Whisper	Rattle
	Loud	Hum	Tone
	Click	Harsh	Clear

Feel	Push	Down
Touch	Embrace	Ache
Grab	Warm	Gut reaction
Hold	Cold	Queasy
Heavy	Light	Float
Sinking	Contact	Shaky
Fuzzy	Wobbly	Ease

In NLP, the senses are often called representational systems because that's what they do - they represent the outside world. They are also used to represent memories - every memory you have is stored in all of your senses - your preferred sense is the one which comes to mind most often.

Can you see your house in your mind, hear a favourite actor's voice, remember what your keys feel like? In order to do this, your mind is using the same sense to represent a memory to you that it would use to represent the outside world.

Your consciousness includes components both from the outside world and from within your memory. When we remember something, we use our preferred sensory system to bring the information to hand. The sensory system chosen is visible externally in things like the language already covered and also in areas like body posture and eye movements.

Motivation Direction

Towards and Away From

We could think of motivation as a thought that compels you to take action. When someone says that they are 'motivated', this often means that they are thinking that they really ought to do something but they're not in fact doing something. Logically, you can't be motivated and take action at the same time. Therefore, truly motivated people don't say that they're motivated, they just get on with it.

If we look more closely at the thoughts that lead to action, we can notice that they fall towards the two ends of a spectrum. Here are some examples of what people might answer when asked the question, "Why did you decide to ..?"

- I wanted to get the project finished

- I couldn't leave it a moment longer

- I just don't like seeing the place look untidy

- I needed to get it right

- I wanted to save time for the future

- I wanted to improve the working environment

Can you see the differences in these reasons? Some of them are 'to get something' whilst others are 'to avoid something'. We can call these two directions 'Towards' and 'Away From'

Broadly, a person will respond to a stimulus by taking action, either because they see an opportunity to achieve something that they want or to prevent or avoid something that they would rather not have.

Motivation direction is very much dependent on context. If you are doing something that you really enjoy, such as playing a sport, and someone asks you if you would like more free time, you would probably focus on what you would like to do more of. If you are doing something that you don't enjoy, such as home maintenance, and someone asks you if you would like more free time, you would probably think, "Sure, if someone could take this off my hands, that would be great".

A person will be predisposed to a certain direction of motivation, which gives you an opportunity to influence them to take action.

For example, if a client is talking about a problem, your natural assumption might be that they want to solve it. It's easy to focus first on the problem itself, but when you really listen to the client's words, you might find that they are focusing on either avoiding the problem or on achieving some change in situation.

If it's not obvious at first, the client's questions or objections can point the way. For example, when you suggest a solution, the client might say, "But will that mean that I have to pay more?" which tells you that they're focusing Away From the problem. If the client says, "And will that mean that I can also use the contract in other situations?" then they are focusing Towards a solution.

As well as adjusting your own focus and language to that of the client, it is very useful to use both forms in your marketing literature.

Here are some examples of benefits expressed as both Towards and Away From motivations.

- "Saves you money and gives you more free time"

- "Don't struggle by yourself, our support can make things easier"

- "Reduce anxiety and increase your peace of mind"

- "No more worrying about the future; we can support your plans and put your mind at rest"

The format isn't 'more of / less of', it's 'what I would take action to avoid / what I would take action to achieve'

To find out whether a person is motivated by moving towards things they want or by getting away from things they don't want, in a specific context, ask:

"What do you want from [action or event]?"

The answer may include something similar to:

Towards	Away from
To get	To avoid
To have	So I don't have to
To become	To get away from
I want	I don't want

Decision Criteria

Similarities and Differences

Even though you might question some peoples' decisions, we do in fact use very specific criteria. Decisions are rarely straightforward, and criteria can have different priorities and consequences which we have to balance.

Decisions are therefore based on comparisons. Is something better than what you have now? Are those curtains darker? Is this carpet as good as the one in your bedroom? Does this colour complement your furniture? Or does this colour make a refreshing change?

What do you notice about these two images?

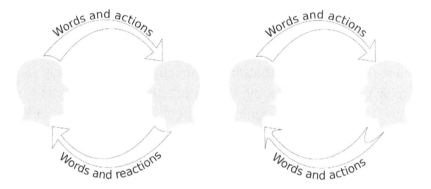

Was your first reaction, "They're the same... oh wait, not quite", or was it, "They're different... basically the same but with five differences".

In fact, whilst the diagrams are neither the same nor different, you can easily focus your attention onto the similarities or differences.

The thinking preference of decision criteria means that people are predisposed to either focus on the similarities or the differences when making a comparison.

In practice, this means that, when you describe a solution to a client, they will either look at how the future situation is similar to their current situation, or they will look at how it is different. In general, people want to preserve what they like and change what they don't like, and in order to make a change, they often have to feel that the future benefits of a course of action outweigh their inertia to keep things as they are.

This doesn't mean that some people are more 'stuck in their ways' or more 'open minded', because if you presented the same decision to them with the criteria switched around, you could see a completely different response.

For example, if their current focus is on what is undesirable about their current situation, then they will most likely label it as a 'problem' and come to you for help. If their focus is on what they want to maintain then they are most likely tolerating their current situation, and if you offer help, they'll reply, "Oh, it's not too bad, really". In order to make these determinations, they are making comparisons of their current situation with what they think is required to change that situation.

Sales people have long understood the power of exploring what the customer likes about their current home or vehicle. Junior staff would say, "Don't tell them how nice their home is! They won't want to sell it!", and more experienced staff would reply, "They have their own reasons for selling, and what they want to buy is a home that is the same but better than the one they have. If we understand what they love about their current home, we'll know what to look for in finding them a new one."

Now, here's something that they don't teach you on NLP Practitioner courses. The process of making a comparison cannot take place in real time, it must involve memory and hence a comparison is always distorted.

To discover someone's decision criteria, ask them about two similar instances. Be careful not to bias them one way or the other with words such as "compare".

What can you tell me about this job and your last job [car, house, partner etc.]?

The answer will likely contain both similarities and differences, the important thing is to notice which one the client gives you first, or which they attribute more value to.

Differences   One was...

Similarities with exceptions They were both, except...

Similarities   They were both...

Decision Process

Options and Procedures

When you cook dinner, do you begin by seeing what ingredients you have, and then think up something that you can make with them? Or do you begin by thinking about what you want to eat and then check to see if you have the ingredients?

Some people, when faced with a decision, will tend to think about what they already know how to do or what they already have experience of. They follow a mental Procedure that they feel best fits the current situation. For example, if you ask them how they would like to proceed with a legal decision, they would reply, "Well, what usually happens next?"

Other people will reply, "What are my options?" They prefer not to follow a set or proven procedure, instead preferring to try a new or different route.

The Procedures thinkers say, "What next?" and the Options thinkers say, "What if?"

This is a very easy thinking pattern to recognize, and an important one to respond to. If you are faced with a very Options oriented client and you talk in Procedures, you'll send them to sleep. However, if you present a very Procedures oriented client with too many Options, you'll send them into a tail spin.

One of the simplest ways to ensure that you appeal to both thinking preferences is to present a number of options and then make a recommendation, or simply say that the next step of the process has a number of options to choose from.

The Procedures thinkers like the security of a proven process whilst the Options thinkers like the security of making a choice.

Some people never seem to do things the same way twice. Others seem unable to innovate or create and will continue to do something the same way until external events force them to change. Options thinkers are good at being creative and thinking up new ideas and ways to do things. Procedures thinkers are good at finishing things and following routines. You wouldn't want procedures people in creative jobs and you wouldn't want options people in jobs that were heavily regulated.

To find out if a person likes to have many options available at each decision point or if that person needs to follow a set procedure, ask:

Why did you choose this job [car, house, computer, course of action etc.]?

Options	Procedures
Answers why, very quickly	Answers how the choice came to be with a story and steps
Clearly defined reasons	

Time Orientation

Time is an abstract concept that applies to almost everything that we do. We group our experiences into three distinct time periods; 'past', 'future', and 'present', and different cultures give these periods different significance.

Some people and cultures are very focused in the past, and have a strong sense of nostalgia, heritage and protecting a legacy. Some are focused in the future, with a strong sense of purpose and creativity. And some are focused in the present, with a 'go with the flow' attitude. They seem to live for the moment, not planning ahead and not valuing the lessons of the past.

From these descriptions, you can perhaps see that different time orientations can affect a person's perception of themselves, of events and of other people. The 'generation gap' certainly plays a part, and if you work with clients across a wide age range, you will no doubt see this in action.

Most importantly, people respond differently to the connection between these periods of time. Much research has been done on this subject, and people from hundreds of different countries and cultures have been asked to complete a very simple research task; to draw three circles on a piece of paper, representing past, present and future. The differences are startling, and bear a very literal relation to what we stereotypically think about different cultures.

Try it for yourself, and ask your colleagues and family to do the same. What do you notice about the similarities and differences? Do they help you to understand the time related areas where you feel more synergy or frustration in a particular relationship.

If you work with clients from many different cultural backgrounds and want to learn more about how they think and communicate, read 'Riding the Waves of Culture' by Fons Trompenaars.

Again, the key is to pay attention to a client's language and behaviour and ensure that you are communicating with them 'on their wavelength'. The exercise above is important because it gets you talking to your friends and colleagues about a subject that you may previously have taken for granted, and understanding them more is the foundation of better communication and better relationships.

24.1 Time Orientation

Try the time orientation exercise from the book 'Riding the Waves of Culture'.

Draw three circles, representing past, present and future.

Mark a cross to indicate where 'you' are in relation to these circles.

What do you interpret from what you have drawn?

Ask some friends and colleagues to do the same. What do you notice?

Look for the relative size of the circles and the distance between them.

Where do you spend most of your time?

Reference Source

Internal and External

Have you noticed how some people just know what it is they want whereas other people are always asking if what they're doing is OK?

Some people just don't seem to take any notice of the world around them whilst others are always checking that everyone else is OK.

Do you instinctively know when something is right, or do you like to keep "to do" lists so that you can be sure that everything's finished off?

The source of reference is: do you use your own internal judgements and benchmarks or do you use other people's?

To find out whether a person is motivated and judged by their own internal ideals and concepts or whether they need external feedback and benchmarking you can ask this question:

"How do you know when what you're doing is right?"

Internal	External
I just know	My boss tells me
Eh?	My colleagues tell me
	I tick everything off my to do list
	I have a pile of certificates

When someone is internally referenced:

If you tell them that they should do something because everyone else in the team is, they might say "so what?".

They might not even understand the question, the thought of asking someone else's opinion being so alien to them.

They may hear instructions as comments.

When someone is externally referenced:

If you tell them that, if they think something is right then, that's good enough, they may get quite frustrated.

They may hear comments as instructions.

> What correlations do you see between the meta-programs? For example, for something to be external, it must be in the present or future, and is therefore a source of possibility rather than certainty.

I'd like to finish this chapter by pointing out that the above metaprograms are a collection of those that you'll find throughout the NLP body of knowledge, although I don't necessarily agree with them myself. While they are part of the SNLP certification criteria, I have an alternative view.

Some people believe that there's enough of everything for everyone, and all that's needed to get through life is a little patience.

Other people believe that there's not enough of everything to go round, so if you don't fight for what you need, you might lose out.

The basic difference is that people who had every need attended to as a baby grow up knowing that the world, and other people, will satisfy their needs, so it's safe to rely on other people. On the other hand, people who didn't have every need satisfied as a baby grow up knowing that if you want something, you have to get it for yourself and you can't rely totally on other people, especially where your livelihood or safety are concerned.

It's not a matter of which is best, as there are pros and cons to each type. Flexibility always wins.

The 'accommodating' people are led by external stimuli, so we could say that's like the 'external' reference metaprogram. The 'competing' people are led by internal stimuli, so we could say that's like the 'internal' reference metaprogram.

I believe that all of the other 'metaprograms' can be derived from these two basic world views, an idea that I explore in more detail in The NLP Master Practitioner Manual.

For now, I just wanted to leave it with you as food for thought.

25 Modelling

Modelling is a very important part of NLP. It is the basis for all of the techniques, because they were modelled from the minds of people who were very good at helping other people to change. Therefore, the techniques are not NLP in themselves, they are the results of NLP.

NLP gives us a process for developing and evolving models of excellence. In order to understand and apply NLP effectively, you need to understand the concept of modelling. NLP's techniques work, some of the time. By modelling the problem first, you'll find that the techniques work first time, every time.

Let's take the fast phobia cure as an example. If you use it with ten people who have a phobia, you might find it works with half of them. This doesn't mean that the technique is only effective 50% of the time, it means that half of the people you used it with did not have a phobia. A common example is "fear of flying". I'll go out on a limb here and say that no-one is afraid of flying. Not a single person in the whole world is afraid of flying. There are, however, a lot of people who are afraid of crashing. This is not a phobic response. A fear of crashing takes a great deal of imagination, and so the first step is to find out how the problem works by modelling it so that you can choose or create an appropriate technique.

In the world of electronics, there are good engineers and there are average engineers. The average engineers will fix a piece of equipment by replacing all the components until they find the one that was causing the problem. If you've ever had a domestic appliance repaired by the main service agent, you will have experienced this first hand. They want you to but the spares up front before the engineer arrives and, if those parts aren't faulty, you don't get a refund. When trying to get my dishwasher fixed, I asked, "Would it be an idea for the engineer to diagnose the fault before ordering the spare parts?" The answer from the call centre was that I could try it that way if I wanted, but I'd have to pay two call-out charges.

Good engineers observe behaviour closely. They know how a piece of equipment behaves when it is working normally, so they know where to start looking when it does not behave normally. Average engineers do not observe behaviour in the same way.

When I was an engineer, I learned to observe behaviour, because it was the only way to fix complex problems. If you don't know what the equipment does when it's working properly, how can you know what is wrong with it when it isn't working properly?

Medical researchers study disorders in order to understand more about them. With NLP, we focus on people who have talents that we want to understand. If we want to create a way of 'curing' a phobia, what we look for is people who used to have a phobia and now don't so that we can figure out what changed. Ideally, this approach is focused on or at least tailored to an individual client.

Despite what some people say, NLP's approach isn't 'better', it's just a different way of looking at things.

Far too many coaches are being taught prescriptive, off the shelf processes which do not benefit clients, because the client is not in the exact situation that the coaching tools were designed for.

If you want to improve the performance of a sales team, it doesn't help to focus on the under-performers, even though that may seem intuitively right. Surely, if the high performers are doing well, we don't need to worry about them. In fact, we need to figure out what the over-performers are doing first. NLP modelling is automatically systemic and ecological. By modelling a successful sales person, we can understand the mindset that works for that team, in that company, in that market, with those products and those customers. Therefore, by teaching that mindset to other sales people in the same team, we have an instantly workable process.

You are an expert. Anything that you can do really well without having to think about it is a talent. Maybe you've had the experience of watching someone do something amazing and asking them, "how did you do that?" to which they reply, "I don't know, I just did it. Doesn't everyone?"

Many people assume that this means the behavioural knowledge required to perform a complex task is locked away and is irretrievable. We get a glimpse of the knowledge through observing behaviour, but there is no way to extract the knowledge itself.

In modelling the hypnotherapist Milton Erickson, Bandler and Grinder wanted to discover what he did that achieved consistent results, and those techniques in turn provided an insight into the workings of the human mind.

Bandler and Grinder were first interested in excellent communicators in the field of personal change, so they went to talk to some of the most outstanding therapists at the time. They found that these people had certain things in common to do with they way that they communicated. By exploring these similarities, a model was developed of the way these people used language to influence patterns of thought and behaviour.

So, techniques such as anchoring and reframing are NLP applied. They are not strictly NLP itself. NLP is the process by which we extracted those techniques from the minds of the original role models.

Modelling is as much a mindset of curiosity as an explicit set of tools that you must use as prescribed. This mindset will help you to learn interesting things from experts, from people you admire and from yourself.

When you watch your colleagues, clients, managers and friends, you will notice that they do certain things in a certain order. You will be able to watch the process by which they individually behave in order to achieve their goals.

There are a number of hallmarks of a talent that seem to be consistent:

- The person is able to get consistent results without having to think about the process or being aware of it

- When asked, the person is a little surprised that the skill is worth modelling

- When you first ask, "how do you do it?" they answer, "I don't know - I just do it"

There are many ways you can approach the modelling process itself, so here are a few ideas that you can use.

General Hints

You'll find that the majority of valuable information that you get from your modelling subject will come when you're paying the least attention to them. It's a very good idea to record the conversation and listen to it several times to glean every last piece of content.

Many people have said that the most valuable information came out after the interview had finished and they were "just chatting", so that should tell you something about the style of interview that gets the most response from the subject!

You should aim to interview your subject somewhere that they feel comfortable, and preferably somewhere they would naturally use the skill that you're modelling so that they have easy access to it.

Spend some time getting your subject into a state where they are fully associated with the skill you want to model. You'll find that the whole process is then much easier. You can do this by asking them very detailed questions about a specific situation until you notice that they are "really there".

And finally, remember to thank your subject and to share the results with them afterwards.

NLP Modelling

Strictly speaking, NLP modelling follows a particular format. The first step requires the modeller to emulate everything that the role model does. At this stage, the modeller does not reject any behaviour, no matter how seemingly irrelevant. The test of this is that the modeller can get the same or similar results to the role model when in the same context without being able to explain what they are doing.

The second step is the to code the behaviour and to remove redundant elements so that what is left is a simple process that can be taught and reproduced at will.

In practice, most people today would begin filtering the information to be assimilated at the uptake stage, for example ignoring the role model's nail biting or poor dress sense. In the strictest application of NLP modelling, we don't know if those are relevant or not, so we copy everything that can be observed.

Remember to check you have a good level of rapport before you start - you may find it useful to frame the meeting with a statement such as, "When I've modelled successful people in the past, I've found the questions I'm about to ask really useful - if they don't make sense, that's fine - just use them as a guide to say what comes into your mind. If I ask similar sounding questions, it's to give you a chance to build on what you've said already"

NLP Modelling is not actually a certification requirement at Practitioner level, however I suggest that it is very valuable, both in learning to adapt the techniques and in learning some useful new skills.

Often, when helping someone change something or solve a problem, just modelling the undesired behaviour will change it for the better. Perhaps this is as a result of bringing unconscious aspects of the behaviour to their conscious attention, perhaps it's as a result of reframing the behaviour as a talent rather than a problem. All I can say for certain is that it is a vital part of any coaching process that I undertake with a client.

Another important application of NLP modelling in business is talent management, or the replicating of talents within a team or organisation.

Most teams and organisations have a handful of "star performers" who effortlessly excel, in sales, customer service, design, management, leadership or any area of a business where intuitive skills rather than business processes play an important part in an individual's performance. In other words, that applies to every area of every business!

By modelling your star performers, you can find out how they are able to achieve the results that they get. You can then help them to refine their own talent and you can also teach it to everyone else as a behavioural model for excellence.

Your organisation is already a proving ground for excellence, and you currently measure it through sales management, appraisals and pay rises. By adding the essential tools and principles of NLP modelling to this, you can accelerate the rate at which intuitive best practice develops in your business and benefits your customers.

Success Factor Modelling

Robert Dilts is probably the most well known and prolific modeller, having modelled people such as Walt Disney and Albert Einstein and produced models of generic skills such as leadership and creativity.

Dilts' Success Factor Modelling approach requires that you find a number of people who appear to share a common skill or talent. The whole modelling process is as follows:

- Interview the individual

- Interview the people they work with or relate to

- Watch them in their normal environment to confirm the model

- Check the model against their peers to benchmark their performance

- Check the model against your own peers to check current research or thinking

- Check the model against the individual or organisation's vision their stated future direction

- Check the model against the individual or organisation's past history

From all of these separate models you can then refine a model of the specific skill that can be used by anyone to achieve the same results.

Strategy Elicitation and the TOTE Model

A strategy is a specific sequence of steps that are necessary to perform a particular task. Simply, you take your subject through the skill, step by step, until you have built up a detailed map of the behaviour. For example, a skill for goal setting might break down into:

1. Visual construct of desired outcome

2. Kinaesthetic check for congruence of outcome

3. Visual recall of current situation

4. Visual construct of steps required to reach outcome

5. Kinaesthetic check for congruence of outcome

In other words, the person imagines what they would like to have, feels good about it, imagines the steps they need to take and, if it feels right, they do it.

The TOTE model adds an extra layer of formality to the basic strategy in that it adds criteria for starting the strategy and ending it. TOTE stands for Test Operate Test Exit, so to the above example it adds "how do you know when you want something?" and "how do you know when you've got it?"

You may also find that your subject has very specific criteria for the Test and Exit stages, for example someone who is scared of public speaking may know to get scared if there are more than 3 people in the audience. If there are fewer than 3, it doesn't count as a presentation so the "get scared" strategy doesn't run (the Operate part).

26 Tips for Practitioner Techniques

You'll know by now that I am somewhat sceptical of coaching models. There's nothing wrong with them in themselves, my concern is that their creators peddle them as the panacea for coaching or the "right" way to coach. Remember, a model is never the thing it represents, so whenever you look at a coaching model, or any model, you have to remember that all of the important stuff has been missed out in order to give it a snappy acronym.

GROW does not work in itself. NLP techniques do not work in themselves. They need an attitude and a relationship around them, therefore the models and the techniques miss out precisely the elements that make them work.

You may be wondering at this point if I can tell you what I think does work, and so I thought I would share some of my top tips with you.

Presuppose success

Don't ask if *anything* has changed, ask *what* has changed.

This does not mean that you must assume that every technique or coaching session will end with a major life transformation. It could mean that a problem is a little less fuzzy, or a relationship doesn't quite seem so distant, or a goal seems somehow brighter.

In pure NLP terms, you are not looking for a change in the client's intention, you are looking for a change in submodalities.

Your clients can, and will, say whatever they want. Sometimes they will say what they think you want to hear. Sometimes, they will want to hide the fact that they have only superficially explored a problem. Therefore, do not ask for the client's judgement or conclusion, only ask them to describe how the situation has changed, and direct them to specify changes in submodality.

Do not say, "How have the submodalities of your representation of this system changed?", because you need to use plain language, not the internal jargon of NLP.

Instead, try something like, "When you imagine the situation now, what seems different? Would you say that it looks a little different? And when you imagine how the conversation will have changed, could you be more specific about what has changed? How does it sound different?"

A change in submodalities is the short term test for you. The test for the client is a tangible change in their life.

High involvement, low attachment

A coach should be highly involved and engaged with the client, but not attached to the outcome. The client's success or failure is not dependent on the coach, and the coach's success is not dependent on the client's. They are connected, but not dependent. If you become attached, you'll start to need the outcome more than the client does.

There's no rush!

You don't have to dive in to quick fixes. You don't have to do techniques at the client the moment you "know what their problem is". Take it easy.

If they didn't ask you to fix it, it isn't broken

Engineers say that if it isn't broken then don't fix it. I say that if the person didn't specifically ask for your help then they didn't have a problem, no matter what you may think.

Trust your hunches

Your hunches come from somewhere, and they represent huge volumes of information that you can't even begin to work out consciously, so don't bother. Simply trust.

Focus on what you want first

You need your own outcomes independent of what the client says they want to work on during a session. Whatever the client presents as their outcome for the session is rarely what they end up working on anyway, so if you use that as your only guide, you'll be dragged all over the place. Your coaching sessions will seem directionless, you'll run out of time and the client won't get the value they want. And remember that you're doing this for your own benefit, no one else's

Are you asking that great question for your benefit or for the client's?

So you have a great new question you want to try out that you read in that newsletter. Does the client need the question, or do you need it more, in which case ask it somewhere else.

You don't need the answers

When you ask a question, the answer isn't for you, it's for the client.

The unconscious always knows what it wants

The unconscious mind, both your client's and your own, always knows what it wants, and always knows what to do, and it will do its best to scream that information at you. All you have to do is pay attention.

Do you need to say it more that the client needs to hear it?

The same goes for advice as for questions. Are you saying it because you have carefully constructed a linguistic pattern, or a hypnotic embedded command, or perhaps a story or metaphor? Or is there just something you want to get off your chest? Or is it a case of "Ooh! Ooh! I've got a better story than that!". Is it a case of the old therapist's, "You think you've got problems? You wouldn't believe what happened to me today…"

You don't have to fix the problem, only break it

If you're planning to fix or solve a problem, it means you have already decided what the right solution is. You never know what the right solution was until the client has put it into practice. Never. Therefore, you cannot solve the problem, you can only break the old pattern of behaviour so that the client has to make a new, more useful choice.

Watch and listen

You wouldn't want a plumber to dive straight in and pull your central heating boiler apart without even making some initial diagnostic checks. Similarly, don't even think about starting coaching until you've spent some time watching and listening to establish some benchmarks, notice some state changes, hear some unconscious signals, that kind of thing.

Everything you need is in the first sentence

When the client first tells you what they want, or what the problem is, they will tell you everything you need to know, in their words, in their non verbal communication, in their metaphors, in their ambiguities, in their pauses, in their hesitations, in their silences. All you have to do is pay attention.

Particularly in the first sentence, the client's language is 'isomorphic' with their problem, meaning that they share a structural similarity. You'll find more about this in Peter's book 'Genius at Work', but you will learn everything you need for yourself by paying attention and focusing on the Meta Model.

The client has everything they need to be everything they want

Maybe they have all the resources they need, maybe they don't. Who knows for sure? But what they aspire to is already within them, otherwise they wouldn't know to aspire to it.

SORT

Your State comes first, then your Outcome. Only then do you establish Rapport and make a connection. And only when you have those three do you even think about Techniques. And of course, your first techniques might be to set your client's state and outcome.

Relationship, Intention, Perspective

I propose to you that a coach is effective, not because of their certificates or fancy coaching models, but because of three simple yet vital factors. A coach has a certain Relationship with the client which implies expertise, change, professionalism and so on. The coach has an Intention which may be to help the client to achieve a goal or make a change. It's a different intention to the client's friends and family, who want the client to feel better, or be happy, or stay the way they are. Finally, the coach can see things that the client can't, not because of any special gift, but because they have Perspective. They're looking at the situation from a different angle, so they have different information available to them.

27 Coaching Tools

SORT

Until you have rapport, there is no point launching into techniques. In an environment where we are practising a number of techniques, it is easy to focus on them and to dive right in once you think you know the "right" technique to use.

If you want to SORT a client's problem out, remember, If you only have ten seconds with a client, get them into a resourceful State. If you have thirty seconds, get them to set an Outcome. If you have a minute, check for Rapport. Only when you have done those things can you even think about a Technique.

Or, to think about it another way, you need to have your State right before you set an Outcome, and only then get into Rapport, and only when you have those three do you go anywhere near a Technique.

State

Outcome

Rapport

Technique

Intuitive Problem Solving

In this exercise, you have to trust yourself to know the answer before your client does, which doesn't mean that you know better than them because you won't be giving them that kind of advice. Wait and see. Work with the same person for the whole exercise.

Describe the Problem

Have your client tell you about a current, genuine problem they have. It can be anything, big or small, the only rule being that that they feel some emotional connection to it, maybe frustration, disappointment, confusion, guilt or even exasperation or anger.

As they tell you about it, ignore their words completely. As nosey human beings, we like to get tied up in the content, offer suggestions, fix people's problems and so on.

Completely ignore their words and instead focus on only three things as you notice what they do when they talk about a particular aspect of the problem, or experience a particular emotional state. Pay attention to:

- Their voice tone

- Where they look

- What they do with their hands

DO NOT interact in any way other than to show you are listening and interested. Do not ask any questions.

When I ask groups for feedback at this stage of the exercise, they say things like:

- I couldn't pay attention to all 3 aspects, only 1 or 2

- I noticed how every time my client said x he did y

- I found it hard not to listen to content

- He looked around a lot

- She moved her hands a lot

- His voice changed when he talked about feelings

Play Back the Problem

Play back your client's problem, concentrating on using the exact voice tone they used, looking where they looked (as if they were looking at something real) and moving your hands in the same way. You don't have to understand what it means, you're just respecting the fact that it means something to them.

When I ask groups for feedback at this stage of the exercise, they say things like:

- I felt like my partner was really listening

- I felt comfortable with my partner

- I felt that my partner really understood me

- I was surprised that I do all of that when I talk

- My partner was very perceptive

What you have done by noticing your partner's voice tone, eye movements and gestures is pick up on the key non verbal communication channels. You have started to focus on the non-verbal elements of communication where someone's true beliefs, reactions and intentions leak out.

Ask Questions

The final thing we're going to do is solve a problem only by asking questions about it. Remember, it's not your problem so it's not your responsibility to solve it. All you need to do is change your client's perspective of the problem. Therefore, it is only important to ask the questions. The answers are not for you, so you don't need to respond to them.

The only rule is that you are only allowed to ask questions that you'll find in The Unsticker, a few pages on from here.

These questions work in a particular way, changing your client's perception of the problem. Since they're carrying around a representation, a model, of the problem in their heads, when their perception changes, the model changes and when the model changes, the problem changes. It doesn't matter if you ask the same question more than once, you will get a different answer each time.

You have 10 minutes each for this, and if you solve the problem with the first question, just move on, don't be tempted to dwell on it for the sake of it. Remember to ask these questions gently, as if you really care about the person's problem, and as if you know that they already know how to solve it, they just haven't realised it yet.

When I ask groups for feedback at this stage of the exercise, they say things like:

- It really helped me to think through the problem

- It helped me to find my own solution

- It changed my perspective of the problem

- I feel differently about the problem

Intuition

For this final part of the exercise, use only your intuition.

Don't rationalise it, don't explain it, don't find reasons for it.

Just tell your client what you feel their problem is *really* all about, and give them one single piece of advice.

Don't sit there and analyse it. Don't worry about whether it is right or wrong. It doesn't have to make any sense. You don't have to explain it. Just say what you feel is right.

- The summary was absolutely spot on

- My partner discovered something really important that I hadn't even mentioned

- The suggestion was really accurate

- My partner told me what I already knew I had to do

- He used the exact words that I have been secretly saying to myself

What you have just done, by trusting your intuition, is allowed yourself access to more of your brain than just by focusing analytically. So if you really want to pay attention to someone, stop listening and allow yourself to really hear.

You will learn more about what is really important to your client, and that creates greater empathy and strengthens the connection between you. That strong connection allows you to ask questions that normally you wouldn't get away with, and those questions help you to change the person's perception.

Changing the other person's perceptions is the basis for changing their opinions, needs and beliefs, and that is the basis for creating a very powerful relationship.

The Untangler

In pairs, interview your client to learn about a problem or other situation they would like to explore. Your intention is to help them resolve it.

As your client talks, notice key words or phrases that they mark out with gestures, state shifts or voice tone changes. Write these words and phrases down verbatim on small cards or pieces of paper.

If you can't fit something onto a card, ask your client to summarise a particular point with a word or phrase that fits.

When you're finished, give the cards to your client and ask them to sort out and organise the cards. They can do anything they want with the cards in order to organise them in a way that makes sense to them.

Do not intervene at this point, just watch and notice what happens.

When they have laid out all of the cards, you can begin to ask questions about the structure and pattern of the cards. Notice any asymmetries, anything that stands out, anything that seems interesting.

Ignore what is written on the cards, just look at the shapes and patterns. As you question the pattern, you may find that your client wants to make changes.

Ask them if any cards are missing, or if there are any that do not belong in the shape, and make any necessary changes. Keep going until the pattern resolves into something new, often a very specific and relevant symbol, that marks a shift in your client's thinking.

The Unsticker

When you have a problem to solve or you feel stuck or indecisive, you can use the world famous Unsticker.

It will make a difference if you get someone else to do the asking, so that you can concentrate fully on your answers. When you're doing the asking, remember that the answers are not important to you, they're only important to the person with the problem. You may or may not get a verbal answer; it doesn't really matter as long as they make sense of the question in relation to their stated problem.

It's very important that you choose questions randomly rather than looking through the list and picking a "good" question. Picking a "good" question means you've found one that fits inside the problem, so it won't help you. I guarantee that if you look for a "good" or "right" question, it will not work.

Do not look at the questions, just choose a number between 1 and 200 and then turn to that question. Then ask away, and see how quickly the problem changes.

People do tend to follow patterns in choosing numbers, probably going to 73 first, avoiding numbers at the start and end and so on. Therefore, use some external aid to help you. Look around you for numbers on posters and signs, or just open the book, close your eyes and point.

You can also access a free online version on The Unsticker's website at www.theunsticker.com which randomises 200 questions for you, and which also links to the free Android version. The paperback book The Unsticker has over 300 questions, and some glorious illustrations too.

1   What is it that you don't want to not have happened?

2   A travelling salesman throws this problem on the floor to demonstrate a new vacuum cleaner. Do you buy the vacuum cleaner?

3   Are you secretly in love with this problem?

4   Do you need anyone else to do this for you?

5   Imagine your best friend has this problem. What is your advice to them?

6   What would happen if this just slipped your mind?

7   If this problem went away right now, what would you do with all that free time?

8   When will you have solved this problem yet?

9   So what?

10 Imagine a close colleague has this problem. What is your advice to them?

11 What do you want most of all?

12 What would happen if you didn't?

13 What does this problem signify?

14 If this problem were a person, where would you hit him/her?

15 What does this problem demonstrate?

16 Where would this problem be without you?

17 Who else does this involve?

18 Who can you turn to?

19 How do you know?

20 If you turned this problem on its head, how would it smell?

21 Imagine your favourite actor/actress has this problem. What is your advice to them?

22 Why not sleep on it?

23 When did you first start to realise this?

24 What shape is this problem?

25 Who?

26 After you've solved this problem, who will you celebrate with?

27 What will you do?

28 After you've solved this problem, what will be next?

29 What would be the best question for me to ask now?

30 Imagine your favourite school teacher has this problem. What is your advice to them?

31 How?

32 What mustn't you do?

33 How slow is this problem?

34 What is the most awkward question for me to ask?

35 What would happen if you did?

36 Are you certain this is your problem?

37 Which part of this problem is the most spiky?

38 As you look back on this, which question was the one that really helped you most?

39 How does this problem help you?

40 How is this a problem right now?

41 If this problem were a shop, what shop would it be?

42 I want to make sure I understand you...what is it that you want to happen?

43 Why?

44 Think of someone you know who you love. What would they do?

45 How would a mouse eat this problem?

46 Who else is concerned about this?

47 What can you do?

48 When did you first know about this?

49 What have you done to earn this problem?

50 What would you do?

51 If this problem were a fruit, what fruit would it be?

52 When you look back on this problem, what will make you laugh most?

53 If this problem were a vegetable, which one would it be?

54 If you painted this problem, what colour would you use third?

55 Think of someone you know who you respect. What would they do?

56 If you saw this problem in trouble, would you help it?

57 What will you do differently next time?

58 What needs to happen for this problem to disappear?

59 What does this problem taste like?

60 What won't you do?

61 How will having had this problem have helped you?

62 Where would this problem hold a tea party?

63 What's the one thing you would like most, right now?

64 What would you do if things weren't the same?

65 What kind of cake could solve this problem?

66 How will having had this problem help you grow?

67 What shouldn't you do?

68 Imagine it's a day from now. How has the problem changed?

69 When did you first start to think this way?

70 What?

71 What did you do differently last time?

72 What does this problem mean?

73 Do you remember that time you were really creative?

74 Was this a problem a month ago?

75 How do you know that this is a problem for you?

76 Do you remember that time you got into so much trouble?

77 If you won this problem in a raffle, would you give it back?

78 What is this problem a symptom of?

79 How shiny is this problem?

80 What extra resource or skill would make the biggest difference to you, right now?

81 What if this was really someone else's problem?

82 When did you last worry about this?

83 As you see yourself with this problem, what makes you smile?

84 After you've solved this problem, will you miss it?

85 Where?

86 Was this a problem a week ago?

87 How could you make money out of this problem?

88 Was this a problem a year ago?

89 When did you last think about this?

90 What colour is this problem?

91 As you step back from yourself, what strikes you as odd?

92 If you donated this problem to a charity shop, what would they say?

93 What kind of animal could solve this problem?

94 What can't you do?

95 As you see yourself, what strikes you as funny?

96 Imagine it's a week from now. How has the problem changed?

97 When do you want this to change?

98 Why don't you?

99 What does this problem sound like?

100 How does this problem benefit you?

101 How light is this problem?

102 How does it feel to know you can laugh about this?

103 If you had a voodoo doll, who would you give this problem to?

104 Who cares enough about you to help you?

105 What if?

106 If the fairies came and took this problem away, what would you spend the

107 As you see yourself with this problem, what strikes you as sad?

108 Imagine it's ten years from now. How has the problem changed?

109 Imagine your child has this problem. What is your advice to them?

110 What should you do?

111 I want to make sure I understand...can you think that from someone else's point of view?

112 Imagine it's a month from now. How has the problem changed?

113 What wouldn't happen if you did?

114 What if you were wrong about this?

115 Think of someone you know who you envy. What would they do?

116 Are you worrying about the right problem?

117 Why bother?

118 Imagine your favourite cartoon character has this problem. What is your advice to them?

119 What does this problem smell like?

120 Is there something more important beneath this?

121 Do you remember when you laughed until you cried?

122 What has been the best thing about this problem?

123 I'm not quite sure I understand. Can you think that from a different perspective?

124 I'm not quite sure I understand. Can you think that a different way?

125 How will having had this problem have improved you?

126 A travelling salesman tries to sell you this problem. Do you buy it?

127 Who stands to gain if you solve this?

128 Was this a problem a day ago?

129 When was the last time you forgot what this problem was called?

130 Which part of this problem is the most ticklish?

131 What do you want to happen?

132 When?

133 As you look back on this, which question made you smile the most?

134 What would be the worst question for me to ask you?

135 Who can you trust?

136 What must you do?

137 When did you first find out about this?

138 What does this problem prove?

139 How many light bulbs could change this problem?

140 Is this problem really a symptom?

141 Can you think of a good reason to keep this problem?

142 How could this problem benefit someone else?

143 What is this problem a sign of?

144 How do you know you're right?

145 Imagine your parent has this problem. What is your advice to them?

146 Is someone up there trying to tell you something?

147 If you drop the problem, does it smash or splat?

148 If a child brought this problem home from school and said "look what I made!" would you pretend to like it?

149 If this problem were a musical instrument, which instrument would it be?

150 How heavy is this problem?

151 What kind of car could run over this problem?

152 How will having had this problem have changed you?

153 Which is worse, that problem or running out of milk?

154 If you came home from shopping and found that the shop hadn't charged you for this problem, would you own up?

155 As you see yourself, what strikes you as curious?

156 Do you secretly enjoy having this problem?

157 Think of someone you know who you hate. What would they do?

158 Will you miss having this problem around?

159 When you have solved this problem, what will you do with all that spare time?

160 What has been the turning point for this problem?

161 What size is this problem?

162 Why are you?

163 What makes you so lucky that you could have a problem like this?

164 If this problem were a piece of music, what music would it be?

165 What does this problem symbolise?

166 Who else knows about this?

167 After you've solved this problem, will the sun shine?

168 Think of someone you know who you trust. What would they do?

169 Imagine it's a year from now. How has the problem changed?

170 Imagine you bought a new pair of trousers and found this problem in the pocket. Would you tell the shopkeeper?

171 What gives you the right to have this problem?

172 As you see yourself with this problem, what strikes you as interesting?

173 What does this problem show?

174 Who can you depend on?

175 What would happen if you simply forgot all about this?

176 What wouldn't happen if you didn't?

177 Who can you rely on?

178 Think of someone you know who you distrust. What would they do?

179 In years to come, how glad will you be that you once had this problem?

180 What would you be doing now if things were different?

181 What would be the easiest question for me to ask?

182 Let me think about that one for a moment...

183 Do you need this problem?

184 If this problem was a bug, would you squash it or put it out?

185 Why isn't this problem rounder?

186 Is this a problem that you need?

187 Was this a problem ten years ago?

188 What kind of rock could forget this problem?

189 As you see yourself with this problem, what do you notice?

190 What wouldn't you do?

191 Who cares enough about this to help you?

192 What does this problem do for you?

193 Is this problem carbon neutral?

194 As you look back on this, which question was the hardest to answer?

195 How fast is this problem?

196 Which part of this problem is the most furry?

197 If this problem were a car, what car would it be?

198 What wouldn't you do?

199 If you found a wallet with this problem in it, would you hand it in to the police?

200 How will having had this problem have helped you develop?

28 Society of NLP Certification Criteria

Society of NLP

The following criteria for NLP Practitioner and NLP Master Practitioner certification are determined by the Society of NLP, the original NLP licensing body which was first formed in 1979, the year in which Bandler and Grinder's first NLP book, "Frogs into Princes" was published.

When you attend a certified training program, you will need to sign a license agreement which ensures that you understand the rights and obligations of certification. You can find all of the SNLP documentation in the Training section at www.geniusnlp.com

NLP Practitioner

Representational Systems

- Detect signs and sequences of representational systems

- Detect submodalities in all representational systems

- Change sequences of representational systems

- Access information in all representational systems

- Communicate in all representational systems

- Translate between representational systems

- Detect simultaneous and sequential incongruities

Rapport Building

- Establish rapport in all representational systems

Pace and Lead

- Pace and lead non-verbally and verbally

- Pace and lead through mirroring, direct matching and indirect matching in all representational systems

Anchoring

- Elicit and install anchors in all representational systems

- Stacking, amplify, collapse and chain anchors

- Disassociation techniques including the Phobia Cure and future-pacing

Language Patterns

- Detect and use the patterns of the Meta Model and Milton Model as information-gathering and information-organizing tools.

Outcome Orientation

- Set well-formed outcomes

Reframing

- Use basic reframing techniques

- Six Step Reframing

Sub-Modalities

- Swish

- Timeline

Strategies

- Basic strategy elicitation skills

Trance

- Basic trance induction and utilisation procedures

- Trance induction using the Meta Model and Milton Model language patterns

NLP Master Practitioner

Multi-level tasking and purposeful multi-level communication, including:

Detect conscious and unconscious communication.

Distinguish between content and structure.

Understand and integrate the presuppositions of NLP.

Understand remedial and generative change.

Customising NLP Practitioner techniques to meet the needs of a client.

Creating states of consciousness and physiology that lead to flexibility and creativity in thinking and action.

Making conscious shifts in perspective, state and behaviour to maintain overall control of the coaching process.

Meta Programs

Elicit Meta Programs and build them into your coaching approach.

Framing outcomes

Understand the difference between an outcome and a direction.

Have a systemic approach to predicting the implications of change over time.

Generalise change through time.

Advanced Language Skills

Detect Sleight of Mouth Patterns.

Reframing at different logical levels using the various Sleight of Mouth Patterns.

Sort incongruities and integrate them conversationally.

Implement the patterns of NLP techniques conversationally, e.g. through presuppositions in questions.

Values and Criteria

Elicit values for the purpose of motivation, setting outcomes, negotiation procedures, conflict resolution, etc.

Advanced Strategies Skills

Elicit, design, modify and install strategies.

Use motivation, convincer, decision, and follow through strategies inside other techniques.

Trance

Recognise, induce, and utilise naturally occurring trance phenomena, also known as conversational hypnosis.

Developing a greater awareness and utilisation of a systemic approach.

29

Certification Sessions

This chapter is relevant for students of my NLP Practitioner training program, where the students work through a number of coaching practice sessions.

For each session you'll be told who you are working with and the pairs are drawn up on a random rotation so that everyone has an equal share of being practitioner and client, and everyone works with someone different each time.

In order to give you as much high quality practice as possible, the timing of this last day is very important. The session start times will be displayed in the room and at the start of each session you'll be told when to be back in the room.

It's easy to get carried away in these sessions and want to carry on all day with one person. If you don't stick to the times given, you are denying yourself the quality practice that you need in order to fully integrate the skills you've learned throughout the course, and of course you are also affecting the sessions that follow. Staying on time is one of the most obvious signs that you are in control of the session.

It's very common that at the start of the day, delegates have an armful of tools and techniques that they know how to use, but they don't know how to choose. This is one of the key outcomes of the day. As you work through the sessions, you will probably find yourself talking much less and listening much more.

Remembering that the client will tell you everything you need to know in the first few sentences, you'll soon find that listening to the client and getting a sense of the structure of the problem or situation will give you all the information you need to choose your approach.

Client

As a client, you have the opportunity to work on some issues that are really important to you. You may have a fear that you want to tackle or a problem to solve. Many people who come to the Practitioner course are running their own businesses - or thinking about it - and this is an ideal opportunity to do some serious planning with the help of a talented group of coaches.

You can spend some time planning the issues or opportunities you are going to explore during the sessions so that you can get the most value from the time. You will learn as much about the process as the client as you will as the Practitioner, so both roles are equally important.

Practitioner

At first, many people find they are so busy thinking about which technique to use that they miss what the client tells them. After a while, they find that spending at least half the time just listening and exploring the issue is time well spent.

As a Practitioner, perhaps your most important job is to maintain an outcome oriented state. You can use all of your rapport skills to lead your client and in many cases, all the Practitioner has to do is sit there and look confident while the client finds their own solution!

NLP's techniques are each built around a particular structure, so by exploring the structure of the problem, you'll be able to choose the most appropriate technique.

Here are a few examples of techniques that you can use and situations where they might be relevant.

Anchoring	To capture useful states or integrate states, and to control and test responses
Collapse anchors	To generate a new state in order to disrupt a strong, undesired emotional response
Fast phobia cure	For a situation where the client's undesired response is too strong for them to explore with other techniques
Future pace	Creating the possibility for change
Meta model	Always vital when exploring and mapping out the issue being presented
Milton model	To gently guide the client towards their desired outcome
Outcomes	To find out what the client wants!
Pattern interrupt	To interrupt an undesirable state
Pacing & Leading	To non-verbally guide the client to an outcome
Perceptual Positions	To bring balance to a past interaction or to explore a future interaction
Rapport	To guide the communication process
Six step reframe	For long-term repetitive patterns of behaviour
Squash	To resolve decisions and integrate undesired emotional responses
Storytelling	To change state or shape an outcome

Strategies	To map the internal process that drives a particular behaviour
Submodalities	Exploring and changing perceptual distortions
Swish	To interrupt habitual behaviours and reactions
Timeline	To explore a future decision or set goals, and to 'fill in the gaps' in a long term plan
Trance	To help the client explore in a relaxed way, free from distractions
Utilisation	Pacing, to connect the client's real time sensory experience with a desired outcome

A technique will be less effective if you concentrate only on the technique. Use the whole time available and let the techniques do the work for you.

State: Choose a resourceful state

Outcomes: Set a direction

Rapport: Get into rapport

Questions: Learn about the problem

Intervention: The technique!

Future pace: Create a future where the problem is solved

Test: Check to make sure the intervention worked

There may be times when you get stuck and don't know where to go next - that's fine. It happens when you're focusing on the technique and not on the client. Here are some ideas for what you can say to get moving.

- That's right

- What would be a good outcome for you in this?

- Where do you believe you are right now on this?

- What would you like to do next?

Finally, and perhaps most importantly, there is no right or wrong course of action and what I am looking for is that you are able to help the client move in the general direction they want to go. It doesn't matter if a technique appears to work or not - what I'm looking for is you acting in the interests of your client, maintaining your state and making the most of the chance to develop your skills.

30 The Beginning

During your journey through the NLP Practitioner program, what have you discovered about NLP, and in that exploration, discovered about yourself?

You may remember the words of one of NLP's co-creators, Richard Bandler: "NLP is an attitude and a methodology which leaves behind a trail of techniques" .

You have now spent some time exploring those techniques, and at this point, some of them may seem unimpressive, others miraculous, and this is an insight into the subjective nature of ourselves. If we could guarantee that a particular technique would work before you had even met the person you're working with, life would be without its rich diversity and exciting challenges. All of the footprints would look the same, and would all lead to the same place.

As you have explored NLP, you have added your own footprints to this journey that we share.

As you develop your ideas and integrate the principles of NLP with the skills and experience that you already have even further, you will serve as a guide to others hoping to make that journey that is our birthright; the journey of self discovery, insight and knowledge.

Some people find NLP through a desire to help others, and some people have something that they want for themselves. Whether you choose to focus your attention on others or yourself, you are part of this evolving system which encompasses us all. When one part of a system changes, the whole must change with it. Balance is always restored.

Therefore, by developing your own skills, achieving what you want from life and living in pursuit of your true potential, you have an impact which reaches father than you may currently realise. You touch the lives of others in every moment, through the expectations you create, the experiences you share and the memories you leave behind. And in this you leave something of yourself with everyone who you work with.

Just as you carry around role models of people who have made a real difference in your life – friends, leaders, entertainers, teachers – so you become a role model in other peoples' lives, and they will forever carry their impression of you with them.

So as you reflect on this part of the journey, these steps that we have taken side by side, you can look back and see how your footprints have mingled and merged, sharing your experiences, your fears and your dreams in order to enrich this learning and growing process.

I want to take this opportunity to thank you for choosing to spend this part of your journey with me and to wish you safe travels ahead as you continue to follow your path and to be open to the new horizons and new possibilities that await you.

31 The Author

Peter first encountered NLP in 1993 while working in the Telecoms industry and has been studying, developing and teaching it ever since.

Author of such well received books as "NLP in Business", "Change Magic" and "Genius at Work", Peter has an unparalleled breadth and depth of experience in applying NLP in business to create measurable performance improvements, such as a 700% increase in profitability for a global engineering company.

Peter has taught NLP all over the world, and has been a "guest trainer" with some of the UK's best known NLP training companies. Today, Peter's focus is on executive coaching and business performance consulting, using a unique talent modelling approach which he has developed over the past 15 years to replicate talent within an organisational culture.

Example Projects and Clients

Engineering/Manufacturing: Two year talent coaching program for 25 high potential future leaders in a project environment. This program achieved a 83% success rate. (Babcock Nuclear)

IT Services: Leadership coaching for a sales director resulting in over £300million revenue and successful team development. (Logica/CGI)

Engineering/Manufacturing: Leadership coaching for a business unit director resulting in a successful merger of Alstec into Babcock. (Babcock Nuclear)

Software: Consultancy skills training program for European professional services teams. (HP)

Engineering/Manufacturing: Executive coaching for selected leaders throughout the business, resulting in one Business Unit Director achieving a 700% increase in profitability in his business unit. (Parker Hannifin)

Charity: Bespoke Leadership program, based around their strategic plan, delivered to all managers. (RSPB)

Engineering/Manufacturing: Worked with the leadership team to identify £16 Million in lost revenue and put in place management strategies to prevent ongoing losses. (Babcock Marine)

Services: Coaching for sales manager and sales team resulting in North America team going from 50% of target to all being over their sales targets. (FGI/Mercer)

Insurance: NLP Practitioner training for training design team and NLP Train the Trainer program for their team of 20 trainers. (Saga Insurance)

Transport/Consultancy: Presentation skills program delivered to over 150 of their stakeholder facing staff and project teams. Bespoke training program created by modelling their highest performing stakeholder managers. (RSSB)

Contact Centre: NLP Practitioner program for their team of 16 trainers. This delivered a doubling of sales conversion rates as a result of their redesign of internal training programs. (Inkfish/D&G)

Health/Leisure: Sales skills, strategy and sales management development with a doubling of sales conversion rates and a dramatic improvement in cash flow. (Fitness Industry Education)

Retail: Consultancy project to identify and 'blueprint' the talents of high performers within the business resulting in a 25% time and cost saving on their graduate training program. (Somerfield)

Banking: Management development training for a Japanese corporate bank. (Mizuho)

Recruitment/Search: NLP training, team building and performance coaching for a global executive search consultancy. (Global Sage)

Telecoms: Consultative sales training program for 250 SME sales people. (BT)

Testimonials

Guy Wood, Director, Sales Development, CGI (Global IT Services company)

"I became General Manager of a Business Development function in a new "intra-penuerial" division. New markets, solutions and team members were all needed. I was looking for support to improve my ability to generate results from and with all these new people, not forgetting my peers in the leadership team and our executives.

Working with Peter gave me techniques which, in many ways used my innate senses, wisdom and abilities to really enhance how I took action. I was able to pace my interactions to those of the individuals and teams I interacted with. Too often our focus on content success, failure and answers confuses our chance to see the other person. Once I was tuned into a client or a team member I could lead with them to the places I needed to us to find together. This really helped developing new business opportunities and it also gave me the tools to be clear and straight forward without complication or conflict. A key strength I gained, through understanding why I was doing this, was the self-belief to stand up and communicate with vision and really lead teams and interactions. Knowing why helps to unearth the natural passion for the challenge and the satisfaction of achieving.

It wasn't all plain sailing, managing and leading never is and the tough issues, exiting poor performers, tricky client situations, tough executive reviews, tense management relationships were all enhanced through my work with Peter.

Peter's support was vital in;

Helping me recruit 25 new team members and bringing almost all of them to quota,

In selling £0.3bn in two years, landing milestone deals in a new market and new technology area,

and in giving our executive confidence in our growth that generated their investment of time and resources."

Matt Prosser, Strategic Director at South Oxfordshire Council

"Peter supported our recent Strategic Management Board away day, looking at our future strategy and vision. His interventions were clear and kept us focussed on the agreed outcomes for the day in an excellent way. He did not shy away from challenging us or giving us some simple tools to bring clarity. We look forward to working with him again in the future."

Andrew Pettingill, Managing Director at Meridian Business Support

"I enjoyed working with Peter in a mentoring capacity which helped my personal development and confidence to take on a much bigger role. I would recommend working with Peter to support in the training and development arena with you or your teams."

Stephen Cordell MCIPD, L&D Manager at Parker Hannifin

"Peter is a highly creative and thoughtful coach with an excellent knowledge of his subject. He has a very personable and pragmatic approach that encourages his clients explore their issues."

Manny Richter, Human Resources Manager, Bostik

"Peter Freeth has a unique approach to putting theory into action. I recommend his book to Learning and Development professionals, HR managers or trainers."

Gavin Muge, Gavin Muge Learning & Development

"Peter is a quality focussed professional who sets and expects high standards of performance. Peter is able to provide real value to clients and deliver courses and learning of a high quality. The knowledge and experience that Peter has enables him to build relationships well and to inspire others around him to produce their best."

Kevin Henderson, Contracts Manager, Oxford Brookes University

"I worked closely with Peter Freeth at Oxford Brookes University, and was very impressed by Peter's knowledge of his subject area, and the attention to detail he gave regarding the terms and conditions of the contracts we discussed. I had great confidence that having agreed the terms and conditions of the contracts with Peter, our interests were well protected."

Ian Wycherley, Programme Director, Oxford Brookes University

"Peter is highly skilled at building business relationships at all levels. He combines strong commercial awareness with exceptionally clear verbal and written communication. In my experience, Peter always delivers on projects that he is involved in, and I confidently recommend him as a business partner."

Reviews for Peter's books

"Hugely practical and refreshingly straight-forward. A must for any coach, teacher or trainer." *David Nicoll*

"A practical, congruent and elegant handbook that I can not praise highly enough … inspiring, stimulating and highly practical" *Stephen Cotterell*

"This really is as good as they say" *Karl Tyler*

"This is one of the most practical toolkits I have found for opening up thinking and creating new possibilities. One of a leader's 'must have' books" *David Nicoll*

"I actually felt that I wasn't reading this book but having a conversation with the author. Peter's style is very much to write to the inner voice, the internal critic that we all have and I found myself answering the questions posed along the way. He has made it a very engaging book indeed - how many books do that now? No doubt you will hear that something is "common sense" without stopping to think what that means. What struck me in this book was that if you want a good idea about what common sense actually looks like in practice, then it's contained within the pages of Change Magic. The principles contained are ideal advice for anybody engaged in change (and who isn't nowadays?) at work, and also to build into training programs which are about personal change or for those who bring it about. I have to say none of this was included in my formal management qualifications but really, it should have been." *Stephen Hopkirk - ESH Associates*

"If I had to reduce my business library to one book, this would be it. Peter's approach is practical, down to earth, and perpetually challenging. This chap is to be counted amongst the business guru's/greats. And he has one great advantage over many of them - his stuff actually works across the whole business not just for 'strategy' people." *David Nicoll*

"Peter gift wraps startling ideas with great entertainment, In the hands of another, less intelligent writer, this kind of book could become incoherent, but Peter has enough intellectual power to make this a 'MUST HAVE BOOK'...Change Magic has conviction, style, knowledge and humour." *Michael Flaherty, Practice Manager (RAMC) 29 Commando Regt (RA)*

"A wealth of new insights and ideas, Change Magic represents a different approach so that you can take away your own unique interpretations and apply them into the real world of organisational change." *Peter Harty, MD, Innervision Performance Coaching*

"A practical and engaging set of everyday problem solving tools which is guaranteed to generate solutions to problems, and leave users with smiles on their faces. Magic!" *Geoff Cook, MD, The Training Partnership*

"Not just another book about how to think outside the box. No check list or recipes to follow but definitely full of ideas that challenge your established routines and conventional thinking. No matter how successful you have been in the business world, a must read for all. Very inspiring book... should be given to all employees and managers at every level of the organization when they come on board." *Jean-Baptiste Gruet, VP Global Sales, Workplace Options*

"Excellent, brilliant, just what I was looking for. The book now looks like I've had it for years and has loads of sticky markers all over it. And you'll be pleased to know (I think) that even though a big chunk of things I already did, I've now become more aware and refined, honed and adapted using the suggestions and tips and I've been using/applying it all over the last two weeks with fantastic results. This week however I've had phenomenal reactions from the sales staff in the classroom sessions I've been running. So a very big THANK YOU." *Karen Stockton, Associated New Media*

"I have no doubt that Peter is on course to be one of the most influential and effective leadership guides of the early 21st century. If you've encountered Peter before, you'll probably already have this book. If you haven't – be prepared for a fundamental shift in your approach to business. He really is that good" *David Nicoll, MD Certax Accounting*

Made in the USA
Coppell, TX
23 January 2023

11554273R00256